MADE IN AFRICA

THE HISTORY OF AFRICAN PLAYERS IN ENGLISH FOOTBALL

ED AARONS

This edition first published in Great Britain in 2020 by

ARENA SPORT
An imprint of Birlinn Limited
West Newington House
10 Newington Road
Edinburgh
EH9 1QS

www.arenasportbooks.co.uk

ISBN: 9781909715929
eBook ISBN: 9781788852838

British Library Cataloguing-in-Publication Data
A catalogue record for this book is available on request from the British Library.

Designed and typeset by Polaris Publishing, Edinburgh
www.polarispublishing.com

Printed in Great Britain by Clays Ltd, Elcograf S.p.A.

CONTENTS

Ed Aarons is a sports journalist for *The Guardian* who has been an expert on African football for more than a decade. He has built a reputation for being one of the best of the new generation of football journalists in the country, with particularly close links to African players in the Premier League.

ACKNOWLEDGEMENTS

This book would not have been possible without the assistance of so many people, not least Nick Walters at David Luxton Associates. It was his suggestion to incorporate a contemporary storyline to run alongside the broader history of African players that convinced me not to give up on something that I often thought would never actually see the light of day.

The idea first came after Didier Drogba's heroics for Chelsea in the 2012 Champions League final, although it took some time to form a proper plan. In February 2015, I made contact with Manny Abbeyquaye, who had established his Heritage Lottery Funded Out of Africa Campaign four years before that in Birmingham. Like Arthur Wharton originally from Ghana, Manny has taken the story of African players in English football to thousands of children around the country via a documentary, touring exhibition and school resource packs.

It was his encouragement that prompted me to begin seriously working on it properly, with Phil Vasili and Edwin Stein in particular providing invaluable help in my early research. The intriguing Steve Mokone story consumed me for the best part of 2016 and 2017, however, resulting in a different book that has yet to be published detailing the full tragic story of South Africa's first black professional player.

I decided to return to the original idea in 2018, but once again found it hard to convince anyone to take on a project that the majority felt was hardly going to attract the massive sales from what was considered a niche subject. Yet it was Nick's faith and understanding about the importance of publishing the book in order to recognise the enormous contribution so many African players have made to our game over the years that has helped finally bring it to reality. I would also like to thank my publishers and Pete Burns for his patience with various late changes and careful guidance through the whole process.

The length of time it has taken to complete this book meant countless hours of interviews, transcribing, reading and writing in my spare time. But it was still only made possible by my understanding bosses at the *Guardian*, like football editors Marcus Christenson and Jon Brodkin. Working at such a brilliant place since 2015 has also introduced me to so many amazing colleagues who have proved invaluable with their help over the years, in particular Nick Ames – who was nutmegged during our kickabout in Mohamed Salah's home town – has always provided fantastic knowledge and support.

It was also vital to meet up with so many different journalists who have shared contacts or information over Twitter and elsewhere over the years during the 2019 Africa Cup of Nations. From my old BBC colleagues, Piers Edwards and Nick Cavell, and those I knew from South Africa, like Joe Crann, Velile Mbuli and Jonty Mark, to others I finally met in Egypt, such as Maher Mezahi, Oluwashina Okeleji and Amadou Makadji, the friendly encouragement and assistance I received was much appreciated. Feet of the Chameleon – Ian Hawkey's masterpiece about African football – was my inspiration in writing this book and it was an honour to be able to discuss my ideas with him in person having both once worked with the late Tony Mashati in Johannesburg.

Then there are those who helped to tell their stories. Shaun Campbell and Howard Holmes were invaluable in relaying their passion for Wharton's life, while Tom Egbers, Don Sabo and Thandi Mokone-Chase were just three of many who gave up their time to discuss the enigmatic Mokone.

Paul Harrison and Albert's daughter, Yvonne Johanneson, offered me a unique insight into one of the game's most important pioneers and it was also an honour to speak to some of my childhood heroes who graced the Premier League during the 1990s and 2000s, including Daniel Amokachi, Lucas Radebe, Christopher Wreh, Mustpaha Hadji and Michael Essien. Hundreds of players are barely even mentioned but each has their own unique experience of how they made it to the pinnacle of English football.

I would also like to thank those who have helped gain access to today's modern superstars. Liverpool's Matt McCann kindly set up the insightful interview with Jürgen Klopp, while Bjorn Bezemer was always on hand to answer endless queries on Sadio Mané and Naby Keïta. Meanwhile, Sascha Empacher, Mostafa Algrtly, Fadi Ashraf and the team at kingfut.com provided fantastic background on Salah.

Finally I would like to thank one of my oldest friends Matt Rowe for helping to proof some of the early versions – I don't know anyone with a better football knowledge than you. Not forgetting my family too, of course . . . I really appreciate all your guidance and support in the past. Thanks too Sarah (and Mollie!). I could never have done this without you.

Ed Aarons

INTRODUCTION

"I love the fact that we have so many African players . . . until the Africa Cup of Nations starts. Then it's 'Oh my God!'" says Jürgen Klopp, breaking into his famous guffaw.

Six weeks to the day since Liverpool's victory over Tottenham in the Champions League ended his personal run of six straight defeats in major finals, Klopp is in his office at the club's Melwood training ground. For once, though, as he leans back on the sofa loading up a new vape, the former striker turned central defender, who has become one of football's most famous personalities, seems to be only half-joking.

"It's still better than it used to be because before they were out in the middle of the season," he adds. "In the past because the Africa Cup of Nations was in the winter it was really a reason not to sign an African player because you would lose him for four weeks in the middle of the season. That was really something we had in our minds always."

In purchasing Sadio Mané, Mohamed Salah and Naby Keïta

in successive summers between 2016 and 2018, Liverpool broke the African transfer record three times. It has certainly paid dividends. Although Keïta – the Guinea midfielder who was handed Steven Gerrard's famous No. 8 shirt when he moved from RB Leipzig in June 2018 for almost £53 million – struggled with injuries in his debut season, the goalscoring exploits of Senegal's Mané and Salah of Egypt helped transform Liverpool from Premier League also-rans into European champions. Klopp's views on the new scheduling of Africa's biennial tournament would be put to the test a few days later when Mané's Senegal side contested the final against Algeria in Cairo – his 55th game of an exhausting but prolific season – just two weeks before the Community Shield against Manchester City. The decision to move the 2021 tournament in Cameroon back to January would later test his patience even further, although the man who spent most of his own playing career at Mainz in the German second division before becoming one of the world's best managers can claim to have played a special role in the story of African players in English football. Klopp admits he has been fascinated by the continent ever since he watched a bulldozing striker from Ghana make his name with Saarbrücken in the late 1980s. Anthony Yeboah, as Klopp and most of Germany still refer to him, was part of Eintracht Frankfurt's exciting young team that was pipped to the Bundesliga title by Stuttgart in 1992, with the striker finishing as the league's top scorer for the following two seasons.

"Yeboah was one of the greatest strikers who played in Germany apart from Gerd Müller. He had a big impact on society," enthuses Liverpool's manager, who also remembers some of the abuse one of the country's first black players had to endure. "In football we never thought about racism. If some idiots were shouting something, you realised it but you were saying, 'Are you mad? What are you doing?' There wasn't social media so it didn't get the awareness of today. It was usually a single person and if he did it, he would get a slap and go home. He wouldn't do it again. But now of course it becomes more – there are more people – and the story becomes bigger and bigger through the reaction. It's a shame that we are still talking about things like this but that's how society is."

In 2014, a wall painting of Yeboah was unveiled on the side of a house in Frankfurt near Eintracht's stadium with the message in German: "We are ashamed of everybody who screams against us". It was taken from an open letter the Ghana international had written 24 years earlier, also signed by fellow professionals Anthony Baffoe and Souleyman Sané, the father of future Manchester City forward Leroy, to protest against racism. Yeboah would later follow in the footsteps of Albert Johanneson, the South African who became the first black player to appear in the FA Cup final 30 years earlier, when he signed for Leeds in 1995. Klopp also admits to a soft spot for Jay Jay Okocha – another African who would also go on to make a name for himself in English football with Bolton after first starring in the Bundesliga.

"He scored the most spectacular goal in the history of German football," he remembers of Okocha's brilliant individual strike for Eintracht against Karlsruhe in 1993 that goalkeeping legend Oliver Kahn joked in 2016 still left him "feeling dizzy". "It took like five minutes of Kahn and his defenders diving on the floor before he put the ball in the net! Some of the world's best players have been from Africa. George Weah. Didier Drogba. Yaya Touré. In their generation they were some of the best players so why should we not sign them? It's great."

The Liverpool side that defeated Spurs in Madrid contained their natural successors in Mané and Salah. Even with Keïta sidelined due to an injury he sustained in the semi-final against Barcelona before the famous comeback in the second leg, the presence of defender Joël Matip – born in Germany to a

Cameroonian father – in his starting line-up certainly underlined Klopp's appreciation of players with African heritage.

And then there was Divock Origi. The striker scored the second goal in the final against Tottenham to complete a fairy-tale story that had seen him almost leave the club the previous summer. Almost 30 years earlier, Origi's father Mike Okoth arrived in Belgium from Kenya to pursue his dream to play in Europe. By coincidence, that was where Klopp's wife had spent three years working as a teacher.

"We are quite . . . as a family. I'm . . . my wife worked and lived in Africa," he explains, stuttering slightly. "In Kenya. In a German school. Our elder son lived there for a couple of years so they are really interested in Africa. She was a teacher. She helped me to understand some of the culture."

Klopp first met Ulla Sandrock while she was working as a waitress at Oktoberfest in 2005 having moved back to Mainz from Kenya. Both had children from previous marriages and they were married within months.

"In Nairobi I had a completely free hand in education," Ulla told German newspaper *Der Spiegel* in 2008. "In Mainz, I first worked as a teacher at a special school, but immediately noticed: I can no longer make friends with the old-established methods. Everything has certain rules to follow; that drives me crazy. I'm like my husband. We 'Kloppos' need our freedoms to realise our potential."

Having left teaching to pursue a career as a children's author, her first book – *Tom and the Magic Football* in 2008 – told the story of "the fascination of the game, the longing for a distant heroic world, the common thrill and, above all, the sense of security that the child feels through the attention of the parents". Or, as Klopp – who wrote the foreword – puts it: "It's like Harry Potter but it's about football. There's no Harry Potter flying on his fucking stick – just football."

A year later, the sequel *Tom and the Magic Football in Africa* was published in which the eponymous hero and his friends travel to Africa to help save his friend Mucawe's village on Lake Malawi from demolition by a Western industrialist who wants to build a hotel complex. Drawing heavily on Ulla's own experiences of life in Kenya, it is a parable of fighting against the odds that her husband believes still applies to many of today's African players.

"What you cannot get any more is a special story which, in the good old times . . . he came from a working family, had nothing," he says. "In Europe it's difficult to find that – maybe in London it's possible, I'm not too sure. But all the African players have this story. It means they are motivated through the roof.

"It's about the story that is behind them," adds Klopp enthusiastically. "If you look at Sadio Mané – running away from home. Mo Salah: driving four and a half hours every day to training. You have these stories there. You don't have these stories here. I read an article about the influence of Mo Salah at this moment in the Arabic world – it's unbelievable!"

***

One of the best memories of my childhood is being allowed to stay up to watch England's World Cup quarter-final against Cameroon in 1990. Inspired by 38-year-old Roger Milla and his famous corner flag wiggle, the Indomitable Lions had already lived up to their nickname by beating reigning champions Argentina in the opening match of the tournament and were within seven minutes of reaching the last four before Gary Lineker equalised from the penalty spot and then scored again in extra time. Despite their defeat, however, Cameroon's success proved to be a watershed for African players in English football.

France and Portugal had a long history of raiding their former colonies for talented players for both their clubs and national teams – Moroccan-born Just Fontaine won the Golden Boot at the 1958 World Cup for the latter, followed by Mozambican Eusébio for Portugal in 1966. Yet England had remained a largely closed shop until the advent of the Premier League in 1992. Aside from exceptions like Arthur Wharton and Albert Johanneson, who were briefly feted during their careers only to fall into obscurity and alcoholism in later years, forgotten and broken by their experiences, it wasn't until the likes of Peter Ndlovu, Lucas Radebe and Yeboah exploded on to the scene in the mid-1990s that things began to change. Just as Klopp and most of Germany had fallen in love with Yeboah a few years earlier, suddenly children in Leeds, London and Leicester were attempting to emulate his two brilliant volleys against Wimbledon and Liverpool in August 1995.

A budding striker myself, I was so infatuated with him that I would spend hours playing as the Black Stars on Sensible World of Soccer, with Abedi Pelé – the father of future Premier League players André and Jordan Ayew – and Nii Lamptey providing the ammunition for the deadly Leeds frontman. As the years went by and icons like Nwankwo Kanu, Okocha and Didier Drogba became Premier League cult heroes who transcended club allegiances, my interest in African football expanded, culminating in the decision to move to South Africa ahead of the historic 2010 World Cup. I still have a shaky video I filmed on a prehistoric digital camera of Luis Suárez's infamous handball in the final minutes of extra time at Soccer City which prevented Ghana from going one step further than Cameroon by reaching the semi-finals. Seeing them eventually lose on penalties felt as painful as any of England's numerous shoot-out defeats.

As well as admiration for some of the unbelievable talents who have graced English football, though, my obsession with African football stems from stories like Arsenal's Christopher Wreh: a refugee from the brutal Liberian civil war who became the first

African to win the league title in 1998. His journey from the slums of Monrovia to the glamour of the Premier League is an exceptional example of what Klopp was referring to: somehow there is something even more compelling about those players who started out with nothing yet still achieved their dreams against all the odds.

These days, you don't have to look far for others. By March 2020, 278 Africans had played in the Premier League, scoring more than 1,000 goals since its inception in 1992. But that has only been possible due to the sacrifices of those who paved the way for superstars like Mané, Salah and Keïta. This book is an attempt to recognise the significant contribution they have all made to our game.

ONE

THE LONG WAIT

On a bright October day in 2014, a 16-foot bronze statue of Arthur Wharton – English football's first African player – was unveiled in the memorial garden of St George's Park. In attendance at the Football Association's new £120 million headquarters were some of the main beneficiaries of his proud legacy, including Viv Anderson who became the first black player to represent England's senior side 90 years after Wharton first arrived in the country from Ghana – then known as the Gold Coast.

"In a way I can relate to him . . ." said the former Nottingham Forest and Manchester United defender, his voice trailing away as he was interviewed by the FA's in-house TV channel, "but I wouldn't like to imagine what he must have gone through in the 1800s playing football."

Anderson was right. For all his experiences of racism on the terraces during the late 1970s and early 1980s when black players were routinely subjected to vicious monkey chants and worse, the discrimination Wharton encountered throughout his life – on and off the pitch – was even more degrading. Designed by acclaimed sculptor Vivien Mallock, the statue of him diving acrobatically to tip a ball over the crossbar is one of the first things current England players of all age groups and races see when they arrive at St George's Park. But the story of how it and six other replica statues – two of which now adorn the headquarters of both FIFA and UEFA – came into existence was, just like his own life and the subsequent history of African players in English football, far from simple.

For more than 60 years in a quiet corner of Edlington cemetery that was once reserved for paupers, just a few hundred metres from the busy A1(M) that connects north and south Yorkshire, the body of one of English football's most important pioneers lay in an unmarked grave. Born in Jamestown, Accra in modern-day Ghana, Wharton moved to Shoal Hill College in Staffordshire, 20 miles from where his statue now stands, in 1882 to begin his training to become a Methodist minister. He was following in the Wesleyan footsteps of his father, Reverend Henry Wharton, who became the first missionary from the Caribbean to arrive in West Africa during the 1850s.

Wharton junior was destined to follow a different path. Within eight years, he had become the first man to record ten seconds flat for the 100 yards dash before emerging as the first black professional footballer in history. Had it not been for a letter published in the *Rotherham Advertiser* in October 1996, however, his remarkable story may never have been told.

"I'd found out quite a lot about his football career by that stage through newspapers and local archives," remembers historian Phil Vasili. "Towards the end, he moved across the Pennines to Stalybridge and the archives there had a team photo with Arthur in. I got totally obsessed with him. I was spending hours in different libraries around the country. All of this was without any funding. I was working as a lecturer for the Open University so I registered the story of black footballers in English football as a PhD but then Arthur took over . . ."

In a desperate attempt to uncover more about the man who began his football career as a goalkeeper with Darlington before turning out for all-conquering Preston North End, Rotherham and Sheffield United among others, Vasili sent out a barrage of letters to newspapers in the areas he had played in appealing for anyone who knew Wharton's wife, Emma Lister, to come forward.

By chance, a 65-year-old from Rotherham called Sheila Leeson happened to see his request. She was the niece of Emma Lister, who had died the previous year. Just a few weeks earlier, Leeson had discovered some intriguing photographs in her recently deceased mother's attic of a young black man with a moustache standing next to a large distinctive trophy. With help from her son-in-law, research revealed that it was none other than the prestigious HH Prince Hassan Pacha Challenge Trophy, awarded to its 100 yards champion by the Amateur Athletic Association of England.

"At first, Sheila didn't know anything about her connection to Arthur," says Vasili. "There was a lot of family folklore that had been passed down through generations. At first, Sheila had no idea that he was her grandfather. She found out that her Aunt Emma, who was Arthur's wife, was not speaking to her grandmother because she had an affair with Arthur and had produced three children. That was why he ended up being buried without a headstone because it was a family that had been divided."

After responding to Vasili's letter with the news that she had found what he was looking for, Leeson was invited to the launch of a new group called Football Unites, Racism Divides (FURD) in Sheffield in 1997, where former Everton and then Sheffield United manager Howard Kendall was the special guest. She revealed that they had identified Wharton's final resting place as the cemetery in Edlington.

"It was the start of the whole thing because that gave us the impetus to decide that we were going to get a proper gravestone for him," recalls FURD's founder, Howard Holmes. "Within a year we had enough to do it. Some of the money came from fans and the rest came from the PFA."

But that was only the beginning. In 1998, aided by research begun almost 20 years earlier by Ray Jenkins – who had lectured on African history at Staffordshire University – Vasili's book *The First Black Footballer: Arthur Wharton 1865–1930: An Absence of Memory* finally told the story of an incredible sporting career that had so nearly been consigned to history.

"Fergie sent along Dwight Yorke and Andy Cole to the book launch and they didn't want to be there. They had faces like smacked bums," Vasili remembers of the former Manchester United strikers. "I don't think they really knew why they were there at that point but then they started looking around the exhibition and realised the significance of it. We gave them a couple of books and by the end of it they had got really interested in it. They ended up staying a bit afterwards to talk to me. That weekend they played against Wimbledon and scored three goals between them as they won 5-1. Afterwards they said, 'We went to this book launch about Arthur Wharton and it really inspired us.'"

***

A career as a sportsman wasn't really an option for most people if, like Wharton, you happened to have been born in Africa during the 1860s. But it was even less likely if you had black skin. His father, Reverend Henry Wharton, who had moved to modern-day Ghana from Grenada a year before Arthur's birth in October 1865, was the son of a Scottish merchant who had settled in Grenada and married a local woman of African descent. Reverend

Wharton would later become the first African-Caribbean to hold the post of General Superintendent of the Gold Coast district of the Wesleyan Missionary Society and arrived in West Africa at a time when the mortality rate of missionaries was extremely high due to diseases like malaria and yellow fever.

His biography was published in 1875 – two years after his death – which explained that Arthur's father had married Annie Florence Grant, whose mother, Ama Egyiriba, was a member of the Fante Ghanaian royal family. Her father had been a Scottish trader called John C. Grant, who was part of one of the most prominent families in the capital city of Accra. It turned out that Wharton's uncle, Francis Chapman Grant, had been the proprietor of the *Gold Coast Times* and an important community leader who had organised campaigns against colonisation by Britain in the 1870s. "Wharton therefore embodied, and was a product of, those destinations of the triangular slave trade route encompassing Britain, West Africa and the Caribbean," wrote Vasili in *The First Black Footballer.*

From an early age, the expectation was that Arthur would follow his father into the Church in a society where young men were encouraged to seek "salvation" through "the trinity of the Cs: commerce, Christianity and civilised education, rather than on the games field." Immediately after Reverend Wharton's death, Grant – one of whose descendants was the former Charlton, Luton and Millwall striker Kim – took Wharton under his wing and arranged for both him and his elder sister, Clara, to move to England to continue their education. Four years at the Burlington Road School taught them both the sensibilities of Victorian life before returning to the Gold Coast at the age of 14. Three years later, Wharton was back. But unlike some of his elder brothers and cousins who attended the celebrated Wesleyan institution Queen's College in Taunton, Somerset, he found himself in the heart of industrial Staffordshire instead.

Shoal Hill College in Cannock may have been chosen due to the presence of headmaster Samuel G. Gwynne – a former teacher at Queen's who had moved north a few years earlier having taught some of Grant's own sons. Three Grants were already there, so the arrival of a dark-skinned gangly teenager in 1882 would not have raised too many eyebrows. Ill health forced Gwynne to close down the school two years later and Wharton moved to Cleveland College in Darlington to finish his formal education. But it was in the north-east town known for its association with the birth of the modern railway system that he displayed an aptitude for a different kind of pursuit.

Freed from the restrictions on sporting activity back home, Wharton had played football and cricket for Cannock, scoring a duck on his cricket debut but later going on to captain the side despite still being a teenager. He soon established himself as a first-choice goalkeeper for Darlington's football club, who had been founded in 1883 and would go on to become one of the original members of the Northern League. Wharton was known for his unusual approach, which included a penchant for punching the ball long distances away from danger and the ability to make spectacular saves. According to Vasili, the father of Herbert Burgin, a lifelong Darlington fan, "used to talk enthusiastically about the exploits of 'Darkie' Wharton in the Darlington goalmouth. He was a very athletic and energetic goalkeeper and became famous for crouching in the corner of the goal until the last minute when he would literally spring into action, diving across the goal to make fantastic saves."

The choice of position seemed strange given his undoubted prowess as a sprinter, which had been established during a series of handicap races held in Darlington not long after his arrival in the north-east. With prizes ranging from a clock to a fruit bowl, Wharton's success encouraged his trainer, Manny Harbron, to enter him into the 100 yards dash at the prestigious Amateur

Athletic Association Championship at Stamford Bridge in 1886. His surprise victory in a time of ten seconds flat made him the first black athlete to win a AAA title and the unofficial world record holder – a forerunner to Jesse Owens, Carl Lewis and Usain Bolt. A song was even composed to celebrate his victory, although Vasili admits in his book that frustratingly the words were never recorded. Another song, this time performed by his teammates to mark his outstanding displays for Darlington Cricket Club, "received cheers of the heartiest, loudest and most enthusiastic in character" in a display of appreciation "of an athlete by athletes".

Wharton's exploits on the track and on the field became big news in the emerging sporting landscape of late 1880s Britain. A series of 'challenges' against leading rivals took place around the country as he dedicated himself to the art of running fast, leading to him retaining his AAA title in 1887 and posing for the picture which Sheila Leeson would come across in her mother's attic almost 110 years later. Yet while his football career also flourished as Wharton was snapped up by Preston North End – the era's most dominant club in 1886 – his academic studies took a back seat. "He chose, as I'm sure most of us would have done at his stage in life, the sweat, dirt and exhilaration of triumph and glory instead of a safe and pensionable post," wrote Vasili in his book *Colouring Over the White Line.* That went explicitly against the path chosen for him by his family back in Accra – a decision that would come to haunt Wharton in later years.

For the meantime, though, he was a celebrated figure of the period, even if his fame also came at a cost. The presence of a black sportsman in the public eye at the height of Britain's empire did not play well with many people and Wharton faced constant reminders that he was not considered an equal. At one athletics meeting he overheard two competitors discussing their new rival, with one boasting, "We can beat a blooming nigger any time." Confronting them face to face to see if they felt the same about their chances in a boxing match, the pair turned down his invitation. Wharton's first victory at Stamford Bridge was not welcomed by everyone in the influential British press either. He was described as "by no means a representative Englishman in appearance . . . he was a brunette of pronounced complexion" who possessed an unusually long heel that was described as typical "of men of colour". It was those kinds of attitudes which would follow Wharton to his grave.

"The local newspapers played him up as a hero because it brought kudos to the area," says Vasili. "But the national newspapers, especially *The Times*, often referred to his ethnicity very early on. A lot spoke about his phrenology and the size of his brain and things like that. It's really sad to see that kind of attitude after he had just won a race."

***

If the reception from his rival athletes and some members of the press was extremely hostile, Wharton's move to Preston had at first provided some encouragement that he would be accepted by his peers. Renowned for secretly paying their players before professionalism was finally introduced in 1886, they reached the semi-finals of the FA Cup with him in goal, only to be beaten by West Bromwich Albion. Wharton was subsequently recommended by a well-known journalist for an international call-up – recognition that would have beaten Anderson's record as the first black man to represent England by more than 90 years had it ever come to fruition.

Preston went one better the following season, reaching the FA Cup final at London's Kennington Oval where they were again beaten by West Brom before going on to become the first side ever to complete the league and cup double in 1889, remaining unbeaten throughout the season. Unlike his teammates in the original 'Invincibles', however, Wharton cannot claim to have beaten Arsène Wenger, Thierry Henry and the rest to the feat because he had left Preston at the start of 1888 to sign a professional contract with Rotherham Town. It was the beginning of a five-year spell with the club which began life in the Midland League before progressing to the newly formed Division Two.

Salaries were obviously nothing in comparison to today's superstars, however, and Wharton's move to Rotherham was an indication that he had made a big decision. While his brother, Charles, was already established with a job in the colonial government back home, becoming a professional sportsman was confirmation that he had turned his back on his family's wishes once and for all. Wharton also announced that he intended to run for money as a "pedestrian", news that was taken in spite of his mother and relatives being "strongly opposed". His hand had been forced somewhat by the closure of Cleveland College that summer but the lure of the track and pitch were too much to resist.

"He was not fulfilling the historical obligation that the West African elite were meant to," explains Vasili. "Men of his class were meant to go back to the Gold Coast and get involved in business, religion or emancipation. Becoming a professional sportsman at the time was a career that was totally populated by working-class people so you had this situation of a very educated black man being more educated than those around him but being the odd one out, because of his class and colour."

In September 1892, Wharton was part of the Rotherham team that was thrashed 7-1 in newly formed Liverpool's first-ever match at Anfield following the departure of previous tenants Everton due to a dispute with owner John Houlding. A few months later, as well as continuing to keep goal every Saturday at Clifton Lane, Wharton was also the landlord of the Albert

Tavern in Rotherham and had begun putting down roots in the south Yorkshire town. His application to join the Gold Coast Government Service that summer therefore appears surprising, especially given that he had married local girl Emma Lister three years earlier in September 1890. The rejection letter uncovered by Vasili from Gold Coast governor F.M. Hodson revealed that he had been turned down for three principal reasons – his "inappropriate status as ex-100 yards amateur champion runner of England, the drunkenness of his brother, Charles and the 'life of ill-repute' of his sister, Clara".

"The irony was that by the 1920s, being a good sportsman was seen as a really good thing to have on your CV," says Vasili. "The very things that were a hindrance to his career in the 1880s became an asset many years later."

With his family now further away than ever before, Wharton turned to his new wife for solace. And her sister. Minnie Wharton Proctor was born on 6 May 1891 to Martha Lister. It is not known why her uncle's name appeared on the birth certificate, although it was later removed. Minnie's sister, Nora, arrived a month after Wharton's application to leave the country was rejected. Sheila Leeson, who is one of Nora's daughters, believes the two events were connected. "Emma didn't have any children but she was banished from the family and we never knew why," she admitted. "It was a secret that my mother took with her to her grave. My mother, her sister and her brother Ben were the three children of Arthur."

While his athletic career took a back seat when he reached his late 20s – a result of what Vasili believes was his growing propensity for alcohol, easily accessible given his status as a landlord – Wharton continued to play football at a high level for more than a decade. At Sheffield United, he was the back-up goalkeeper to William 'Fatty' Foulke, who would go on to represent England, and became the first non-white player to appear in a First Division match against Sunderland in 1895. Later that year, with his stock now beginning to fall as he approached his 30th birthday, Wharton signed for Stalybridge Rovers and also joined the Cheshire town's cricket club. His versatility in several sporting disciplines was not unusual at a time when C.B. Fry represented England at both cricket and football, as well as equalling the world record for the long jump, although Wharton remained a celebrated – if still mysterious – figure in the local press.

"Stalybridge have bagged a real nigger as goalkeeper in Wharton, who is none other than the 'Darkie' who used to guard the North End citadel," wrote the correspondent of the local newspaper on the day he joined. Rather than being a racial slur, however, this term was often applied to describe him in affectionate terms – a reflection of Victorian attitudes that treated the few black players of the era as an 'exoticism'. Whether the same can be said for Wharton's experiences in wider society is doubtful though.

"The attitude to Arthur's colour was a great burden on his shoulders," believes Vasili. "But it's a riches to rags story and the search for identity is at the heart of it. He was almost alienated from both cultures: in West Africa he was seen as European, in Britain he was seen as black."

Jenkins uncovered numerous occasions when he was racially abused during matches by supporters, while newspapers continued to refer to him in language that would be considered derogatory in the 21st century. According to Vasili, he "was not a man to accept such things with a shrug of the shoulder and a forced smile – at Rotherham he had numerous battles with the management committees and at Stalybridge and Ashton."

Based in the market town three miles up the road, Ashton North End had fielded a certain Herbert Chapman in attack the season before his arrival in 1897. But while Chapman went on to lead first Huddersfield and then Arsenal to league titles as a manager, Wharton opened a tobacconist's shop on Old Street and also occasionally turned out on the wing for the club in the Lancashire League – finally using some of his natural speed to his advantage on the football pitch. A series of financial problems forced North End to fold in 1899 and he returned to Stalybridge, subsequently joining his eighth and final club, Stockport County, in 1901.

At the age of 36, his best days were long behind him but Wharton still managed to make several appearances in the Second Division for County, scoring two goals. Unfortunately that did not prevent them from finishing third from bottom, forcing the club to apply for re-election to remain in the league. They were allowed to stay, but Wharton's football career had reached the end. Vasili believes years of alcohol abuse eventually took its toll, even if he remained an active sportsman until well into his 40s after moving back to Yorkshire in search of work.

"I don't know when it started but certainly there was evidence of it during his football career," he says. "One newspaper report says that he was expected to play but he was 'otherwise disposed' and I think a few times his performances may have suffered. The evidence is circumstantial but it's almost certain that he did have a drink problem because it's mentioned so many times. That's probably why he became a publican in the end. We went to the British Legion in New Edlington and met two guys who had remembered Arthur when they were kids. He was still running around the track in his late 40s!"

A court listing which described how Emma Wharton had been beaten up indicated some of the problems Wharton encountered after his retirement. Having chosen to turn his back on his well-heeled family in Africa, the reality of working-class life in a northern English industrial town must have been something of a shock. Desperate to support his family, they made the move back across the Pennines in 1911 and he became a haulage hand at Yorkshire Main Colliery, which opened two years later. With war raging in Europe, he was also a member of the Home Guard but was too old to serve on the front line – unlike Walter Tull, the grandson of a Barbadian slave who played for Tottenham and Northampton before being killed during the Spring Offensive of 1918.

Wharton's own death came 12 years later at Springwell Sanatorium in Balby. Taken around 1928, the last known picture of him on his way to a shift down the pit showed a puffed-up face ravaged by years of excessive drinking, with epithelioma – a form of cancer – and syphilis later listed as the causes of death. It was a far cry from the powerful and lean athlete who had posed with the Prince Hassan trophy 40 years earlier and had been tipped for an international call-up. Unfortunately, that fate was to become a recurring theme for many of the first African players to arrive in English football.

"Arthur embodies the struggle," admits Vasili. "Had he continued on the path chosen for him, he would have probably had a really successful and fulfilling life in the civil service or as a missionary. But because he chose his own path, he ended up in a pauper's grave with nothing. There are some parallels with players who came later, there's no doubt about that."

***

Even now, Shaun Campbell still has to pinch himself about the events of 10 September 2008. "Weeks after I remember sitting up in bed and saying to my wife, 'Was I really on stage with Stevie Wonder?'" he recalls. "It only took me 56 hours from thinking of the concept to actually getting on stage with him. It was remarkable really."

A musician and artist from Leeds with Barbadian ancestry, Campbell studied ballet and contemporary dance in London but came to visit Darlington for a week in his 20s and has stayed ever since. He had come across Arthur Wharton's story while he was giving a talk for Black History Month at Middlesbrough Town Hall a few months earlier.

"I was reading a brochure about Arthur and trying to remember when I had heard his name before. Somebody asked me to play 'Redemption Song' and throughout the whole song I was thinking, 'Where have I heard that name before?' Just at the end I remembered it was a friend of mine had mentioned it to me but I'd never done anything about it. I went and looked further into it and I couldn't believe this man had achieved so much and had received so little recognition. I thought, 'My God, I've got to do something.' So I went back to my shop and I picked up this piece of very heavily grained wood. I'd already started putting some marks on it by just following the grain of the wood and I'd already painted a Scottish saltire. It was fate because of Arthur's Scottish heritage."

A customer came in and asked what he was working on. Campbell explained it was a tribute to English football's first African player who had died penniless and forgotten. Suitably impressed, the customer made contact with local newspaper the *Northern Echo*. "The story came out in the paper under the headline 'Local businessman starts campaign to honour Darlington sporting hero' but that wasn't strictly true," Campbell laughs at the memory. "I hadn't actually started a campaign. So that's how it all began."

By then, it was almost ten years since Vasili's book had finally established Wharton's name in history. But aside from the new gravestone in a more prominent part of Edlington cemetery and a few talks about his life organised by FURD, there had been precious little attempt to honour his memory.

"Black Americans are very proactive at championing their heroes. But the black community in Britain is much more reserved and less committed to stirring the waters," says Campbell. "I had to create momentum. I had to kick doors in. Sometimes tapping isn't enough. It was a troubled journey with a lot of sacrifice and even some abuse. In a meeting with my MP, Jenny Chapman, the local chairman of Darlington Cricket Club and the body which is in charge of Feethams (the former ground where Arthur made his name, which was demolished in 2006 after falling into disrepair) sat next to me and literally used this term 'nigger in a woodpile'. When this sort of thing happens it has a negative impact on you and you have to work out ways to challenge that form of innate racism that some people have."

Campbell enlisted the support of former Sunderland defender Gary Bennett and legendary Leeds striker Brian Deane as his campaign to have a statue of Wharton erected at either the former site of Feethams or outside the newly built Darlington Arena on the outskirts of town built up momentum. "It was difficult because who was I? I'm basically just a shopkeeper so I had to get the ear of my local community first," he remembers. "I wanted them to understand what Arthur should have meant to Darlington. His most significant achievement – that of beating the 100 yards record in 1886 – was run under the banner of Darlington."

Born in Nkawkaw, eastern Ghana, in 1975, George Boateng grew up in Rotterdam after moving to the Netherlands with his family as a child. The midfielder signed for Coventry City in December 1997 and had spent more than a decade in English football by the time he joined newly promoted Hull City in the summer of 2008, having played in the UEFA Cup final for Middlesbrough two years earlier. It was then that Campbell made contact with Boateng in an attempt to get him behind the Arthur Wharton campaign. To his surprise, he agreed. "In bringing in George, I was saying, 'Hey look, we've got the support of a football superstar and he's willing to support the campaign to celebrate your rich history and past.'"

Even with a Dutch international in his corner, though, Campbell still struggled to make the breakthrough. That's when he had his brainwave. Knowing that Wonder had collaborated with UB40 for their cover of his song 'Never Had a Dream Come True', he made contact with their label manager, Ray Williams of Crumbs Music. Williams discovered and helped to launch Elton John's career in the late 1960s. By then, he was living in North Carolina and had become one of the leading film and television music producers on the planet.

"I wouldn't be in the position I am today if it wasn't for the faith he showed in me," admits Campbell. "I left a message and he called me back to say it was a fascinating story. It turned out that his grandfather was Billy Death, who played for Sunderland, so he had an interest in football. I asked whether it would be possible to speak to Stevie Wonder so he gave me the number for somebody who I could get in touch with."

Incredibly, having made contact with him via Keith Harris of Motown Records, Wonder agreed to meet Campbell before his show to discuss how he could help. But with less than 24 hours until he was due on stage in Birmingham, Hurricane Ike – a Category 4 storm that caused $37 billion worth of damage to the eastern seaboard of the United States and the Caribbean – meant he was still in New York. Eventually, he arrived in England's second city with just an hour to spare, not making it to the venue until 45 minutes after he was meant to have started. Campbell and Boateng, who had flown in especially for the concert from Amsterdam, where he was being treated for an injury, were waiting backstage and only had a brief moment to introduce themselves.

"I remember quickly writing down on a piece of brown paper all the salient points to do with Arthur Wharton – what he stood for and how he had been almost forgotten," Campbell recalls. "Stevie went on stage and did a few songs before he started talking about Arthur. George had tears in eyes. He mentioned the foundation, which we weren't at the time. So Stevie was the founder of the foundation. If it wasn't for him putting it out there in front of 12,000 people, I wouldn't have thought of it. We were then invited on to the stage and I went on and spoke a little to the crowd."

The reaction was unbelievable. 'Wonder-ful support for Wharton statue' proclaimed the *Northern Echo*'s front page that week. "To be on the same stage as Stevie Wonder, celebrating Arthur Wharton, is testament to how far the campaign has come," said Boateng. But that was just the start of a journey that would end with the unveiling of the statue outside St George's Park.

"It gave me a level of confidence that I didn't have before," says Campbell. "If it was good enough for Stevie Wonder then it was good enough for anyone whose door I knocked on. What I didn't want to happen to me was what had seemingly happened to Phil, Howard and everyone else who was championing Arthur and to get complacent. I don't mean that in any disingenuous way, I just mean the natural energy ran out slightly, obviously because they were doing other things as well. But it's not about any of us. It's about Arthur Wharton."

Having registered the Arthur Wharton Foundation in the weeks after the concert with the primary aim of promoting racial harmony through sport, his first stop was UEFA's headquarters in Switzerland. They donated £17,500 to the cause which allowed Campbell to step up his planned educational campaign to spread the word about Wharton's unique achievements. His message even reached the Football Association and in March 2011 they invited him and Sheila Leeson to Wembley to be guests of honour for the friendly between England and Ghana, who nine months earlier had come within a Luis Suárez handball of becoming the first African side to reach the World Cup semi-finals.

"At first, I thought having UEFA's support behind me would make it easier to approach the Football Association based on my understanding of what they were like," Campbell says. "A lot of people doubted whether I could get the FA to pay tribute to a black man but that gave me extra motivation. But I never had any resistance from them. [Then FA chairman] Lord Triesman was behind me straight away but then he left and I had to forge a new relationship with David Bernstein. He was behind it from the off and we presented him with their statue at the House of Commons."

It was officially unveiled by the FA in a ceremony before the match, which ended in a 1-1 draw thanks to Asamoah Gyan's injury-time equaliser. "It feels absolutely marvellous," admitted Leeson afterwards.

Later that year, FURD received funding from the National Lottery to carry out school, community and wider awareness-raising work about Wharton's story and achievements, while a blue plaque in his honour was unveiled at the Tameside Stadium in Ashton in September 2012. Campbell was not finished there. Having commissioned seven of the statues because Wharton had once played a marathon seven games in ten days for charity to help feed the poor in Darlington, he went about delivering them to the doors of some of the most powerful institutions in the game including UEFA, the Professional Footballers' Association and Ghana's Football Association.

In June 2012, Campbell travelled to Zurich to present then FIFA president Sepp Blatter with their memorial to the first African player to play professional football. "At the first time of asking FIFA came on board," he recalls. "Later on, we needed funding for the big statue at St George's Park and so I got in touch with Greg Dyke. He was happy to support us so I can only say that the FA from day one have been excellent."

That afternoon in October 2014 was the culmination of

more than 20 years' hard work that started with Ray Jenkins, subsequently consumed the lives of Phil Vasili, FURD's Howard Holmes and, finally, Campbell. "The demands on my time have been ridiculous," he admits. "I've had to foot a lot of the bill myself and that ultimately cost me my business. I was so focused on Arthur that I took my eyes off the ball. But that was a sacrifice I was willing to make. I don't think anyone realises quite what sacrifices I made. But we got there in the end."

At the unveiling of the statue, David Sheepshanks, chairman of St George's Park, described it as a "historic" but also a "future" day. "[It] is going to inspire a whole new generation of young players and in particular young coaches to want to reach for the top and be the best they possibly can be," he said. "When you look at what this man achieved it's simply extraordinary. Imagine the courage he had to display to achieve what he did in those days. We often talk about how hard it is for young people from black and Asian minority backgrounds to get into top jobs today, so imagine what it was like then. Certainly not enough people know about his story and we're going to embrace it in the tour programmes of all the young people and schools that come here."

For Vasili, who had a written a screenplay with university friend Irvine Welsh in 1996 that was commissioned by Channel 4 but never made, it was confirmation that Wharton had taken his rightful place in the history books. "I feel privileged and extremely lucky," he reflects. "You get a warm feeling inside when someone mentions Arthur because now he is getting the recognition he deserves. The best thing about it is that I have a picture of Pelé, the man I've adored for my whole life, holding a copy of my book."

The story is still not over. As well as a trophy to honour Wharton that was presented to the International Association of Athletics Federations (IAAF) in 2013, Bolt is among a number of celebrities who will feature in a forthcoming Netflix documentary about his predecessor's life. Campbell also has kept two of the smaller statues initially produced in reserve. One is earmarked for what he calls an "extraordinary individual", with Yaya Touré, Bolt and Colin Kaepernick among the names to have come under consideration so far. "There's a few people we've got in mind but we're waiting for the sportsperson who stands head and shoulders above everyone," he explains.

The remaining statue is intended for Wonder, who helped to turn his ambitious dream into reality. "This is the year," insists Campbell, although he has already decided who will present the award. "There's nobody better than Barack Obama to do that and I've got my links for him."

TWO

THE BOY FROM BAMBALI

"Of course, I am very proud of Sadio," stressed Mady Touré down a crackly mobile phone line from his home in Paris. "But he is not my player. He's my son. Today we talk about Messi and Neymar but honestly I believe Sadio Mané can be as good as them."

Speaking to Touré from my flat in Forest Hill, south London in October 2014, I did a double-take. "Did he really just say that?!"

My admittedly somewhat rusty French had already been put to the test by Mané himself two years earlier when I met him for the first time while covering the Senegal team at the 2012 Olympics. Based on the lush playing fields of the Manchester Grammar School ahead of their opening match against hosts Great Britain at Old Trafford, he could not keep a straight face when I attempted to interview him after one training session. "At that time I didn't speak English," he laughs now at the memory.

The 20-year-old would end up joining Red Bull Salzburg from Metz after the tournament and was also brimming with cockiness in a brilliant performance two days later as they surprised Stuart Pearce's hosts by drawing 1-1. Featuring a number of players who would also later establish themselves in the Premier League including Cheikhou Kouyaté and Idrissa Gueye and managed by former Birmingham City midfielder Aliou Cissé, they ended up being eliminated 4-2 after extra-time after a thrilling match against eventual gold medal winners Mexico at Wembley.

"The Olympics was a really good experience for me and my teammates," recalls Mané. "I had never played for the national team before so it was very important. I think that was a really big step in my career because it made many people know me and helped my transfer to Red Bull."

Eighteen months earlier, he had arrived in Europe after being spotted by Metz youth coach Olivier Perrin during a match for Touré's Génération Foot academy in Dakar. A former player himself in France who was born and raised in Guinea, Touré's career came to a sudden halt following a knee injury in the mid-1990s before – thanks partly to funding from his friend, Youssou N'Dour – establishing his facility on the outskirts of Senegal's capital city in 2000.

The singer best known in the United Kingdom for his 1994 collaboration with Neneh Cherry on '7 Seconds' also spent time as special advisor to Senegal president Macky Sall after briefly threatening to stand against him in the elections but recognised an opportunity when he saw one.

Dedicated to Touré's father, Amadou, the academy strives to help children from deprived backgrounds follow their dreams of football stardom by offering a place to stay and a guaranteed three meals every day – not always a given in a country where 46.7 per cent of the 15 million population are estimated to live in poverty.

"I started with a table and two balls," Touré remembers. "I started from scratch and I embarked on a project that was a little crazy. Few people believed in this project during the launch. I had my road map and my goals to reach. Before the creation of the academy, when I brought young African players to Europe, I was always told that they were missing something. So I created the academy to bridge those gaps and give the players the best conditions to succeed in Europe."

The results have been nothing short of spectacular. A partnership established with Metz in 2003 – the year after Bruno Metsu's Senegal side reached the quarter-finals of the World Cup in Japan and South Korea – has enabled more than 30 players to establish careers at European clubs including Papiss Cissé and rising star Ismaïla Sarr, who joined Watford for a club record £30 million fee on the eve of the 2019/20 season. As well as the Diambars academy which was founded in 2003 by local businessman Saer Seck with help from Senegal-born Arsenal captain Patrick Vieira, it has helped the country become the 16th-most prolific exporter of players in the world, with an astonishing 203 now plying their trade in 147 leagues around the globe.

For now at least, though, for the children playing football on every street corner of the football-obsessed nation, there is only one player they aspire to be.

***

Sadio Mané's journey to becoming one of the best players in the world a little more than a decade after leaving his home village is a remarkable story of persistence and dedication that makes just about anything seem possible. Born in Sédhiou in the remote Casamance region that is 500 miles south of Dakar but cut off from the rest of the country by The Gambia, in those days, it was easier to access Bambali by boat than road, with the River Casamance close to the disputed border with Guinea- Bissau to the south. Giant mangrove trees and paddy fields dot the landscape until you reach the United Nations-protected Foret du Boudie – home to endangered Guinean baboons and the Cyclops roundleaf bat – with the region's fertile soil traditionally having produced half of Senegal's rice, cotton and corn.

An independence struggle led by the Movement of Democratic Forces of Casamance which began in 1982 has left thousands of people unemployed, unskilled or displaced from their villages, with thousands more killed in the conflict. In 2012, the World Bank estimated that 68.3 per cent of families in the Sédhiou province were living in poverty, with almost 60 per cent of those under the age of 30 unemployed.

"Life was hard there," Mané recalled in the documentary Made in Senegal, which was released in April 2020. "You could only become a farmer. There is no other work there."

Mané father's was an Imam at Bambali's mosque in a country where 90 per cent of the population is Muslim. By the age of seven, his son was already showing the skills that would lead his friends at school to christen him 'Ballonbuwa' or ball wizard, even if they often lacked even the most basic equipment. "We had a really hard time getting hold of a football. Sometimes we picked grapefruit and tried to play with them. Since I was two or three years old, I remember always being with the ball."

Yet it was as he prepared for a kickabout with his friends after class one day that Mané's life changed forever.

"We were about to play on the field when a cousin approached me and said, 'Sadio, your father passed away'," he recalls. "I replied, 'oh really? He's joking..' I couldn't really understand it. Before he passed away, he had this kind of sickness for weeks. We brought him some traditional medicine and it kept him calm for three or four months. But the next time it didn't work and because there was no hospital in Bambali they had to take him to the next village to see if they had medicine that could save his life. But it was not the case."

The political situation in Casamance meant it was too dangerous for his father's body to be brought home and he was buried in the neighbouring village without any of his family present.

"I remember when I was young my father was always saying how proud he was of me. He was a man with a big heart. When he died, it had a big impact on me and the rest of my family,' adds Mané. "I said to myself: 'Now I have to do my best to help my mother.' That's a hard thing to deal with when you are so young."

His growing passion for football would eventually prove to be his salvation. In 2002, when Senegal shocked reigning champions and former colonial masters France in the opening match of the World Cup in Seoul, an awestruck 10-year-old had woken up early to watch them do it.

"There was big excitement in the village," Mané recalls, "But it was already only football for me before that."

The Teranga Lions emulated Cameroon's run to the last eight in 1990, equalling the furthest any African side had ever progressed, before falling to Turkey after extra-time in Osaka.

"None of them came from an academy," remembers Seck, the Diambars founder who is now also a vice-president of the Senegalese Football Association. "A few came from France but most were players who had come from clubs in Senegal and made it to Europe. It was amazing. This shows that Senegal has enough talent. But we have very talented boys."

Senegal's success persuaded Liverpool manager Gérard Houllier to purchase Salif Diao and El-Hadji Diouf after the tournament. Neither exactly lived up to expectations: Diouf was banned for spitting at a supporter during a UEFA Cup match against Celtic in 2003 and left Anfield two years later under a cloud having scored only six goals in 80 appearances and fallen out with almost everyone – including Steven Gerrard and Jamie Carragher – while Diao moved to Stoke in 2007 having spent the previous two years out on loan. But they had showed Mané what was possible.

There was only one problem: his family. Just as Wharton had been 120 years earlier, Mané was urged to concentrate on his studies and forget his dream of becoming a professional.

"His father was an Imam, which means you have to be a good example," explained childhood friend Luc Djiboune. "You're not allowed to play football. Instead you are forced to go to school and become successful."

"It was a tough, tough, tough moment for me," Mané adds. "But I was convinced that was what I wanted to do."

Eventually, after much persuasion, his family allowed him to make the 15-mile journey to Sédhiou to play in the navétanes – a series of sporting events that take place in the rainy season and was established in the 1970s by former long jumper and IAAF president Lamine Diack. Widely acknowledged as the best young player in the region, when a friend suggested that Mané try his luck with a friends team in Dakar two months before he turned 16 it was no surprise that he jumped at the chance. "Just hearing that name Dakar, I thought, 'That will be great for me. I'll seize my opportunity'. In my head Dakar was like Paris. But there was no way my family would let me go."

With help from Djiboune, who was sworn to secrecy, Mané devised a plan to catch a bus to the Gambian border at 6am one morning before making his way to Dakar.

"I prepared everything down to the minute, knowing that I did not have any money at all," he told France Football in 2019. "At sunset, I hid in the tall grass, in front of my house, my sports bag with my things so that I wasn't surprised when leaving. And early the following morning, at around 6 o'clock, I brushed my teeth and didn't even take a shower. I walked for a long time to meet up with a friend who loaned me some money so that I could take the bus to Dakar."

Mané used his student ID at the border because he had yet to be issued with a passport before making his way to the capital, where he stayed with the family of his contact for two weeks. Back home, his absence hadn't gone unnoticed.

"My parents were looking for me everywhere," he remembered. "They were convinced that my best friend knew."

Djiboune refused to tell them anything but he was eventually forced to return home after coming to an agreement with his family.

"His mother was very worried and the family were not at all happy," his uncle Ibrahim told the Athletic website in November 2019. "Sadio said to us, 'I want to be a footballer. I believe I can become a star. I want to show you I can do it.'"

"The day I returned to the village was the worst of my life," Mané says in Made in Senegal. "I felt hate for my family. I said, 'I'm returning to the village on one condition: that I only have one more year of school. That's it'. And they respected my decision. It was tough because I didn't have anyone behind me to push me to achieve my dream. But I never stopped dreaming. It was really brave to leave my family in the village and go to Dakar to try and be successful but I knew that i could be successful. After that, my family started to take it more seriously and knew that I didn't want to do anything else. They knew they had no choice so they helped me."

"I don't know exactly how it worked with Sadio but obviously he had to cheat a little at home to tell them this and then doing that," admits Jürgen Klopp. "But that probably makes his story even more special."

At the end of the school year, Mané's uncles arranged for their nephew to attend a trial at Génération Foot, although he remembered coach Abdou Diatta was not impressed by his tattered old boots.

"I will never forget this, and it is funny now, but when I went to try out there was an older man that looked at me like I was in the wrong place. He asked me, 'Are you here for the test?' I said I was. He asked me, 'With those boots? Look at them. How can you play in them?' They were bad, really bad – torn and old. Then he said, 'And with those shorts? You don't even have proper football shorts?' I told him what I came with was the best I had, and I only wanted to play – to show myself. When I got on the pitch, you could see the surprise on his face. He came to me and said, 'I'm picking you straight away. You'll play in my team.'"

Touré was also impressed by his young protégé's commitment to training and it was not long before he was firmly established as one of the academy's most promising young players.

"Sadio was an attentive and very wise young boy," he says.

"When his story was explained to me - how he came from a poor family and had lost his father - I treated him like my child. He knew there was only football to help him."

In Made in Senegal, Perrin recalls watching Mané for the first time and describes how he intercepted a ball in his team's penalty area before running the entire length the pitch before providing the assist for a goal. "It almost looked like a video game. It wasn't normal. It just wasn't normal."

***

Metz's renowned youth system has previously produced international stars such as Robert Pirès, Emmanuel Adebayor and Louis Saha. Yet Mané's dream of following in their footsteps was almost shattered within weeks of his arrival in northeastern France on 11 January 2011. Having initially signed a six-month internship contract, he made his debut for the club's youth team as a substitute but was withdrawn after just 20 minutes. "He couldn't accelerate... he was unrecognisable. I thought is it the cold or what?' But he said nothing," Perrin says.

It turned out that Mané had been carrying a serious hernia injury he had picked up in Senegal while still at Génération Foot and need an operation immediately.

"I feared that if i told them they might send me back to Africa," remembers Mané. "Olivier Perrin was yelling at me. I felt humiliated. I entered the changing room and cried like a mad man. It could have been the end of my career."

When Mané eventually returned eight months later, Metz were struggling at the foot of Ligue 2 and in desperate need of inspiration. He made his professional debut as a substitute in January 2012 against Bastia alongside future international teammate Kalidou Koulibaly, with he giant defender born to Senegalese parents in eastern France having taken the new arrival under his wing.

Thirteen months older but still developing into the commanding player he would become at Napoli after moving to Italy via Belgium, Koulibaly had been jettisoned by Metz at the age of 15 for being "too introverted", in the words of the club's academy head Denis Schaeffer. He returned two years later having cut his teeth in the rough and tumble environment of France's amateur leagues playing for local side Saint-Dié and had been established in the first team for more than a year when Mané joined the club.

Having initially started in the reserves, Metz's struggles prompted coach Dominique Bijotat – the son of Algerian immigrants and who had represented France eight times during his own playing career – to turn to the teenage Senegalese forward. The 5-2 defeat on his debut against Bastia began a disastrous run of form that would eventually lead to Metz being relegated to the third tier for the first time in their history. Koulibaly's broken foot was the catalyst, with the defender moving to Genk at the end of the season.

"I think that this experience was good for them, even if it was in an unfavourable context," admitted Bijotat in 2018. "They developed psychological qualities that might not have happened if they hadn't suffered in the same way."

With 12 starts and 19 appearances in total as he turned 20 at the end of the season, Mané had already caught the eye of scouts from several teams including nouveau-riche Austrians Red Bull Salzburg as he linked up with Senegal's Olympic squad in Manchester. Coached by Cissé – the tough-tackling midfielder who was the heartbeat of the 2002 World Cup side and went on to play for Birmingham and Portsmouth – they were making their debut at the Under-23 tournament having defeated Oman in a play-off. Nobody gave them much of a chance of coming through a group containing Stuart Pearce's Great Britain and a Uruguay side featuring both Luis Suárez and Edinson Cavani as overage players.

Yet after Moussa Konaté earned a share of the points against the hosts in their opening match, a 2-0 victory against Suárez and co. took Cissé's exciting young side into the quarter-finals, where they were beaten 4-2 after extra time by eventual winners Mexico in front of 80,000 supporters at Wembley. Starring in the No 10 role, Mané certainly caught the eye of Houllier – the man who had brought Diouf and Diao to Anfield a decade earlier. Now working for Red Bull in a lucrative consultancy role, the former schoolteacher recommended they did whatever it would take to sign him.

"What I liked was his speed and ability on the ball. It was fantastic for a boy of his age," Houllier said in 2017. "I quickly discovered that Metz would be willing to sell for financial reasons. Salzburg agreed to buy him and we paid €4 million. The potential was there and we just had to make sure he was well looked after."

"We had some interest from other clubs but in the end Red Bull paid a lot of money so it was decided by Metz that he would go to Austria," says Mané's agent Björn Bezemer, a former lower-league player from Bremen, Germany who established his arena11 sports group in 2007. "The league there is OK but you have to find the point to leave. If you are there for more than two years there is a danger that a player will get used to the rhythm and lose their opportunity to make progress. Sadio is the best example of this because he has continued to improve every season."

Mané was placed with a French-speaking family in the city that was more renowned for being the birthplace of a certain Wolfgang Amadeus Mozart rather than any footballing heritage. Established in 1933 after a merger of Salzburg's two biggest clubs, Hertha and Rapid, Austria Salzburg had to wait until 1994 to win their first Bundesliga title in a season when they were also losing finalists to Internazionale in the UEFA Cup. They won three more titles in the mid-1990s but were floundering in mid-table obscurity once more when Red Bull owner Dietrich Mateschitz purchased the club in 2005. Their declaration that "this is a new club with no history" did not go down well with supporters and nor did the decision to change the club's colours from purple to red and white, with some fans eventually forming their own breakaway club.

But thanks to huge investment from Mateschitz, the Red Bull juggernaut began their domination of Austrian football that has since yielded ten league titles and counting. Central to their success has been the recruitment of promising young stars from around the world thanks to an impressive global network of scouts that has become the envy of other European clubs. The purchase of New York club MetroStars in 2006 was followed three years later by another investment in German fifth division side SSV Markranstädt, with the rebranded side RB Leipzig moving into the Zentralstadion – once one of Europe's biggest arenas that had been renovated for the 2006 World Cup having previously fallen into disrepair.

Despite his relative lack of experience, Mané was an instant success in the Austrian top flight. Nineteen goals in his first season helped Salzburg to win the double before ending his second campaign as player of the season with 23 goals. A 3-0 win in a mid-season friendly against Bayern Munich alerted the reigning European champions to his vast potential, along with the manager of their arch-rivals, Borussia Dortmund, whom they had beaten in the Champions League final in 2013.

"I misjudged the personality of Sadio," Klopp admits more than six years on. "I saw him at Salzburg and there was no doubt about the quality. But Sadio came into Dortmund and had his . . . 'cool' attitude. Sadio is not really a 'cool' person – he is a very serious person, really thoughtful."

"But he comes in and has the baseball cap here," adds Liverpool's manager, pointing his hands at an angle away from his head as he spoke. "It was this kind of blasé attitude but you could see he was acting a little bit, which is mostly because you are a bit insecure – especially when you are meeting me! He played that role of a cool guy and . . . oooof. I didn't get it. Nice fella, obviously. But now

I think I really misjudged it. The problem was that I usually have these meetings alone and there were like ten people around. Alone with Sadio and after ten minutes I would have known much more about him than I would in this half an hour. So sorry Dortmund for not signing Sadio and not signing Son [Heung-min]. I did sign a few good ones as well though!"

Mané now admits their meeting just made him more determined to prove him wrong: "He said I was like a rapper! I always wear my cap all the time… But I think I gave my best so what can i say? That's part of life. You never know how you are going to get along with people. But I think he was wrong for sure! It was an experience for me as well though. I knew I had to show him more until we met again…"

***

While Bayern would also come to regret their decision to look elsewhere, it was Southampton who eventually took the plunge on the final day of the transfer window. Mané had controversially refused to play in Salzburg's crucial Champions League play-off against Malmo after rejecting a transfer to Russian side Spartak Moscow, instead heading for the south coast of England.

"There were lots of clubs interested but Red Bull were asking for €15 million and that created a small problem," Touré explained when making his bold prediction a couple of months later. "Sadio refused to play because he wanted to leave and that's when Southampton came in. It's a great opportunity for him to show what he can do and I can assure you he will be a revelation in the Premier League. But I'm sure he will not spend too long at Southampton because there are lots of clubs in Europe who would like to buy him. When Sadio went to Metz, I said he wouldn't spend very long with them and it was the same when he went to Red Bull. He has the talent to play in the Champions League."

For a while, it seemed Mané may even achieve that at Southampton, who had been languishing in English football's third tier as recently as 2011. Ronald Koeman was appointed to replace Tottenham-bound Mauricio Pochettino at the start of the summer of 2014 and spent the best part of £90 million attempting to replace the holes left by the expensive sales of Luke Shaw and Calum Chambers to Manchester United and Arsenal respectively, as well as Adam Lallana and Dejan Lovren – both of whom had joined Liverpool. Mané arrived on the recommendation of Saints' chief scout Bill Green and, as predicted, soon hit it off with new teammates Graziano Pellè and Dusan Tadic in an all-action front three, even if he later admitted it had not exactly been his dream destination.

"That transfer was tough and complicated," he said in June 2019. "I'll tell you the truth. Southampton is a very good club, but I didn't want to go there."

"Sadio had offers from places like China and Russia but also bigger clubs in Europe," Bezemer recalls. "We said, 'No, now is not the time to make just big money or sitting on a bench in a top club, we want to take a career step,' so he accepted the offer for less money from Southampton because we felt this was the right move at that stage. I had a few conversations with the manager and director of football there and they gave us a good feeling. Sadio trusted in the right people and, in the end, it paid off. Our plan for Sadio has always been to make him Africa's best player. The most important thing was to manage him to take the right decision. It's easy to make a fast deal but we prefer to have a long-term relationship with all of our players."

Mané made his first league start for Southampton in the 2-1 win over Queens Park Rangers at the end of September – a victory that lifted them to second place in the table. By contrast, Liverpool were struggling down in 14th under Brendan Rodgers having come so close to winning the title a few months earlier. The

Northern Irishman never really recovered from that hangover, with Suárez completing his £65 million move to Barcelona in the summer. His former side crashed out of the Champions League in the group stages after losing to Basel and ended the season being walloped by Stoke 6-1 as they finished sixth.

Meanwhile, goals in successive matches against Crystal Palace, Arsenal and Chelsea around the turn of the year helped Mané end the season with ten in the league as Southampton finished just two points behind Liverpool in seventh. The only blemish had been when he turned up late for the home match against Rodgers' side at the end of February and was left out of the starting line-up for the 2-0 defeat. But after such an impressive first season in English football that ended with Mané breaking Robbie Fowler's Premier League record for the fastest hat-trick in just 176 seconds against Aston Villa on the final day, already the vultures were circling.

As well as a £20 million bid from Manchester United that was swiftly rejected, approaches from both Liverpool and Tottenham were also resisted by Southampton as Morgan Schneiderlin and Nathaniel Clyne were sold instead for a combined £53 million in the summer of 2015. Perhaps distracted by the attention, Mané eventually scored his first Premier League goal of the new season against Swansea at the end of September. But it was his performance in Klopp's first home game in charge of Liverpool a few weeks later that really rubber-stamped the German's desire not to miss out on him this time.

Rodgers had been sacked following a 1-1 draw in the Merseyside derby at the start of October that left them tenth in the table after eight matches, with the former Dortmund boss immediately installed as the favourite to succeed him. Klopp was taking a breather after leaving the German club following seven successful years that yielded two Bundesliga titles but didn't hesitate in accepting the challenge. Introducing himself as 'The Normal One' in stark contrast to José Mourinho's 'Special One' in his first press conference a week later, the Klopp era began with a 0-0 draw against Tottenham on 17 October 2015 before Southampton visited Anfield.

While Divock Origi laboured in attack before being replaced by Christian Benteke at half-time, Mané was a constant threat on the break as Liverpool struggled to find a way past star defender Virgil van Dijk. A thumping header from Benteke, who moved to Belgium to escape the civil war in the Democratic Republic of Congo as a two-year-old, looked to have earned Klopp his first win since taking over until he was denied when the Senegal star bundled the ball in at the back post with just four minutes left. Mané was shown a red card as the clock ticked into injury time after receiving a second caution but still left Merseyside with his reputation richly enhanced.

Another goal against Liverpool after just 34 seconds in the League Cup quarter-final at the start of December was yet another timely reminder of Klopp's earlier error of judgement, even though his side went on to thrash Southampton 6-1. In what was beginning to feel like more than just a quirk of fate, Mané then ended a 20-match run without a goal in the Premier League by coming off the bench to score twice as Koeman's side overturned a 2-0 deficit at half-time against the same opponents in March 2016.

"That was the Sadio we like," said the Southampton manager after his side's 3-2 victory. "Sadio had a difficult time the last few weeks so I hope it gives the boy a boost, his performance."

An incident when he turned up late to a pre-match team meeting before the game at Norwich at the start of January had stretched Koeman's patience to the limit. Mané was dropped to the bench – the only Premier League match he didn't start that season – as Southampton lost 1-0 at Carrow Road.

"It is the most difficult situation I have faced until now, of course," fumed an exasperated Koeman. "Everything was going well, we had a lot of positive critics. That was the message to the players – it is so easy when everything is going well but now we have to keep togetherness. That is what I expect and that is not what we showed today."

The usually ice-cool Dutchman appeared to lay the blame for the defeat on Mané, who he revealed had already been warned about "not being focused" during training the previous week. Koeman was asked if he felt his attitude was linked with the opening of the transfer window. "Ask him," he demanded. "Ask him really why. Ask him – I don't know."

The obvious truth was Mané's head had been turned, with United not the only side to have kept in touch with his agent Bezemer. After his virtuoso performance at St Mary's that saw him miss a penalty four minutes after coming on at half-time before making amends by scoring twice – including the winning goal just before the final whistle – Klopp was even more convinced. Bezemer kept his options open, even taking Mané to meet Pochettino at Tottenham's sparkling training facility near Enfield. But his client's heart was set on working with the man who had – unbeknown to him – rejected him two years earlier.

"I knew Jürgen Klopp from Germany and thought that he could be the right coach to take him forward after Southampton," says Bezemer. "You never know what will happen so it can be a bit of guesswork. We tried to find out about Liverpool before he committed himself to them and it is not only the coach, the whole club is very professional. I think it worked out pretty well."

On 28 June 2016, five weeks after Liverpool had been beaten by Sevilla in the Europa League final, Mané was unveiled as Klopp's first major addition for £34 million – a new record for an African player. "I have followed Sadio since his impressive performances in the Olympics in 2012," said his new manager. "Since I came here I have spoken to the staff a lot about him and have always felt he could be a very good signing for us. He has a lot of quality, works hard and has a very good goalscoring record."

Mané himself described it as "the best day of my life".

"Liverpool is one of the biggest clubs in the world," he added. "When I was younger, I watched Liverpool against AC Milan [in the 2005 Champions League final]. It was amazing and I was very, very, very happy for Liverpool. This club has great players and great legends like Gerrard, Carragher and many other players. The dream has come true."

***

Following in the footsteps of compatriots Diouf and Diao, Mané became the 14th African international to represent Liverpool in the Premier League when he made his debut against Arsenal in August 2016. Legendary Zimbabwean goalkeeper Bruce Grobbelaar had been the first, followed by South Africa's Sean Dundee, Titi Camara of Guinea, Cameroon's Rigobert Song and then another six in the new millennium – Moroccans Oussama Assaidi and Nabil El Zhar, Djimi Traoré and Mohamed Sissoko of Mali, Ivory Coast's Kolo Touré and Nigeria's Victor Moses, who spent a season on loan from Chelsea.

The arrival of Joël Matip, who was born in Germany but had represented Cameroon through his father, a former player himself, from Schalke a few days after Mané would prove to be just the beginning of Klopp's African evolution at Anfield. The defender was kept on the bench for the see-saw encounter at the Emirates Stadium which saw Liverpool score four goals in the space of 18 minutes either side of half-time after Theo Walcott had given Arsène Wenger's side the lead following Alberto Moreno's blunder. Mané's strike, a trademark run that ended with him arrowing a shot past Arsenal keeper Petr Čech to make it 4-1, looked like being decisive before Alex Oxlade-Chamberlain and Calum Chambers set up a frantic finale.

"I played a big part in the excitement of the last half-hour, because it's not allowed to celebrate the fourth goal like this with 35 minutes to go," admitted Klopp afterwards. "At this moment, we switched off the machines. The game was not over. Arsenal lost, but we gave them a path back into the game. We can always score goals and we can defend much better. It's the Premier League and nothing should be easy in this league. Nothing is easy."

Not that anyone had told Mané that. Four more goals in the matches against Leicester, Hull, West Brom and Watford yielded another four wins and convinced some Liverpool fans that they could have another Ian Rush on their hands after many had been dubious whether he had been worth such a large fee in the first place. Liverpool's record of not losing when the Welshman scored stretched for seven years and 145 matches but Mané's luck ran out in another kamikaze display of defending against Bournemouth in December. The 4-3 defeat ensured Klopp's side missed the chance to move into second spot, one point behind leaders Chelsea, although their dramatic victory in the Merseyside derby a week later kept up the pressure.

In the fourth of eight minutes of stoppage time, Mané's awareness and phenomenal speed off the mark after Daniel Sturridge's shot came back off the post enabled him to reach the ball ahead of two Everton defenders to tap home the only goal of the game at Goodison Park and become an instant legend to those of a red persuasion. "I was a little bit lucky but I wish to always be lucky and score goals for the team," he said self-effacingly afterwards. "I'm thankful and very happy to score the winning goal."

Victories over Stoke and Pep Guardiola's Manchester City left Liverpool second in the table at the halfway stage, six points behind Antonio Conte's Chelsea side. The Londoners had equalled Arsenal's record with a 13th successive Premier League victory in the same season that day but any hopes of catching them faded quickly after the turn of the year. Mané scored to put them 2-1 up at Sunderland but then gave away a penalty for handball as the hosts secured a 2-2 home draw. His subsequent departure for the Africa Cup of Nations in Gabon proved to be disastrous as Liverpool failed to win any of their five league matches in January and were knocked out of the FA Cup by Wolves after scraping past Plymouth in a replay.

Just how much they had missed Mané was underlined by his mesmerising display in the 2-0 victory over Tottenham at the start of February 2017, with the Senegal star taking just 16 minutes to find the net on his return before adding a second almost straight away. "They couldn't win without him," admitted Match of the Day pundit Ian Wright that evening. "Mané is the one with that bit of pace to get in behind and I didn't think they were doing that recently and that's because he wasn't there. He is phenomenal. He senses the danger. Spurs couldn't deal with him."

Such had been Liverpool's desperation for him to return when they were also beaten over two legs of the EFL Cup semi-final by Southampton that the Fenway Sports Group, the club's American owners, arranged a private jet to fly him back to Merseyside hours after Senegal's elimination in the quarter-finals to Cameroon on 28 January. Mané had to be helped from the pitch after missing the decisive spot kick in a penalty shoot-out as his country's quest for a first continental title continued and he was inconsolable in the dressing room.

"It's definitely made him stronger," admits Seck, who was Senegal's chef de mission in Gabon. "He has learned a lot from that experience. But he also knew that anyone could have been in that situation. After the game we were on the pitch with him telling him, 'Don't worry, you have only missed a penalty. If we had won it would have been because of you.' He was protected, even if we didn't need to do it that much. Most people in Senegal knew it was just football and he is our most important player."

That view was not shared by everyone, however. A few days after their defeat and as Mané was preparing to make his comeback as a substitute in the 1-1 draw with leaders Chelsea, vandals broke into his uncle's house near Dakar causing serious damage to his car – an incident he later admitted had been "a big surprise".

"Sadio was still quite upset when he got back because he feels a responsibility for his country but we tried to explain that these things happen in football and you can recover from them quickly," recalls Bezemer. "Maybe it helped that the Chelsea match was the next day and Liverpool needed him. The most important thing for me was that he wasn't sitting at home alone just staring at the walls."

The victory over Spurs ensured Liverpool went into the last third of the season with their hopes of qualifying for the Champions League in their own hands. With Chelsea ten points clear at the top, the rest were left to fight it out for the remaining three spots and, after losing at Leicester, Mané's 12th Premier League goal of the season secured a 3-1 home triumph over Arsenal to spark a seven-match unbeaten run. But the win against Everton, which saw the Senegal forward score after just eight minutes at Anfield before limping off in the second half after a collision with Leighton Baines, proved to be his last appearance of the season.

Mané had damaged cartilage in his left knee and required surgery, ruling him out for eight weeks. His campaign was over. Without their top scorer, Liverpool maintained their top four challenge despite the defeat to Crystal Palace at the end of April that proved to be their last at home in the league for nearly three years (and counting). Needing to beat already-relegated Middlesbrough on the final day, a second-half blitz resulted in three unanswered goals to book a return to European football's elite competition, much to the relief of their manager. But as Liverpool's players went off for a well-earned break and Mané continued his rehabilitation over the summer, Klopp was already planning his next big signing.

THREE

A CLOSED SHOP

"People call him the father of Egyptian football," says journalist Fady Ashraf. "I obviously never saw him play but they say he was a bit like Mohamed Salah."

More than a century before Salah's arrival at Anfield from Roma for Liverpool's then club record fee of £36.7 million in June 2017, a slightly built player from the land of the Pharaohs with a wand-like left foot had already made his presence felt in English football. Fulham's 3-1 Second Division victory over Arthur Wharton's old club Stockport County on 11 November 1911 featured a brilliant goal from Hussein Hegazi, who had become known as 'Nebuchadnezzar' among supporters after the legendary first king of Babylon in tribute to his dazzling dribbling skills for non-league side Dulwich Hamlet.

An engineering student at London University, the 20-year-old was the son of a wealthy rural aristocrat from Kremlah in the Sharkeya province of Egypt, east of the Nile Delta, who had been crowned national 400 metres and 800 metres champion in his schooldays. Having learned the game by playing with British soldiers garrisoned near his home, Hegazi approached Hamlet to see if they would take him on when he arrived in the British capital to study. Despite his lack of size, he was an instant success in the hurly-burly of non-league football and was invited for a trial with Fulham within weeks.

Hegazi's dazzling appearance against Stockport ended a decade-long wait for the second African to play in the English league after Wharton. Fulham were suitably impressed to select him for their next Second Division match against Leeds, with the resident poet at one newspaper even penning a devotion to the exotic star. The final verse referred to the looming dispute between the two clubs, given that Fulham's professional status was at odds with Hegazi's ambition to continue his studies. "Fulham was proud of her player from Cairo/Fulham was just like a dog with two tails/Dulwich, you'll find in a terrible ire-o/If for high amateur honour she fails/But at such prospect all Dulwich-ites smile/Backing the luck of this lad from the Nile."

"I was in a difficulty," Hegazi admitted to the newspaper a few weeks later. "For I wanted to play very much in League football, and at the same time I did not want to leave Dulwich Hamlet who have been very good to me. So I have decided to play for the Hamlet. I am sorry if Fulham are disappointed."

Remaining an amateur allowed the London FA to select him for the match against Middlesex the following month – the first of five games for the representative side. A brief flirtation with Millwall lasted just two matches in the Southern Alliance League before his return to the Hamlet side to help officially open their new ground on Champion Hill in suburban southeast London on 21 September 1912. At the end of the season, he enrolled at St Catharine's College, Cambridge to study Arabic and history and won a Blue before returning to Egypt. "Hegazi's departure was English football's great loss," wrote Jack McInroy of TheHamletHistorian website. "Had Hussein Hegazi remained on these shores for the duration of the war he would have qualified for a place in the great Corinthian side of the 1920s. Instead he headed home before the hostilities began."

Back in Egypt, he continued to play football and became one of Cairo giants Al Ahly's star players, also – like Salah 92 years later at London 2012 – representing his country in the Olympics in 1920 and 1924, before retiring at the age of 40. "Hussein Hegazi displayed exemplary sportsmanship on the pitch," remembered writer Naguib Mahfouz, the Nobel Prize winner for Literature in 1988, when asked about one of his childhood heroes. "Throughout his career, Hegazi never committed a foul."

He was swiftly followed by Tewfik Abdullah, another engineering student from Egypt, who became known as 'Derby's Dusky Dribbler' when he scored on his debut against Manchester City in October 1920. Abdullah played 15 times for Derby before being shipped out on loan to Cowdenbeath in Scotland's Second Division and ended up starring in the fledgling American Soccer League. According to Nick Harris in his book *The Foreign Revolution: How Overseas Footballers Changed the English Game,* "his time in Britain and his subsequent move to America were illustrative of the growing international market in players" in the early 1920s. It would not last long, however.

Prompted by Arsenal's signing of Dutch goalkeeper, Gerry Keizer, a few months before Wharton's death in 1930, the Football Association introduced a two-year residency rule to clamp down on clubs buying in foreign players which remained steadfastly in place until 1978. They were strongly supported by Ramsay MacDonald's minority Labour government, with the decision ruthlessly slamming the door on any new signings from Europe or beyond.

A total of 24 South Africans graced the Football League in the period between the wars but many – like Liverpool's prolific striker Gordon Hodgson – were descendants of British émigrés and none came from the black community. Hodgson was born in Johannesburg and moved to Anfield after starring for Transvaal against a touring Liverpool side in 1924, going on to score an astonishing 240 goals in 378 games for the club and playing three times for England. But it was the performances of George Robledo – a striker born in Chile to an English mother who had moved to Yorkshire at the age of five – for Barnsley and then Newcastle after conflict had finally ended in 1945 which signalled the start of a new era. Over the next five years, players from Bermuda, Italy, Jamaica, Hungary, Iceland, Latvia, Norway, Poland, Sweden, Spain and Switzerland had all made their bows in English football. Then the Ferenc Puskas-inspired 6-3 thrashing of Billy Wright's England by Hungary in 1953 in what became known as the 'Match of the Century' served notice that their perceived dominance of the game they had created was over.

Clubs began to search far and wide for new talent, with Charlton manager Jimmy Seed identifying South Africa as a particularly rich source of players. Restrictions on non-white immigration from the Commonwealth at the time dictated that all had European heritage, however. Harris estimates that 52 made their debuts between 1946 and 1960, with a quarter – including striker Eddie Firmani and defender John Hewie – turning out at the Valley. But it was the success of Eastern Cape-born Eddie Stuart at Wolves that would eventually lead to the arrival a very different type of player to these shores.

***

As part of the deal that saw Stuart move to Molineux in January 1951, Wolves had agreed to play a friendly against his former club Rangers in Johannesburg at the end of the season. A star of the whites-only league that had long been established even before the arrival of apartheid three years earlier, he had not come across the teenage sensation starring up front for the South African Bantu XI given the restrictions on interracial sport. With Wolves manager Stan Cullis watching on in a match against their 'coloured' counterparts, Steve 'Kalamazoo' Mokone scored twice and earned a penalty in a 3-1 victory. "'You played a marvellous game,' [Cullis] told me earnestly," wrote Mokone in his autobiography, *Kalamazoo!: The Life and Times of a Soccer Player* several years later. "'Would you be willing to join Wolves on an extended trial basis, if I invited you?' Surprised and elated, I managed, 'I'll ask my parents.' But when I told my father about the offer, he said, 'No.' I went back to school."

Born in Doornfontein in Johannesburg on 23 March 1932, Mokone's parents Paul and Emily had moved the young Steve and his two sisters to the then-thriving neighbourhood of Sophiatown 20 minutes to the west of the city centre just as war broke out in Europe. Known as a hotbed of music, art and liberal politics during the 1940s, it was also, as Mokone repeatedly referenced in later life, where he learned to play "the beautiful game". His father ran a taxi firm, "dabbled in real estate" and preferred cricket, while his mother, who called Steve by his middle name 'Madi', liked to play tennis. But there was only ever one sport for their son.

In an interview in 2012, Mokone remembered how he used to steal his mother's tennis balls and attach a piece of string to them "so I could always practise kicking even when I was talking to people". He soon progressed to playing in local street matches with his friends for a small wager, invariably emerging victorious. Having moved when he was 11 to the administrative capital, Pretoria, he began starring for his school Kilnerton and joined local side Methodist FC, becoming a regular in the first team by the age of 15. He was the youngest-ever player to represent the Pretoria and District Bantu XI – mistakenly referred to as the South African Black National XI in his autobiography – a year later. Separate federations for each racial group had existed since the 1930s, and, although there were no restrictions to stop non-white groups competing against each other, the onset of apartheid meant he rarely faced a white player until his arrival in England.

Mokone left Kilnerton at 16 with a newly acquired nickname due to his love of the song 'I've Got a Gal in Kalamazoo' from the Glenn Miller film *Orchestra Wives*. "I suppose I must have whistled and hummed it more than anyone else because soon everyone was calling me 'Kalamazoo', just as some of my pals were nicknamed 'Stanley Matthews' and 'Joe Louis'," he said in Charlie Buchan's *Football Monthly*. The story is given a slightly different slant in his hugely entertaining autobiography, where Mokone states it was adopted as the theme tune for Durban Bush Bucks, whom he joined in 1951 having moved to the prestigious Ohlange Institute to complete his schooling. More than 40 years later, it was where Nelson Mandela famously cast his vote in South Africa's first free election and, in 1901, had become the first school in the country to be founded by the black community.

Despite his father's wish that his son would become a doctor, news of Mokone's exploits on the field spread. A year after he turned down Wolves, who would go on to win three league titles between 1953 and 1959, a representative from Newcastle United also tried their luck. "I couldn't understand what he was saying to me," Mokone told Phil Vasili in a phone interview in 1997. "These people sounded as if they came from another planet. At the time, of course, they did."

Undeterred, he applied for a passport to enable him to one day leave South Africa. However, the authorities soon discovered that on his return to Pretoria in 1952, he had become an active part of the fledgling ANC Youth League through his new side Pretoria Home Stars. Mokone's association with some of the more radical members of the black community did not help his case for a passport and he was told in no uncertain terms to forget about going overseas. Instead, he enrolled at the Bantu Normal teacher training college in Vlakfontein, where Desmond Tutu and singer Miriam Makeba were two of his classmates.

In keeping with so much of Mokone's story, there are conflicting accounts of how he ended up as South Africa's first black professional player in English football. The romantic version, as told by popular magazine of the era *Football Monthly* anyway, goes like this: after first contacting Wolves to see if they would be interested in signing him, the editor of the local evening paper, Mr L. Jenkins, had convinced him to try his luck with a Third Division club "where he thought I would get a better chance. And that is why I landed at Coventry. Running through the names of the English Third Division (South) in the results and scorers of an English newspaper one day, I noticed the name 'Coventry City'. The title fascinated me and I wrote to Highfield Road right away. I had a very encouraging reply from the Coventry club and I finally decided to make the most significant move of my life."

But that tale appears to have just been inspired by his ghostwriter's imagination. Mokone has also said that it was Buchan – the founder and editor of *Football Monthly* – who was instrumental in smoothing his passage to England thanks to his contacts at Coventry, which is probably much closer to the truth. What is certain is that former Sunderland, Arsenal and England striker Buchan also contributed £100 towards his fare and a payment to the government as their safeguard against Mokone returning in a "destitute condition".

Interestingly, he makes no reference to the circumstances surrounding his arrival in England in his autobiography – other than mistakenly stating he left South Africa in 1955, while the official records show he actually joined Coventry a year later.

But in the *Football Monthly* article, published in January 1957, Mokone describes the arrangements he made to take care of his family having persuaded his father to allow him to pursue his dream. "My parents were not too keen, at first, of my travelling 6,000 miles to take a wild chance of making good at a game but I finally won them over and arranged for my wife, Betty, and four-month-old son Archie to stay with them." There is no mention of Ronnie Sello, born a year before his departure to a nurse Mokone had met in hospital after being involved in a car accident. "I had no intention of marrying her. I had slept with her only once," he wrote in his autobiography. "I was going overseas, but Mavis wouldn't hear of an abortion. In June 1955 my son, Ronnie, was born. Later he was to play a very negative role in my life."

***

It didn't take long for Mokone to make his presence felt in his new home. He was met at the airport on 9 August 1956 by a man representing Buchan – referred to as "Buchanan" in his autobiography – and taken to stay at the Strand Palace Hotel in Piccadilly Circus. The culture shock was immediate. "I'd never been in an all-white environment before," he remembered. "I had no one to talk to, no one to confide in."

Even settling into the hotel proved slightly problematic. He was bemused at the large wooden box in the corner of his room – "I didn't know how it worked or even how to switch it on" – because televisions were yet to be introduced in South Africa for another 20 years. Mokone also had trouble coming to terms with being served by his white maid. "She came to make the bed and took my shoes away afterwards. I thought, 'Why the hell is she taking my shoes away?' But I couldn't say anything because she was white and because I was afraid of the implications of confrontation. The cleaning lady told me they took them away to polish them and I didn't believe her. After that I took them and hid them under the bed. I just wasn't sure."

Not everything was such a culture shock, however. That evening, Mokone went out on the town and writes in his autobiography that he was propositioned by a "lady of the night", eventually ending up at a hotel in Victoria with her and her friend. "I, who had never before gone to bed with a white woman, was confronted by two white women. Unnerving! What had begun as an erotic adventure turned into a nightmare as first one then the other made demands on me. There was simply no let-up to it. Meanwhile, they fought each other for their turn, scratching and pulling one another's hair. Finally I begged for mercy. This was rape, and I was the one being raped!"

With no money to pay for the room after they had abandoned him in the early hours, he made a run for it while the "frowsy" landlady "phoned the police". The next day, Mokone was taken for a photo shoot with Queens Park Rangers' new signing, Teslim Balogun, at the offices of Buchan's *Football Monthly* magazine on what was a historic day for African football. A member of the Nigerian select team that had played a number of leading English amateur sides on their pioneering tour in 1949, Balogun made 13 appearances that season for QPR in the Third Division (South) before returning home to coach the national side in later years. They were both treated to some "on the spot" training from Buchan, who still remains Sunderland's leading scorer of all time in the league with 209 goals.

Buchan accompanied Mokone on the train to Coventry, where they were greeted by chairman Mr W. Erle Shanks. The next day's paper had a picture of Mokone wearing an oversized duffel coat and smiling nervously as he shook hands with him. Asked about his first impressions of England, he reflected that "the people are very friendly but not the weather". The article also says Mokone had two burning ambitions: "to make good as a footballer and meet his great hero, Wolves and England captain Billy Wright . . . if he comes up to the standard required it is expected he will be offered professional terms. If so he will become the first native coloured player to play for an English league club."

Coventry had arranged for him to stay with a devout Christian family who lived on Allesley Old Road in the west of the city and were members of the Committee of African Organisations. Based in London, it offered support to exiled politicians from the continent. The eldest daughter was married to an Indian who had recently graduated from university, while another was dating a "West Indian" student. But Mokone still admitted feeling uncomfortable using the same cups and the same toilet as a white family, despite later acknowledging that it was a problem of his own making due to his "cultural baggage".

Teammates Roy Proverbs and Alf Bentley were also staying there and accompanied Mokone to his first training session. It was only then that he met manager Harry Warren for the first time. Having spent 16 years in charge of Southend United, his arrival two months earlier had certainly put a few noses out of joint. George Raynor was demoted to first-team coach just six months after he was recruited from Italian side Lazio at great expense. Raynor, the man who led Sweden to the gold medal in the 1948 London Olympics and third place in the 1950 World Cup, was known as a football purist. But those ideas did not chime particularly well with Warren's more direct approach.

Mokone was thrown into the action immediately. Just 48 hours after his arrival in England, he scored a goal at Highfield Road for the reserves in a practice game against the first team. "Mokone showed good ball control and an agile football brain, but obviously found the conditions strange – he has not played on grass before," wrote Derek Henderson, the *Coventry Evening Telegraph's* columnist under his pseudonym 'Nemo'.

"I was not at my best, really, but I shall soon settle down to English conditions and style," added Mokone. "I am not worried at all about making good." Although he said it was too early to judge whether their new prospect could play for the first team, Raynor – who would go on to lead hosts Sweden to the 1958 World Cup final, where they were beaten 5-2 by a Pelé-inspired Brazil – felt he showed promise and "flicks the ball in a continental fashion but he must develop a more powerful kick".

Reg Matthews, recently capped by England despite the club's lowly status, was in goal for the first team and Mokone "sold him a dummy before flicking the ball into the corner of the net". According to Nemo, Matthews did manage to save two of his penalties, although Mokone gained revenge at the next day's training session.

"I recall some press folk asking me to take penalty kicks against Reg. At first I was reluctant, but [they] persuaded me to take some," he wrote in an email to Mike Young, membership secretary for Coventry City Former Players Association, in 2014. "With my first shot, I sent Reg diving the wrong way. With my second shot, I again sent Reg diving the wrong way. Reg was getting upset because he was the England keeper. But you see, Reg was watching my leg/foot and as long as you did that, you would never know which way the ball was going to go. I used to practise that trick dozens and dozens of times with a tennis ball. I recall walking into the dressing room shaking because I had shown up Reg."

Matthews later sought him out and made an effort to congratulate him for making a good impression, but the other players did not know what to make of their exotic new teammate. He made his first official appearance for Coventry's reserves against Birmingham two weeks later alongside club stalwart Lol Harvey, who remembered Mokone refusing to wear shin pads because he said they would "hamper his style". Once again, he scored as the home team won 2-1 and "certainly pleased the crowd". Yet to be offered a professional deal, Mokone was given a job on the club's ground staff with a small wage. "I still found it a struggle to keep myself and send money home," he admitted. Director J.R. Mead eventually found him a part-time job as a clerk in his office on a wage of £5 a week to ease the burden and allow their overseas recruit to concentrate on his game. It paid dividends.

Despite suffering an ankle injury at the end of September, Mokone impressed on his return and was selected to play in a Thursday night friendly against Nottingham Forest on 4 October. Warren was at Highfield Road to watch two prospective signings who were included in Coventry's side as guest players and he saw his South African trialist set up the opening goal with a deft through ball. Two days later, the first team slumped to a 3-1 defeat against Torquay to leave them in 13th place in the division. Mokone's big chance had arrived.

"High commotion and excitement at Highfield Road on Saturday when Steve 'Kalamazoo' Mokone touched the ball," wrote Nemo in the following week's match report of the 2-1 defeat against Millwall. The attendance of 20,261 was around 4,000 more than had watched Coventry's previous home match two weeks earlier against Reading and there was no doubting whom they had all come to see.

"He had pace and could dribble – it was so exciting to be there," says Bobby Gould, who remembers being in the crowd as a ten-year-old that day and would go on to play for Coventry before two spells as manager. "I can still see him playing that day when I close my eyes."

"When I was a schoolboy, I just remember how exotic he was. He just seemed like a breath of fresh air," adds Young.

An impressive assist was the highlight of his Football League debut, despite a disastrous third successive defeat for Coventry.

Receiving the ball in his own half and skipping past his man, Mokone delivered a perfect pass for Ray Sambrook to lob the ball over the stranded Millwall goalkeeper. "Mokone's form was a revelation, I think, to all of us," purred Nemo. "On Saturday's display alone, it would not be hard to say that the coloured South African boy is the best right-winger the City have played this season. He created opening after opening only for his colleagues to fritter them away. He showed excellent ball control and positional sense, and was always ready to shoot first time."

Warren was also suitably impressed. Two days later, Mokone scored twice for the reserves against Nottingham Forest and was summoned to his manager's office when he reported for training in the morning. "Big and beaming, [he] greeted me with the magic words: 'Well Steve, we're going to sign you as a professional,'" Mokone wrote in *Football Monthly*. "So, with the Coventry secretary Bernard Hitchener looking over my shoulder to make sure everything was in order, I signed the form that was to turn me from an anxious but enthusiastic coloured boy from Pretoria into an English professional league footballer. In a way, I suppose, I am something of a football ambassador for my people and I know they are watching my progress very closely."

However, it appears the reality was actually different to the picture painted by the magazine. Aside from Raynor, club captain Noel Simpson and Matthews, Mokone later said he was subjected to "paternalistic racism" from the rest of his colleagues. "After training we would go into a big bath in the changing rooms," he remembered in 2013. "With all those white people naked and I'm naked . . . they sort of sit to the side and I'm on the other side. I'm thinking things but I can't say it. We come out and we take our towels and then go to the lounge to eat. I would sit at a table on my own because no one would come and eat with me."

In his nine months at Coventry, Matthews was the only player to invite Mokone to his house and, when the goalkeeper was sold to Chelsea for a record fee of £22,000 in November, he became even more isolated. In fact, it seems that he suffered from racism from the very start. Earning just £5 a week, Mokone wrote in his autobiography that he was "unable to socialise" with his teammates as a result. When he went to ask Warren if he would be given professional status, he was told, "That's the trouble with you people. You're never satisfied." "The phrase 'you people' had so many connotations for me," Mokone later acknowledged knowingly.

***

The picture in the *Coventry Telegraph* of a grinning Mokone, pen in hand, and his manager as he signed his first professional contract on 16 October 1956 may have masked the reality but he made no secret of his disdain for Warren – and English football in general – in later years. After one training session, he was castigated for performing too many tricks and told to "get a job in a circus". Despite their personal issues, however, Warren knew Coventry were in desperate need of inspiration from somewhere. Defeat against Brighton a few days after Mokone signed his contract was their fourth in succession as the new recruit from South Africa found his opposing full-back – future England defender Jim Langley – "too much for him" in a 2-1 defeat. After another poor display for the reserves, he was written off by Nemo as "not quite ready for week-by-week League duty". Five days later, though, Mokone turned on the style.

The first hour of Coventry's match against Gillingham at Highfield Road had been a dreary affair until Dennis Uphill headed the home side in front, only for the visitors to equalise immediately. Peter Hill restored Coventry's lead in the 73rd minute and the points were sealed soon after. Mokone "sent the crowd wild" as he raced on to a pass from John Walton and placed a shot in the far corner to register his first league goal. Hill rounded things off just before full time to complete a 4-1 victory and finally bring an end to Coventry's barren run.

"There is no doubt about Steve Mokone being a crowd-pleaser," wrote Nemo. "His goal could hardly have been more popular had it won the City promotion. I am sure this likeable coloured player will soon realise, however, that 'foot-fluttering' over the ball may look very good to the spectators but not always to his colleagues who have run into position for a quick pass or centre. But Kalamazoo promised well in those final 15 minutes, when he got a better service of the ball, and, indeed, the whole team was remarkably transformed."

Retaining his place for the following week's match against Swindon, Mokone set up Coventry's opening goal as they battled back from a 2-0 deficit to earn a draw. It was to be his final league appearance for the club. Having played seven games in the space of just 16 days, Warren decided to give him a rest. Raynor was then replaced as coach by former England and Arsenal hardman Wilf Copping, who had a reputation for being a disciplinarian. Injury and illness brought on by his first winter in England meant Mokone quickly drifted out of the first-team picture at Highfield Road. Even after his recovery and as the team struggled, Warren and Copping refused to turn to their South African import, who became increasingly isolated. By the first week of January, disillusioned with the lack of opportunities to play for the first team, he submitted a transfer request. Warren reacted furiously, mainly because Mokone had also gone to the national newspapers to complain about his treatment.

"After the trumpets had sounded and the enthusiasm for the novelty which I was had passed, I found myself unwanted and alone," he told the *Daily Mirror*. Accusing Coventry of failing to develop him as a player, Mokone said the club had gone back on the promises they had made to him when he arrived. Charlton Athletic, who had sold Firmani to Sampdoria in 1955, were also reported to be interested in signing him.

The next day, Warren summoned Mokone to his office again. He was told his transfer request would be granted at the end of the season and he would be allowed to leave for free. Had Raynor still been around then things may have been different. Having signalled his intention to leave, Mokone became even more of a peripheral figure in his final months in England and was reduced to turning out in minor cup competitions and for the reserves. At the start of March, Mokone scored the only goal for Coventry's reserves in a friendly win played in foggy conditions under floodlights against Danish club Akademisk Boldklub – a match he remembered later for comments made to him by a teammate. "At half-time one of our players said to me, 'Steve, you should have scored that goal because the opposition players could not see you.' That hurt. I don't know whether I was being ultra-sensitive, but I thought he meant because I was black. It hurt. But I never said a word."

His performances still couldn't persuade Warren and Copping to give him another chance as Coventry eventually limped home 16th in the Third Division (South). The dream move had turned sour. On 22 April 1957, Mokone played his last match for the club in a 3-1 defeat for the reserves against Swansea at Highfield Road.

There are several different versions of how he ended up at Heracles – a club then marooned in the Tweede Divisie B – the third tier of Dutch football. In Mokone's autobiography, his spell in England is covered in less than four pages and claims that despite being frozen out of the picture at Third Division (South) Coventry, he was wanted by no less than Valencia and Racing Club de Paris, at that stage one of France's biggest clubs.

He even claimed to have travelled to Spain to meet officials from Real Madrid, only for the move to fall apart after they sent along a secretary who couldn't speak English to translate.

Heracles were the next to make contact. Mokone says he met a representative of the Dutch side from the remote town of Almelo situated not far from the German border in London and was promised he would be "paid handsomely" to play in a series of exhibition matches. His contract with Coventry still had a few months to go but Mokone had "ensured that they could not hold me hostage after that by demanding a huge transfer fee".

However, according to Tom Egbers, a Dutch journalist who has written two books on Mokone's life, his arrival in one of European football's outposts was pure chance. "The Heracles manager was given a football magazine from England in which the names were published of 20 players who were free agents," he told me. "He decided to write to all of them inviting them to play a trial match in Holland. At that time, the view was that England was the Mecca of football so anyone playing there would boost the attendances. They had one reply, from a certain Steve Mokone of Coventry City."

***

Like most of the stories in *De Zwarte Meteoor* (*The Black Meteor*) – Egbers' account of Mokone's three years in the Netherlands – his arrival on Dutch soil for the first time on Sunday, 19 May 1957 is described in vivid detail. Born in Almelo in October 1957 to a Dutch father and a mother from Preston with Irish heritage, Egbers, who has presented the Dutch version of *Match of the Day* for almost 20 years, became a regular at Bornsestraat from the age of four, accompanying his father to Heracles matches "hand in hand". Egbers admits he always had a soft spot for the few foreign players to pass through the club in the years following Mokone, often wondering why on earth they had chosen to come to Almelo, of all places, to ply their trade.

But it was the only player about whom his father "would grow lyrical" who illuminated his childhood dreams. "I used to go to the club as a small boy and my father also played for them, as did my grandfather," he remembered in our first conversation back in 2014. "My father always used to tell me about this wonderful player who joined the club in the 1950s who was a black man – something that was unheard of in our part of the country."

Without even seeing him play – or even having seen a photograph – Mokone became his hero by the age of ten. Having spent the majority of their existence in the lower leagues, Heracles' fortunes later began to improve and the club had spells back in Holland's top flight during the 1960s but the name Mokone still provoked widespread adulation from "otherwise level-headed supporters", as well as a sense of mystique.

After studying journalism in Utrecht, Egbers joined the Netherlands' public broadcaster NOS in 1984 and also worked for respected Dutch football magazine *Voetbal International*. Following a brief spell at a rival broadcaster, he returned to NOS and began anchoring its TV coverage of Holland's national side. One day, a colleague handed him a present taken from an old petrol station collection – a colour photograph of the 1958/59 Heracles side. "I looked at the card and, at first glance, received a shock. Between all those beefy farmers' sons stood a small black man. That was, that must be . . ."

Finding Mokone became his obsession. "Up to that moment he had been no more than a shadow, a sort of mirage," he wrote in *The Black Meteor*. "I had to know everything about him. How he had ended up at Heracles, what kind of man was he, whether he was still alive and, if so, what was the name of his particular Muncie?"

Egbers discovered that in the years since leaving Heracles,

whom he helped win promotion in his first season before abruptly departing in July 1959 citing "personal problems", Mokone had been very busy indeed. Notice of his death in March 2015 later published by his family even contained the claim that he "was voted Europe's best soccer player" that year despite a nomadic period in his career that would take him to eight different countries over the next five years. Quite what the late Alfredo Di Stéfano would make of being deprived his second Ballon d'Or we can only speculate.

A short spell at Cardiff, where he scored the first goal in a 3-2 home victory over Liverpool on the opening day of the Second Division season in August 1959, ended after just a few months when Mokone fell out with the manager, Bill Jones. In February 1960, he was sent off in a tempestuous Welsh Cup sixth-round match against Swansea after wrestling on the ground with opponent Harry Griffiths before throwing mud in retaliation.

Mokone eventually ended up at Marseille – where he failed to make a first-team appearance and instead opened a shop selling football boots that went bust – via Barcelona or Sporting Lisbon, depending on whom you believe. "I had left Heracles and signed on with the Barcelona Football Club," he wrote in his autobiography. "Because they had their quota of foreign players, they loaned me to the Marseille Football Club in France. As a foreign star, I attracted large crowds to these games. (Actually, I always pulled in large crowds wherever I played)."

In February 2016, I contacted Barcelona to verify whether he had ever been on their books. Given that General Franco's Delegación Nacional de Deportes had banned clubs from taking on foreign players other than in "extreme circumstances" back in 1953, it seemed unlikely. "After checking the information with our Club History Department, we are sorry to inform you that Mr. Steve Mokone never signed for our club," confirmed the reply.

Egbers' version was that he was taken on by Portuguese side Sporting after a trial, only for them to have exceeded their limit on foreign players and thus losing him to Marseille. Whatever the truth, when Mokone turned up at Italian side Torino in 1962, he had already completed his third and final brief spell in English football – consisting of just one appearance for Barnsley in their League Cup first-round match against Southport on 13 September 1961 – and moved to Zimbabwe to take up a job in a brewery.

Despite the security of a regular job after several years spent scratching a living around Europe, it appears Mokone still yearned for another opportunity to make it at the highest level. His chance came in the form of Otto Gloria, the former Sporting coach who would go on to lead a Eusébio-inspired Portugal to third place at the 1966 World Cup. He had a history of encouraging African-born players to succeed in Europe and had been approached by one of Torino's directors offering him the job for the forthcoming 1962/63 season. The director was eventually overruled and Argentine Benjamin Santos kept his post for another season, although not until Mokone was requested to attend a trial on Gloria's recommendation.

Once again, the impact he had is open to debate. "My arrival in Torino had proved to be something of a sensation," Mokone wrote in his autobiography after a long description of his admiration for "well-dressed" Italian women. Despite suffering from toothache, the trialist scored five goals in an exhibition game against Verona 24 hours after his flight from Zimbabwe had landed and was dubbed "The Maserati of soccer" by journalist Beppe Branco. "Now that was a classy comparison," Mokone commented.

Yet despite the existence of a photograph which he claims shows him scoring the last of his five goals, it seems that is actually taken from a practice match between the Torino first team and reserves which featured in *La Stampa*'s Piedmont edition on 9 November 1962. In fact, Italian social historian Marco Bagozzi discovered in his article, 'Mokone: the pioneering legend and the reality' that no match against Verona even took place, although the South African – referred to as "Mokoni" by the paper – did impress the reserve-team coach by scoring three goals. However, the presence of Spaniard Joaquín Peiró and Gerry Hitchens, the former Aston Villa striker who had replaced Denis Law in the summer having joined from Internazionale, meant Torino's two permitted overseas spots for that season were already filled. Mokone was told he would only be selected for friendly matches but that there may be an opportunity next season if he could prove himself. It never came.

By the end of 1964, Mokone had enrolled for a degree in psychology with political science at the University of Rochester in New York State after an ill-fated spell coaching in Australia. His daughter, Thandi, was born in 1966 to his wife Joyce, whom he had married in London five years earlier. As well as studying in the United States, Mokone played an active part in the attempts to keep apartheid South Africa out of the Olympics. Having travelled to the 1960 Games in Rome with South African Dennis Brutus, who would go on to found the South African Non-Racial Olympic Committee (SANROC) in 1962, they were reunited eight years later during the Committee on Africa's successful campaign to ensure South Africa was formally banned from competing in Mexico City.

But while his status as a pioneering hero among black South Africans back home continued to grow, Mokone's home life was beset with problems. Tensions with Joyce steadily increased and, by the time that Ronnie Sello arrived to live with his father in 1973, they had almost reached breaking point. A year later, the couple flew to Santo Domingo in the Dominican Republic after agreeing to get divorced. But Mokone admits they were both too scared to make the final break because "there was security in knowing that the other was there". The reunion didn't last for long.

In that same year, Joyce later claimed Mokone had beaten her up so badly that she had to seek medical attention for two badly swollen eye sockets, although her husband insisted in his autobiography that it was him who ended up in hospital. "My father drank a lot so it was often when he was drinking that he could become quite argumentative and the violence would escalate," remembered Thandi when we first spoke in September 2015. "I recall frequently the police being called to the house."

They finally got divorced in September 1977. Three months later, Mokone's life changed forever. In his autobiography he remembered returning home to find a note from Ronnie which said the police had taken him and Thandi to East Brunswick police station in New Jersey. "Shocked, I rushed to the station. Thandi was asleep on a bench and the police were interrogating Ronnie about me. I was told I was under arrest for credit card fraud!"

Bailed after claiming he had been badly beaten up by the police, Mokone was arrested again three days later. This time, it was for an acid attack on his ex-wife, which had allegedly taken place on 20 November. Describing the assault in her statement, Joyce said her "mind saw nothing but the body of a man that I have known for 16 years and to me that sure was my husband's stature". Joyce was lucky to escape with minor injuries to both eyes and a cut to her chin when she fell. Most of her hair also fell out and she had scars down her right-hand side which never left her.

Joyce's attorney, Ann Boylan Rogers, had not been so lucky. Just six weeks earlier as she returned to the Manhattan apartment she shared with her husband Ed Rogers, the 36-year-old of Irish descent had sodium hydroxide – a liquid more commonly known as lye or caustic acid which is used to make soap, among other things – thrown over her face by an unknown man. Boylan Rogers lost the sight in her left eye and was permanently disfigured.

It would be almost a year after his arrest until Mokone was finally sentenced for the attack on Joyce. But the case never even went to court. Under pressure from his lawyer to accept a plea bargain given the wealth of evidence against him, he began a 12-year term in Rahway Prison in East Jersey. He was later also convicted for the attack on Boylan Rogers after a lengthy and complicated trial that saw Ronnie provide crucial and disputed evidence against his father, eventually moving to the notorious Attica Prison – where he was placed in the same cell block as the boxer Rubin 'Hurricane' Carter – in 1985.

Egbers tracked Mokone down a decade later and vowed to uncover the true story behind his imprisonment, culminating in his second book, *Twaalf Gestolen Jaren* (*Twelve Stolen Years*). "Good men sometimes do bad things," wrote journalist Jonathan Wilson in an article for *The National* newspaper in the United Arab Emirates on the eve of the 2010 World Cup in South Africa that told the story of one the country's most famous players. "But the inconsistencies and procedural flaws in the trials uncovered by Egbers, and the fact that, whether it was acted upon or not, there was some level of conspiracy against him, suggest that Mokone, having begun as a pioneer for black South African sport, ended up as a martyr to it."

As conspiracy theories went, it certainly ticked all the boxes.

***

"I read the article by Steve's daughter Thandi Mokone-Chase!" began Don Sabo's email in late September 2015. "I had never seen this declaration and I am still absorbing her indictment of Steve. As a pro-feminist man I learned long ago to listen closely to and to believe women's claims about domestic violence. I am stunned. Men's violence against women has always been hidden behind convention."

It was six months since Mokone's death in Washington at the age of 82. I had made contact with Sabo, a sociology professor and expert on the American prison system, in an attempt to find out what had happened to South Africa's first black export to English football while he was behind bars. They met during Mokone's stay in Attica in the late 1980s and remained in touch after he was finally released in August 1990. His response to Thandi Mokone's article published that July in the *New York Times* entitled 'Father, Apartheid Trailblazer and Domestic Abuser', in which Mokone had been accused of "physically abusing and sexualising" his own daughter, showed the accusations had clearly come as something of a surprise.

"Was Steve yet another man who kept his violence and aggression carefully hidden behind a quiet and heroic persona?" asked Sabo rhetorically. "The standard and sardonic quip made by educators, counsellors and volunteers who worked in the prison environment was that 'everybody behind bars claims to be innocent!' Was Steve yet another prisoner who created a story that exonerated him and, by extension, preserved his heroic sport legacy? Answering this question appears to be a key motivation for your journalistic inquiry. After reading his daughter's article I'm inclined to conclude that the answer could well be 'yes'."

Having published an article for *The Guardian* about Mokone's remarkable story a few weeks after his death, I had spoken to Thandi in September 2015 to hear her side of the story, resulting in a piece headlined: 'A club divided: high-flying Heracles haunted by ghost of Steve Mokone'. It described how his former club's brilliant start to the new season that saw them briefly top the Eredivisie had coincided with Thandi's claims about her father.

"I am very shocked by the news," responded Heracles chairman Jan Smit. "They are nasty accusations. He is now deceased, and the case should be properly sorted out after that incriminating letter. Whether a stand in our new stadium will be renamed after him is now part of government consultation."

At the time of writing, there is still no Steve Mokone stand at the Polman Stadion. Thandi's version of the story has since been strongly disputed by Egbers and Mokone's widow Louise, with a new book celebrating his achievements on the field released in 2018. Whatever the truth, the controversy after his death was still a sad footnote to the life of a man who, despite his brief stay, had been such an important pioneer for black African players in English football.

FOUR

THE JEWEL OF THE NILE DELTA

It wasn't supposed to end like this. But as he hit the turf face first in the 25th minute of the 2018 Champions League final, Mohamed Salah felt a sharp pain in his left shoulder and knew his dream debut season was over. Tears immediately welled up in the eyes of Liverpool's 44-goal man, finally accepting defeat four minutes later having tried gainfully to carry on at Kiev's Olimpiyskiy Stadium. Sadio Mané was the first to offer his condolences, placing an arm around his teammate's shoulders as he left the pitch, followed by Cristiano Ronaldo and then his devastated manager, Jürgen Klopp.

A joyous campaign that had proved all the doubters wrong and had the distinction of being the most productive in terms of goals by any African player in the history of English football had come to a shuddering halt. And there was only one man to blame: Real Madrid's Sergio Ramos. Never a stranger to controversy having received a European record 25 red cards in his career, the European Judo Union would later describe the Spaniard's actions in pulling Salah to the ground by holding on to his armpit and ensuring he landed on top of him as they fell as a perfectly executed example of the 'waki-gatame' technique that has been banned in the sport for several years.

After Ramos somehow but predictably escaped punishment from Slovenian referee Damir Skomina, there was a sense of inevitability about what happened next. Mané briefly provided hope that Liverpool could defeat Zinedine Zidane's double reigning champions even without Salah when he equalised Karim Benzema's opening goal within four minutes of the second half. But two goals from Gareth Bale, the second the result of an extraordinary blunder from goalkeeper Loris Karius that saw him inexplicably spill the Welshman's shot from distance over the line, finally dashed their dream of a sixth European title. (It was later discovered the goalkeeper had suffered concussion shortly before Benzema's goal having earlier taken a blow to the head from, you guessed it, Ramos.)

Salah was already on his way to hospital as the post-match celebrations began, with a victorious Ronaldo hinting he had performed his last act in a Madrid shirt. Scans later confirmed the Egyptian had sprained ligaments in his left shoulder and was in real danger of missing out on his country's first appearance at a World Cup finals since 1990. Still not fully fit, he ended up playing a bit-part role as The Pharaohs were sent packing after the group stages, even suffering the ignominy of losing to Saudi Arabia in their last match.

A €1 billion lawsuit against Ramos was later launched by an Egyptian lawyer, not to mention a petition which called on FIFA to take action against the Spain defender who had "used tricks that defy the spirit of the game and fair play" which garnered more than half a million signatures. Meanwhile, the second African player to be crowned as the PFA's Player of the Year tried to forget by going fishing at his favourite holiday resort of El Gouna on the Red Sea with his brother, Nasser, and childhood friends.

On his return to Cairo, more than a thousand supporters turned up at Salah's home when his address was leaked on

Facebook, delighting them when their hero emerged to sign autographs. "People can relate to him – he's like one of us and he made it out," admits student Yussuf El Dsuky. "He's also opened the door for a lot of players to follow in his footsteps."

Yet – as his manager would acknowledge a little incredulously 12 months later – there were still those who felt Salah had something to prove in English football.

"After the first season when he scored an incredible number of goals, people were questioning whether he was a one-hit wonder," remembers Klopp. "But I'm not sure where they got this idea from? I think it's only about his stature. It's about that. Because he is so quick in all the movements but they think, 'Yeah, next time I will get him.' But he is very strong in both the body and the mind."

***

"Many coaches will say that they made him famous but I know it was down to me," insists Said El Shishiny. The man who first met Mohamed Salah when he was a slight teenager playing for El Mokawloon's Under-16 side as a defender is not alone. Everywhere you go in Egypt these days there is someone claiming to have played some part in his meteoric rise, especially in Salah's home town.

Situated in the agricultural hub of the Gharbia Governorate, slap bang in the middle of the Nile Delta, Nagrig has become the setting for endless articles and news reports documenting the childhood of the local boy who became a superstar. Salah's arduous nine-hour bus journey every day to training in Cairo and back again has become the stuff of legend since his breakthrough season at Anfield.

Given the endless number of journalists who have visited Nagrig in recent years to document the childhood of the local boy who became a superstar, at first my arrival after a bumpy three-hour journey in a hire car barely raised an eyebrow in the small town with a population of around 12,000. But it didn't take long before I was being taken on a guided tour by an enthusiastic 11-year-old called Mustapha, making my way from Salah's family home to the pitch where he honed his skills in his youth accompanied by an excited group of around 20 children. Many were wearing Liverpool shirts – none, you suspect, purchased from the club's official online shop – with the name and number of their hero on the back.

"Of course I saw him play here. He was my neighbour so I know him well," says Mrs Amene, who now works in the youth centre which was renamed in Salah's honour a few years ago. "He was always a very respectable child. We are very proud of him."

Situated next to the dusty pitch overlooked by the town's mosque and surrounded by paddy fields, the two rooms inside the centre sometimes also host other activities like karate but usually most of the attention is on what is happening outside. Overlooked by a giant mural of Salah on the wall, an impromptu match breaks out that basically involves each player trying to keep the ball for as long as possible before they lose possession and join the chasing pack. Mrs Amene watches over them earnestly as she speaks to me, making sure nobody is acting out of turn as one of the children – much to their delight – deftly nutmegs my friend.

Salah started playing here at the age of eight and immediately caught the eye of coach Ghamri Abdel-Hameed El-Saadani. "His talent clearly showed from the beginning," he recalled in an interview in 2018. "But talent is not everything – Mohamed's success is also a product of a will of steel, effort and determination."

Having made my way on to the roof, I am looking out over the jasmine fields that surround Nagrig as dusk starts to fall when a shout comes from the pitch below: "Mohamed Salah!" It is one of the children trying to attract my attention.

"Mohamed Salah!" I shout back.

"Mohamed Salah! Mohamed Salah!" several of them reply in unison.

It became a customary greeting during my stay in Egypt, with even stony-faced customs officials and police officers softening when his name is mentioned. This is a player who has transcended his sport like no other in football-crazy Egypt's history. The next stop on the tour takes us to Nagrig's new medical centre, where Liverpool's star striker has paid for two kidney dialysis machines and various other equipment. Then there is the school down the road which also bears his name which has received extra funding ever since his move to Europe, extended in 2018 to create the Azhari Institute for Girls so they no longer have to take the long journey to the next town for their education. The Mohamed Salah Charity Foundation has also donated land and the best part of £400,000 to build a sewage treatment works on the outskirts of the town, guaranteeing Nagrig has an abundant supply of water all year round.

"Family is everything to him," says journalist Mostafa Algrtly from Egyptian website masrawy.com. "If a friend needs help he will always try to do it. He feels a duty to his country to try and give something back. That's why he is even happy to walk about without any bodyguards sometimes."

Maher Shetia, the mayor of Nagrig, has a Mohamed Salah chant as his ringtone and these days doubles as an official spokesman for the family given his father's request to stay out of the limelight. Salah Ghaly was a respected member of the community for many years before his son's rise to fame and, along with his wife, worked in an administrative role for the government as well as – like many of Nagrig's residents – trading in jasmine.

"Mohamed was a very ordinary child – like all the other children in this village," the mayor says. "He inherited his love for playing football from his father and uncles, who played with the village's Amateur Youth Centre's team during the 1980s and 1990s. Salah's father noticed his son's talent and had him join the Ittihad Basyoun team when he was 12 years old. One day, Reda El-Mallah, a football scout, came to our village to watch another child named Sherif and possibly persuade him to join one of El-Mokawloon's small teams in Tanta. He asked the children to play against Sherif so he could assess him. But watching the match there was one player who stood out – Mohamed Salah."

It wasn't long until his talent caught the eye of El-Mokawloon's coaches and he was invited to join their Under-15 side based in Cairo. In stark contrast to his future teammate Mané's family at the same age, his father actively encouraged him to pursue his dream despite the huge distances involved.

"I would complain that I didn't want to travel four hours to training," said Salah in 2018. "But he stood by me and told me that all great players go through this. The price for him was very high, and I'll never forget the role he played in my career."

Yet while his father's support enabled him to attend training in the short term, there is no doubting El Shishiny's crucial role in his early development. With Salah by then in his second year at the club, he had arranged for the young prospect to stay with his family in Cairo for one or two nights a week to allow him to rest properly from their training sessions rather than make the long trip back to Nagrig every day. But even that was not getting the best out of him. Concerned that Salah could fail to reach his potential, his coach came up with a plan. "He was travelling a long way every day so I asked the president if we could help by giving them a room in the club's lodgings," he recalls. "I told him that we needed to look after one of our best young players."

El Mokawloon is also known as Arab Contractors due to its ownership by the construction company, which is one of the region's biggest road builders. The legend goes that the club president called Ibrahim Mahlab, the CEO of Arab Contractors – who would go on to serve as Egypt's prime minister for 18 months – to ask his permission and the decision was swiftly made.

El Shishiny also has another claim to fame, although this one has been disputed by various others over the years. "I'm the coach who recommended him for the first team," he says convincingly. "Mohamed was playing as a left-sided defender for our team but I thought he could be better further forward. At the time, he wasn't the main player in his position as we had another four who could also play there so I decided to try something different and put him on the right wing. He was always very quick and was getting into good positions, even if he was missing some of the chances.

"We had a match against ENNPI when we won 4-0 and Mohamed had three chances to score but missed every time," continues El Shishiny. "After the match I went to the changing room and he was crying, so I asked him, 'Why are you crying?' He said, 'Because I didn't score today.' . . . Everyone else in the team was happy because we had won but he was so upset. I told him, 'Don't worry, you will be the top scorer in our team next season.' He ended up scoring 30 goals!"

Salah's impressive performances in his new attacking role at youth level saw him promoted to the first-team squad after much persuasion from El Shishiny. A year later in May 2010, a 17-year-old Salah made his debut for El Mokawloon in the Egyptian Premier League against El Mansoura in a 1-1 draw, scoring his first goal seven months later against giants Al Ahly. It was the first step of the process that would eventually lead to Anfield via Switzerland and Italy, although Salah had to deal with a major setback early on when he was publicly rejected by the president of Al Ahly's big rivals Zamalek.

"He has always been very brave," says Fady Ashraf, who is a reporter for Egyptian website FilGoal. "That sort of thing has happened to many players in Egypt because it is the ultimate goal to play for one of the big two clubs. But he picked himself up and rose up. That's what he does – every time you think he is struggling he comes through. He has always had this fighting mentality."

Salah himself has admitted that things could easily have turned out very differently. "What if I had joined Zamalek? I think if I had signed for Zamalek I would not be where I am now," he admitted in 2018. "Al Ahly and Zamalek do not allow their players to leave easily, so I believe I would have stayed in Zamalek for not less than four years."

But after starring at the Under-20 World Cup in Colombia during Egypt's run to the last 16 to help his country qualify for the Olympics for the first time since 1992, there would soon be other suitors waiting in the wings.

***

On 1 February 2012, Salah was at home recovering after his side's 2-0 defeat to Al Ahly a few days earlier as he watched the reigning champions' next league match against Al Masry at the Port Said stadium. A 3-1 victory for the hosts quickly turned to tragedy as 74 Ahly supporters were killed and more than 500 injured when Al Masry fans stormed the pitch. Several members of the police force were later sentenced to death after being found guilty of failing to open the gates and allow the visiting supporters to flee to safety. It was later alleged that the riot had been orchestrated as a last throw of the dice by recently deposed leader Hosni Mubarak, who, six months on, was sentenced to life imprisonment for corruption before later being released.

With the domestic league cancelled, Salah's immediate future looked bleak. Yet the intervention of Sascha Empacher would end up changing his life forever. Almost six years earlier, the tall German agent who was once a football journalist before setting up his firm, SPOCS, had been invited to watch Egypt's international friendly against Argentina in Cairo by two local students, Yahia Ali and Ibrahim Azab, who had recently signed up several players to their own agency.

"They came from a different angle to normal agents because Yahia is an engineer and Ibrahim is an accountant," Empacher recalls. "The day after I went with them to see the match against Argentina, I found myself on morning TV because everyone had heard that I was interested in taking some of these players to Europe. At the time nobody was going to Egypt. It's a complicated market with a different mentality that is difficult for western European clubs to handle."

The establishment of an Egyptian arm of his agency with Aly and Azab in 2007 at last created a pathway for several prospects to try their luck in Europe, with Empacher heavily involved in the deal that saw Amr Zaki join Wigan on a season-long loan from Zamalek a year later. Despite chairman Dave Whelan's initial misgivings, the striker initially proved a roaring success and a brilliant acrobatic volley against Liverpool at Anfield – his second of the game and seventh of the season – took him to the top of the Premier League's goalscoring charts on 18 October 2008.

It was the last goal he scored from open play, however, as Zaki's fall from grace was as rapid as his rise had been. Despite ending the season with ten goals, Wigan manager Steve Bruce labelled him as "the most unprofessional player I have ever worked with" after he failed to return on time from an international break and opted against making the signing permanent.

"All the Egyptians were supporting Wigan back then. It's like with Salah and Liverpool today . . ." remembers Ashraf. "But I'm not sure how much those disagreements counted against the overall reputation of Egyptian players."

Ibrahim Said's short-lived stay at Everton certainly hadn't helped either. Arriving at Goodison Park in January 2003 on loan, he failed to make a single appearance for the first team after an ill-judged decision to dye his hair red before their meeting with Liverpool at Anfield. Nonetheless, Zaki's initial success and fellow striker Mido – who joined Tottenham from Ajax in 2006 before moving to Middlesbrough – had proved Egyptian players could make the grade in one of the world's toughest leagues and encouraged Empacher he was on to something. So when Azab contacted him at the end of 2011 urging him to take a look at a young wiry winger with curly hair who was starring for El Mokawloon, he didn't hesitate to snap him up.

"I sent him to a couple of clubs in the Bundesliga and then Belgium. Everywhere," Empacher remembers. "But no one wanted him because Egyptian players didn't have a good reputation. Clubs only think in the moment and not about the future. You often have to find clubs that are not in the top five leagues who are willing to take a risk on an African player. It's a really tough way to reach the top because you need to be very patient. That's not easy when there is a lot of pressure on you back home to become a superstar. That's something that Mohamed handled very well. He showed it was possible."

Luckily for Salah, Swiss champions Basel had also been keeping tabs on the emerging talent ever since his performances at the Under-20 World Cup. They arranged to play a friendly against Egypt's Under-23 side at the club's training ground that saw Salah score twice in a 4-3 victory. He was then invited to stay behind for a week's training in the medieval city on the

River Rhine that, in sporting terms, is most famous for being the birthplace of Roger Federer.

"In his five days of training, he only really convinced us on the fifth day," Basel's sporting director Ruedi Zbinden told Simon Hughes in his book *Allez Allez Allez*. "I had doubts because he had technical deficiencies; he couldn't cross the ball with his right foot and his crosses from the left and his shots weren't very good either. We thought, 'That's not the same guy from the video.' But in the very last training session – a five-a-side – he exploded!"

Salah impressed so much that Basel offered him a four-year contract, although it took a few months to find his feet in what were strange new surroundings.

"The most difficult was at the beginning when you have to explain the way of life in Europe and the language barrier," says Empacher. "Yahia would fly to Basel every couple of weeks and I would be there regularly but the club were also very good at helping him to integrate. He was in the right place at the right time."

Salah's experience at that summer's Olympics was also to prove invaluable, not only for his football career. As well as several members of the side that would go on to qualify for the 2018 World Cup such as his best friend Ahmed Hegazi, Egypt's squad also included the legendary playmaker Mohamed Aboutrika, a three-time winner of the Africa Cup of Nations and Salah's hero. It was less than five months since he had cradled a dying supporter on the dressing room floor of the Port Said stadium. "Captain, I'm glad I got to meet you," had been the 14-year-old fan's last words.

Aboutrika reversed his initial decision to retire in the aftermath and helped Egypt reach the quarter-finals at London 2012, despite the fact that most of the squad were fasting because competition fell during Ramadan. Both he and Salah found the net in a thrilling 3-2 defeat to a Neymar-inspired Brazil at Cardiff's Millennium

Stadium, repeating the trick in the final group stage match against Belarus after Salah had also scored against New Zealand. Three weeks in the company of the man who had become an icon of the previous year's Arab Spring that ended the rule of Mubarak and installed the Muslim Brotherhood president Mohamed Morsi as president just a month before Egypt's first match was bound to have an effect on the 20-year-old Salah. "He looked up to him as a player and as a man," remembered former Egypt coach Bob Bradley. "You could tell he wanted to learn from him and do things the right way."

Morsi's reign as president lasted almost exactly a year before he was removed from office by the military-backed Abdel Fattah el-Sisi and placed under house arrest as he awaited trial. He eventually died in custody nearly six years later on the eve of the 2019 Africa Cup of Nations that was due to be hosted in Egypt. The subsequent crackdown on Morsi's supporters by el-Sisi was thorough and often brutal, with Aboutrika's endorsement for the former president leading to the country's most famous players being exiled after being placed on a terror list. It was a reminder that sport and politics are always closely linked in Egypt.

Aboutrika spent a decade at Al Ahly despite several attempts from European clubs to lure him away. But his successor returned to Switzerland brimming with confidence after his performances at the Olympics and scored in each of his first three league matches for Basel. Despite adding only two more as Basel won the league title for the fourth year in succession, Salah was the inspiration behind their run to the Europa League semi-finals under manager Murat Yakin, scoring the opening goal in the second leg of the previous round against Tottenham as they beat the Premier League side on penalties. Salah also found the net against Chelsea in the second leg of the last-four match at Stamford Bridge – the first of many on English soil – but saw his side go down 5-2 on aggregate.

After just one season in European football, Basel rejected several offers to sign their Egyptian prodigy in the summer of 2013. But two more goals in surprise victories against Chelsea in the group stages of the Champions League at the start of the next campaign ensured that almost every top club in England had registered an interest in Salah by the start of the January transfer window.

"In the beginning, scoring goals was a big problem for him but he learned very quickly," says Empacher. "Then we had the Champions League draw against Chelsea and the marketing began."

Having first made contact with his agent 15 months previously, Liverpool – then managed by Brendan Rodgers – were gazumped when Chelsea offered £11 million up front, £3 million more than their rivals.

"We had an offer in November but they never met the asking price," admits Empacher, who describes the club's then chief executive Ian Ayre as "a complete amateur" in their negotiations. "The first offer was £5 million and the salary was very low. At this time I could see that Mohamed was feeling under pressure because everyone in Egypt was talking about Liverpool. But the problem was their bid hadn't been accepted. English teams are always very slow."

It was at that moment that José Mourinho's side made their move, much to the annoyance of their Merseyside rivals. "The guys in Liverpool never understood it," admits Empacher, "but football transfers are very complex."

The lure of working with Mourinho was also hard to resist. In an attempt to persuade him to move to Stamford Bridge rather than Liverpool or Arsenal, the Portuguese manager had called him and sent a text message but initially received no reply.

"I hadn't paid my Egyptian phone bill so I couldn't call him back," remembered Salah in a television interview in his homeland in 2015. "I didn't know what to do; I couldn't call him on Viber . . . so I sent him a text on WhatsApp asking him to call me back. He called me and that phone call had a huge effect. It was a long conversation. He told me I was a player he needed, and a player that will have an important role. He also told me that Chelsea's style of play will suit me, and . . . that's enough."

Mourinho had recently returned to London for his second spell at the club and was in the process of attempting to rebuild the side in his image when Salah arrived in January 2014. Less than a week earlier, young Belgium midfielder Kevin De Bruyne had been sold to German side Wolfsburg after failing to impress but the Egyptian hoped he would fare better than him, not to mention much-maligned compatriots Zaki or Mido.

"All players are respected; I don't like to criticise any player. I'll just keep concentrating, and hopefully God will help me," he added. "The things any Arabic player needs the most to play in Europe is to have ambition, determination and to have a goal. My advice to young players is that if you have a dream, hold on to it, and do your best to achieve it."

Sadly, however, it just wasn't to be at Stamford Bridge. Despite scoring in a 6-0 win over Arsenal in March, the following season saw Salah play just half an hour of Premier League football as he was slowly frozen out of the picture by a manager who had offered him so much. A key moment came in October after a League Cup match at Shrewsbury when he and fellow winger André Schürrle were criticised for making Mourinho's selection for the next league match "easy" due to their poor performances. A goal from Didier Drogba – also back for his second spell at Stamford Bridge – set up a 2-1 win but it was clear that Salah was struggling to make an impact, seeing one of his shots fly so far off target that it went out for a throw-in.

"Because he was always sitting on the bench, people were making memes that were telling him to follow the example of

Ahmed Elmohamady [then playing for Hull City having moved to England in 2010 with Sunderland] because he was an ever-present player. Salah was seen as overrated," says Ashraf. "This is something that only locals can understand – if you don't play for Ahly or Zamalek then you don't have this fan base behind you. Elmo managed to do it eventually. But for Salah it was much harder."

***

The opportunity to join Fiorentina on an 18-month loan in January 2015 could not have come sooner for Salah. Moving to Italy proved to be his coming of age. Choosing the shirt number 74 in tribute to the supporters who had died at Port Said, he proceeded to score on his debut against Sassuolo and ended the season with six goals in 16 league appearances in Serie A.

"When he went to Fiorentina, no one was interested," says Ashraf. "Everyone said it will be two or three years before he will be back in Egypt. That has been the usual way for our players before then so that's what we expected."

As well as scoring both goals to ensure Fiorentina ended Juventus's 47-game unbeaten home run with a 2-1 victory in the Coppa Italia, his performance in another Europa League victory over Tottenham was further proof that Salah's confidence had returned after his nightmare spell in London. But the decision to join Roma instead on another loan deal at the end of the season did not go down well in Florence. Fiorentina reported Chelsea to FIFA having claimed their agreement contained a clause which allowed them the right to purchase him that summer but their attempt to receive €32 million in compensation was rejected in June 2017.

The complicated legal wranglings of the case saw Salah contact Ramy Abbas, a half-Lebanese lawyer who was born and raised in Colombia but is now based in the United Arab Emirates, for assistance. As well as attending university in Leicester, Abbas had started out as a translator for Elson Becerra – the former Colombia forward who had tried to save Marc-Vivien Foé's life when the Cameroon midfielder suffered a heart attack during the Confederations Cup semi-final in 2003 – when he moved to Emirati club Al Jazira in 2003.

"He was the first player from the Colombian national team to come and play at the UAE and was my idol," Abbas told *GQ* in June 2019. "I started helping him with whatever he needed, travelling back and forth from England to the UAE whenever I had the chance. Then as my studies progressed, he asked me if I could help him negotiate his contract – I was sort of a mediator between him and his club. Unfortunately, his story ended badly. Becerra got involved in an altercation at a nightclub in Cartagena and was shot and killed. Colombia can be a very violent place."

Having graduated in 2005, Abbas immediately began working in football and went on to represent a string of high-profile clients including former Brazil forward Rivaldo in cases at the Court of Arbitration for Sport in Lausanne. But it was his role in the transfer of Hussein Yasser to Manchester City later that year which eventually paid dividends. A Qatar international of Egyptian heritage, the attacking midfielder had begun his career as a youth player at Manchester United before Stuart Pearce was persuaded to sign him for City by Algerian playmaker Ali Benarbia, who had played with him in the past. While he would end up making just one appearance for the club, against Doncaster Rovers in the League Cup, the move and his work at FIFA and CAS had cemented Abbas' growing reputation in the Middle East. Nearly a decade later, it was to him that Salah turned to resolve his dispute with Fiorentina.

"He contacted me around the end of January or beginning of February in 2015, looking for legal advice," remembered Abbas.

"We met for the first time in London. Looking back, I think that was the most important milestone of my career."

A disagreement with Yahia Ali suddenly left SPOCS out in the cold, with Salah taking to Twitter to hit out at Empacher's business partner Oliver Kronenberg, a former head of FIFA's legal department. "Please don't take any news from my ex-agent Oliver Kronenberg and don't believe any of his words," he wrote before the move to Florence was finalised.

Six months later and with Fiorentina keen to exercise an option to purchase him from Chelsea as part of their 18-month loan agreement, it was Abbas who smoothed his path to Roma.

"I think he was badly influenced by other people and didn't understand the way of professional football. This is a matter of fact," says Empacher four years on. "What I can say is that without me, Yahia or Ibrahim, there would be no Mohamed Salah."

***

It's way past 10 o'clock on 8 March 2016 and BT Sport's pundits are discussing the action from the evening's last-16 ties in the Champions League. Top of the agenda is Roma's 2-0 defeat to Real Madrid that saw Luciano Spalletti's side crash out of the competition after losing the first leg by the same score despite creating a hatful of chances in both matches.

"I like Salah – he causes a lot of problems – but you do not have any confidence when he is in front of goal," says former England striker Michael Owen.

"He actually looks a world-beater," interrupts Rio Ferdinand. "He looks a world-beater until he has got to make a decision on passing or shooting."

With nine goals in Serie A already including two in the two league matches to rub it in against Fiorentina as the legal dispute rumbled on in the background, Salah had made an encouraging start to life in the Eternal City as Spalletti's side finished third to qualify for the Champions League again. A permanent move was eventually rubber-stamped in August, with Roma paying around £15 million to Chelsea after he ended the season with 15 goals in all competitions.

Yet the public criticism of Salah had got Abbas thinking. How could he be more effective in front of goal? That summer, the lawyer appeared as a guest on Colombian TV channel Win Sports alongside legendary goalkeeper Faryd Mondragón and Juan José Peláez, the respected veteran manager. Five years after the team bankrolled by infamous drug lord Pablo Escobar had made history by winning the Copa Libertadores, Peláez had become the manager of Atlético Nacional. After winning the Colombian title in his first season, he almost repeated that success in 1995 when his side was beaten by Brazilians Grêmio in the final.

Despite the murder of club captain Andrés Escobar after the AC Milan-bound defender scored an own goal that eliminated Colombia from the 1994 World Cup, Atlético's squad still contained the likes of maverick goalkeeper René Higuita and a teenage Juan Pablo Ángel, who would go on to play for Aston Villa. Jaime Pabón – a journeyman who played as an attacking midfielder or striker – started in the first leg of the final that saw Mario Jardel score in the 3-1 victory in Porto Alegre but was dropped to the bench for the second leg back in Medellin as Atlético were held to a 1-1 draw.

More than two decades on, Pabón had developed a reputation as one of the best striker coaches in the business having worked closely with Jackson Martínez at another of his former clubs, Independiente Medellin, before Martínez's move to Europe. He was recommended to Abbas by both Peláez and Francisco Maturana – the manager of Colombia at both the 1990 and 1994 World Cup finals who also worked in the UAE – and Salah agreed to begin working with him.

In the summer of 2016 as Sadio Mané was unveiled as Liverpool and Africa's new record signing, Pabón travelled to Rome to meet Salah for the first time. "I did an initial assessment, analysed it, and then gave them a report about his strengths and the areas where there was room for improvement," he told Yahoo Sports.

Reporting back that Salah's acceleration was exceptional and that he possessed a good shooting technique, the coach recommended that he should not drop so deep in search of the ball – instead pushing up the pitch as far as possible to minimise the journey to goal.

"Whenever he was about to score, he didn't make the best decisions. He didn't breathe," added Pabón. "So he was out of breath at the end, after taking such a long time to get there. I recommended to shoot earlier, to look at the ball, to make good choices, with angles that were more difficult for the goalkeepers. We did a lot of repetitions, employing that advice."

Setting up a training pitch in the back garden of the house Abbas had hired for Pabón, five minutes from Salah's place in Casal Palocco just outside the Italian capital, he spent hours honing his finishing technique after returning from training. By the time Roma faced Bologna at the start of November, he had managed five goals including one in the opening game of the season against Udinese and a crucial strike in a 3-1 away win over Napoli. A hat-trick at the Stadio Olimpico which helped Spalletti's side maintain their attempt to pursue perennial champions Juventus illustrated Salah's new coolness in front of goal thanks to the breathing tips provided by Pabón.

The Colombian provided welcome company after a training ground collision with teammate Thomas Vermaelen left him on the sidelines for three weeks in December 2016 due to ruptured ankle ligaments. But despite continuing his sessions in Pabón's back garden after regaining his fitness, Salah failed to score again in Serie

A until February. Meanwhile, Edin Džeko racked up the goals, ending the season with 29 as Spalletti's side finished as runners-up. Salah, who had still managed a creditable 15, was given the honour of being replaced by the legendary Francesco Totti in the final game of the season against Genoa. The last-minute winner that clinched second spot was a fitting goodbye to the man who had scored 307 goals in 786 games in 25 years at Roma.

Unbeknown to him as he left the pitch that afternoon, it was also to be Salah's last appearance for the club. Liverpool's interest remained from their previous attempt to sign him in 2014, with the head of scouting and recruitment, Dave Fallows, Barry Hunter – the chief scout – and sporting director Michael Edwards all keen to make a new approach to Roma. Having initially targeted Bundesliga-based trio Christian Pulisic, Julian Draxler and Julian Brandt instead, Jürgen Klopp was initially not so sure despite first having seen Salah in the flesh when Borussia Dortmund played Basel in a friendly four years earlier.

"Mo was lightning," recalls Liverpool's manager with typical enthusiasm. "He was unreachable for us at that time but it was one of these games that you never forget. It's not that you follow these players but I was always aware of him. He went to Chelsea and it didn't work out, which is completely normal. Then going to Italy was a smart move: Fiorentina, Roma. He had to convince people in a different way."

Salah was confirmed as Liverpool's new record signing on 22 June 2017, with the £36.9 million fee making it the second successive summer that Klopp's side had also broken the African transfer record after the purchase of Mané from Southampton 12 months earlier. While a £53 million agreement that would surpass it yet again a year later was being struck with RB Leipzig for Guinea midfielder Naby Keïta, the club's first Egyptian player made a blistering start to life at Anfield when he scored in the 3-3 draw with Watford on the opening day.

That was the first of an astonishing 32 league goals in Salah's debut season, ensuring he became only the second African player in history to win the Premier League's Golden Boot after Drogba. But having proved emphatically that Mourinho had been wrong to allow him to leave Chelsea, his run-in with Ramos in Kiev and the critics who doubted whether Salah could hit such heights again were to provide extra motivation as the new season loomed large.

FIVE

FAR FROM HOME

"His body was found on Friday by policemen who entered his tower block flat in Leeds," wrote Rob Hughes in the *New York Times* in October 1995. "It may have been there for two days but, though Johanneson was only 55, the death certificate will read 'Natural Causes'. That is an official lie. Albert Johanneson, born black in South Africa, was a man, a star, who was born and died a victim of apartheid."

It had been 30 years since the lightning-quick winger from Johannesburg made history by becoming the first black player to play in the FA Cup final. Johanneson was signed by Leeds United in January 1961 after being spotted playing for the 'Coloured XI' in the Kajee Cup – the same competition that had launched the sporting careers of Steve Mokone and a certain Basil D'Oliveira, who would soon become the centre of controversy involving the England cricket team.

But while the 'D'Oliveira affair' that would lead to South Africa being excluded from Test cricket for more than two decades after the talented all-rounder was left out of England's touring squad in 1968 proved to be a spur for the anti-apartheid movement, Johanneson's impact on English football was almost forgotten. After a disappointing performance in the 2-1 defeat to Bill Shankly's Liverpool at Wembley three years earlier, he played only ten more games for the Yorkshire club.

It was only when the true extent of his subsequent descent into alcoholism was revealed that people began to take notice of his tragic story. Rather than two days – as stated by Hughes – police later estimated that he had actually passed away five days before his body was finally discovered. As well as his daughters Alicia and Yvonne, among those present at Johanneson's funeral in October 1995 was current Leeds player and fellow South African Lucas Radebe, who had joined the club the previous year.

"Lucas was injured so he managed to go along to the funeral but I was involved in a match," his compatriot Phil Masinga told me in 2015, four years before the former striker's own untimely passing at the age of 49. "I was a little bit sad because of the circumstances of his death. I wish that I could have met him before he died because I never had an opportunity to shake hands with him."

"It was so sad when he died," adds Johanneson's biographer, Paul Harrison. "It broke my heart. He didn't deserve to die like that after everything he had done and everything he had achieved – to be left in a flat and not be found. Where were his other friends? It's just so horrible."

By the time we spoke in 2017, it had been five years since Harrison's book, *The Black Flash: The Albert Johanneson Story*, was published. I had finally managed to make contact with the former policeman-turned-author and lifelong Leeds fan after several attempts to track him down when he moved back to his home city from the remote Orkney island of Sanday.

Having grown up in the club's golden era under Don Revie, Harrison first watched Johanneson from the stands at Elland Road as a schoolboy. He was only ten when the winger known as 'Hurry, Hurry' in South Africa touched down on English soil for the first time and became an instant hero for his exploits on the wing. It wasn't until a chance encounter in a local pub in 1980 that Harrison finally encountered Johanneson in person to begin a friendship that lasted until his death, with their last interview taking place just weeks before he passed away. "It felt like a huge part of me had been taken away," he wrote in the introduction to *The Black Flash*.

***

April 1961 was an extremely significant month in the history of English football. As the Football League finally relented and lifted the restrictions that had imposed a maximum £20-a-week wage on all professionals, the selection of Albert Johanneson and Gerry Francis in the Leeds side that met Stoke in their Second Division fixture at the Victoria Ground represented a new landmark for African players. "It caused quite a stir in the press at that time," remembered Francis in 1998.

A former cobbler, he had arrived at Elland Road in 1957 after being recommended for a trial by Johannesburg schoolteacher Barney Gaffney. Francis was the Leeds representative at the meeting to discuss removing the wage cap with Football League secretary Alan Hardaker three years later that was also attended by Jimmy Hill, Stanley Matthews, Tom Finney and Bobby Charlton. "He told us we would never win," the South African later admitted. Hardaker was wrong.

The significance of the development would become clear when Fulham's Johnny Haynes became the first £100-a-week player, although Francis would never see those kinds of riches as he quickly dropped into non-league with Tonbridge Angels before becoming a postman and then moving to Canada. But his largely forgotten role in Johanneson's story should not be underestimated.

The son of an African father and Indian mother, Francis had, like D'Oliveira, also played for the 'Coloured XI' in Johannesburg before saving up enough money to make the trip to England just a few weeks after Steve Mokone left Coventry. On arrival, one of his first acts was to appear in the same cricket side as John Charles in the Yorkshire League just before the giant Welshman moved to Juventus for a British record fee of £65,000. A rapid winger capable of playing down either flank, Francis was initially signed as an amateur but impressed enough during his first six months to be handed a professional contract, with a signing-on fee of £10 and weekly wages of £12. "It might sound nothing much by present-day earnings but it was a good wage at that time," he recalled.

More than two years passed and, after making just one appearance for the first team in the FA Cup under Raich Carter, Francis was finally handed his league debut under Revie's predecessor, Jack Taylor. His presence in the starting line-up against Manchester United on 9 September 1959 made him the first black South African to play in the First Division. It wasn't a match to remember, however, as Leeds were thrashed 6-0 at Old Trafford, with Bobby Charlton scoring twice. To compound his misery, Francis also picked up an injury and did not return to the team for a month.

His home debut against Everton was much more satisfying. Despite a nervous start in front of a "thin" crowd of 19,000 at Elland Road, the *Yorkshire Evening Post* rated him as "easily United's most penetrative forward" as he scored the home side's second goal in a thrilling 3-3 draw. "Francis can certainly expect to keep his place at outside right," read the match report. "He came out of a subdued start splendidly and used his intelligence and his pace and his swerve well on the firm going. He opened his league scoring account with as fine a cross drive as I have seen in years." A cartoon depicting Francis smiling while kicking a ball and entitled 'A Springbox of tricks' also appeared in the newspaper that day. Leeds supporters had found themselves a new hero.

Another brilliant goal in the next game against Stanley Matthews' Blackpool appeared to confirm that, although the 3-3 draw at Bloomfield Road left Taylor's side struggling at the foot of the table with just three wins from their opening 13 matches. Like Mokone at Coventry, however, the blistering start for Francis was short-lived as he found himself in and out of the team over the next few months as Leeds continued to find life hard in the top division. He also admitted that life as one of the few black players in the game was far from straightforward.

"I was told that apartheid did not exist in England, but I realised quickly that there was still a little," said Francis. "The public racist insults or from opponents were common but they were mistaken if they thought that would destabilise me. On the contrary, it made me stronger. But Leeds fans adored me; I never experienced any racism from them."

Despite a 1-0 away victory at Turf Moor over eventual champions Burnley in December, they found themselves level on points with Birmingham in the second relegation spot as the season ticked into March. The emergence of a flame-haired Scottish teenager called Billy Bremner had restricted Francis to just a handful of appearances since the turn of the year, with the man who would go on to become the symbol of Revie's Leeds initially handed his chance on the right wing. Two goals from their future manager and one from Bremner secured yet another a 3-3 draw, this time against Birmingham, before a famous victory over Manchester City lifted Taylor's side out of the relegation zone. By the time Francis scored his third goal for Leeds in the 2-1 victory over Preston in mid-April, however, they were back in trouble and ended the season being relegated by a single point.

In the Second Division, Francis made 31 league appearances and scored six goals during the 1960/61 season. He was also selected in Revie's first game as manager at Fratton Park against Portsmouth on 18 March 1961. Two months earlier, Johanneson had joined his compatriot at Elland Road and was already beginning to push for a first-team place of his own. Once more, it was Gaffney who had persuaded Leeds to take a chance on the flying winger who had been starring for Germiston Callies in his homeland. Turned down by Newcastle United, Johanneson was eventually invited for a three-month trial.

"Barney was great," remembered Johanneson in *The Black Flash*. "He discussed the situation with my family and said that he would find some money to help get me there. He expressed a real belief that I had what it takes to be a professional footballer in Europe."

***

Signed from Sunderland three years earlier, by the time he took over as Leeds manager Don Revie was winding down his playing career having previously scored four goals in his six appearances for England. Relinquishing the captaincy to Freddie Goodwin after their relegation, the powerfully built striker from Teesside had been mooted as a potential replacement should Taylor depart and was asserting his growing influence when Johanneson turned up at the end of January. "I admit, I didn't like [Revie] when I first arrived," the South African told Harrison. "He had an arrogant sort of way about him, an aloofness that made him different to many of the other players. He was so much bigger than I was, and even when I was standing in front of him, he would talk over my head, ignoring my presence."

On his arrival at Elland Road, Johanneson was taken on a guided tour of the stadium by Taylor, who warned him that integrating into life in English football would not be easy. "You are unique not only in Leeds, but across the entire profession here in Britain," said the manager. "Many white people have a fear about your kind of people coming here; they will see you as being very different to them. Somebody has already asked me if you are a witch doctor. I have put that person straight and in his place. Your colour is going to be a big problem, Albert, just don't let the bigots get to you."

Shaken but thankful for Taylor's honesty, Johanneson was taken to lodgings around the corner in Beeston, where he was to stay with landlady Edna Wineley. As well as being shocked by his manager's revelation, he soon realised that none of the clothes he had brought with him would be suitable to keep out the cold of a Yorkshire winter. "In those early days, Leeds seemed such a miserable place, cold, dank and depressing," he told Harrison. "I questioned whether I would ever be able to live in England, a place where black people were a rarity and clearly, in parts, not welcome."

Nonetheless, Johanneson made quite an impression once he became used to wearing boots. An incredulous Bremner thought he was joking when the fact he preferred to play with bare feet emerged during his first training session, but despite a couple of heavy 'Welcome to Leeds' challenges that left him sprawling in the mud, the Scot would become a trusted ally in those early days. Full back Grenville Hair, who would make 443 appearances for Leeds in a 16-year career, also took Johanneson under his wing as he attempted to show his worth. But a number of racist incidents marred his early days in England, including being barred from entering the stadium when Leeds travelled to face Sheffield Wednesday in an FA Cup tie. The Hillsborough steward only relented when Bremner appeared and threatened to "knock his block off" if he didn't let his teammate pass.

The experiences certainly left their mark and Johanneson

told Harrison that he had considered returning to South Africa on several occasions. With Francis there to help him settle in, though, the process slowly became easier as he began to exhibit some of the skills that had made his name. Taylor's resignation after he had been informed the board had run out of patience was a blow, with the appointment of Revie as player-manager seemingly an ominous sign that his and Francis' time was almost up. Despite his concerns, Johanneson burst into tears when he was offered a professional contract at the end of his three-month trial. "I'm taking a huge gamble on you delivering," he was told.

Within three days of signing the contract, Johanneson made his first-team debut against Swansea on 7 April 1961 at Elland Road. Despite being subjected to racist insults from the away end as he warmed up, it proved to be a memorable occasion as a pinpoint cross for Jack Charlton to head home in only the second minute gave Leeds an early lead. "He won't forget his first league kick in a hurry and nor will any of the 12,000 who saw it," wrote the *Yorkshire Evening Post*'s correspondent. But Swansea's players had also taken exception to his presence on the pitch. "Bloody hell, Leeds must be desperate – they've got a darkie playing for them," remarked one before kick-off.

Their hatred of him was confirmed a few minutes later when a scything challenge from behind took out Johanneson in full flow, with his aggressor calling him "a nigger" and warning that he would be "kicked back to South Africa" if he tried to humiliate him again. The referee waved away his complaints. "You are black, you are different, I promise you'll take a lot more of that before your career here is finished," he said. "If it happens again, tell him to fuck off; it's only words and words won't kill you." The game ended in a 2-2 draw and afterwards Johanneson was thrown into the communal bath by his celebrating teammates having at first been reluctant to share it due to his skin colour. Once more, it was Bremner who persuaded him otherwise.

Eight days later, on 15 April 1961, Francis and Johanneson were selected for Leeds' trip to face Stoke. It would be the first time in the history of English football that two black African players had appeared on the same side. "That particular week in training, Gerry and I seemed to excel," recalled Johanneson. "We were motivating each other, running at players and past them. The boss told me he had seen nothing like the pair of us when we were in full flow."

Revie confirmed the news the day before the match. Francis was to play on the right flank, with his compatriot lining up on the opposite wing. Stoke's supporters had a reputation for being some of the most hostile in the country and both players were warned to expect the worst. The abuse began even before Johanneson had reached the changing room when a fan confronted him and asked if he was there to "clean shoes". That was only the start. Nonetheless, as the teams prepared to kick off, he remembered looking across the pitch and seeing Francis "looking every bit a professional footballer and not a random black person making up the numbers. We were both there because we deserved it."

In difficult conditions, Leeds struggled to create many chances and the 0-0 draw was another disappointing result as they ended the season in 14th place despite the 7-0 thrashing of Lincoln City – yet another match that Johanneson remembered for receiving a racial slur from an opponent. "Fuck off, nigger boy," he was told afterwards after attempting to make a joke. "I'll always be more of a winner than you ever are. I'm no blackie!"

Like Francis, he was also subjected to numerous prejudicial attitudes away from the pitch – including one occasion when a shopkeeper refused to serve him and called for help to throw out the man who had starred on the wing for the city's football team the previous weekend. When his friend was sold to York two months into the new season as Revie began the process of rebuilding the side in his vision, it left Johanneson feeling "vulnerable". Johanneson started the first seven games of the new season before losing his place but he did score his first goal from the penalty spot in a League Cup defeat against Rotherham. A generally disappointing campaign ended with another goal in a 3-0 win over Newcastle as Leeds finished 19th. But while his place in the side was under threat, Johanneson admitted that year was the happiest of his life. He met Norma Comrie – a chemist who lived locally – and married her in 1963. Francis was his best man. Hair also provided support from the sidelines when nerves kicked in about his speech.

The next season, Johanneson missed just one league game as Leeds ended up fifth. The seeds of revival were in place. Yet, of course, the racism continued. His solitary absence had been caused by a particularly violent approach from Sunderland's players to try to take him out of the game. Punched, kicked and abused throughout, the South African remained on the pitch but was forced to sit out the next match due to the injuries he sustained. That proved to be a significant moment when Revie dropped him for the following season's match against Sunderland saying he would be bullied by his opponents again – an experience that Johanneson later said spoiled the achievement of winning the Second Division and achieving promotion. "I was upset by the manager's reaction," he told Harrison. "It wasn't the first time I ever took drink, but this time I went out and drowned my sorrows with alcohol. I felt rough for several days after and vowed never to drink again."

Harrison insists the Leeds manager's attitude towards his South African winger was a contributing factor in his eventual downfall.

"Don Revie was racist, there's no doubt about it," he says. "He had issues with Albert and with Gerry. Billy Bremner said there was a side to Revie that no one will ever know about because it was all kept in the changing room. There was the story about when they used to go and get fish and chips and Albert would have to sit in the back room. Don Revie used to go. Why would he allow the owner to make him sit in the back just in case he stopped other customers coming to eat?"

***

By the end of the 1964/65 season, Revie's Leeds were the talk of English football. They had begun the new year top of the table after a blistering start to life in the First Division that included a 2-1 victory over Aston Villa on the opening day, when Johanneson scored the equaliser after his team had trailed at half-time. Bremner would later identify that day as a significant moment in their development into championship contenders. Two more goals against Everton at Elland Road in a match where he was repeatedly abused by the travelling supporters at the end of March maintained their tussle for the title with Chelsea and Manchester United until the end of the season, only to agonisingly lose out to United on goal average in the end.

Their appearance in the FA Cup final against Liverpool at Wembley in May 1965 was the first time Leeds had contested English football's most famous match. It was also the first time a non-white African player had stepped foot on the hallowed turf – a fact that has come to define Johanneson's life. But the day itself was one that he later admitted he would have rather forgotten.

"It was clear that while other players appearing in the same game were individuals, I was represented as an object," he told Harrison. "I went to tell Don Revie to pull me out of the team because I wanted to protest and make a stand so people could see that what they were doing to me was wrong. He didn't want to hear about my feelings. 'I'm not listening to you. You are capable of winning this game for us; that is why you are playing. It's a shit pitch for fancy football, so use your pace, run like the wind and don't let the jungle bunny chanting get to you. This isn't a black man's game but you might just shock them if you run at them aggressively with a ball, so run at them whenever you can. If you get muddy make sure your teammates can still see you, shout for the ball whenever you want it, don't disappear.'"

Having spent the majority of the next hour in the toilet being sick, Johanneson's trembling legs finally stepped into the tunnel. Insults from the Liverpool players rained down on him and, just as the two teams were about to emerge on a drizzly afternoon, Shankly whispered in his ear. "I thought I got hell's abuse for being Scottish," said the Liverpool manager. "But son, you've got no chance looking like you do, our fans will murder you." He was right. What Johanneson described as "a cacophony of Zulu-like noises" greeted him on the long walk to the pitch. "I wanted to run back down the tunnel, but I filled my thoughts with how proud my entire family and friends would be at seeing me play at Wembley," he later admitted.

Bogged down by the muddy pitch, however, Johanneson struggled to have an impact on the match as Leeds went down 2-1 after extra time and – rather than being frustrated by the narrow defeat – was instead just relieved when it was all over. "It felt as though I had let down everyone who'd ever known me," he said. "If I am honest, my relationship with Don Revie was never the same after that game. I may have made black football history, but I still look back on that game with much despair and sadness."

"I think he felt like the performing monkey who would get out there and do all his tricks to help Leeds win or lose the game," reflects Harrison. "He put that pressure on himself as well. So on the one hand, you've got everyone remembering him for that day and on the other, him saying, 'It destroyed me'. That's quite a juxtaposition."

Revie purchased winger Mike O'Grady from Huddersfield in the summer and the player who had been one of the standout performers in the previous two seasons quickly found himself surplus to requirements. Frustrated by his diminished status, Johanneson played just a bit-part role for the club in his final five years and increasingly turned to drink as Leeds continued to contest for major honours, eventually winning the First Division title in 1969 after four successive top-four finishes.

"Revie could have stepped in much earlier because he knew Albert was drinking quite heavily to calm his nerves before games," says Harrison. "Bremner and Johnny Giles would have a quick drink before they went out and Albert was just drinking what was left . . . I felt sorry for him because Albert didn't understand what was happening and when you piece all the pieces together you can see that Revie didn't like him and didn't want him there in the first place. But it's difficult without putting him on the spot."

Johanneson's eldest daughter Yvonne agrees that her father's descent into alcoholism could perhaps have been avoided.

"As I've said to several people, my dad did not drink when he met my mum," she insists. "He didn't even have champagne at his wedding. He had orange juice instead. She didn't know him as a drinker but, on the other hand, his family did have a history of alcoholism and was that a contributing factor? For much of his life he recognised that this was something that he could be afflicted with and didn't want to go down that road, to the extent that he was drinking orange juice on his wedding day. That indicates that the pressures were there to submit to the drink and unfortunately his genetic predisposition helped to create a dependency."

Johanneson's last appearance for Leeds the following season came against Burnley after he had been out drinking until the early hours. After yet another heavy challenge, the once-sprightly figure lay prone on the ground as Eddie Gray scored one of the most famous goals in Leeds' history, skipping past several defenders before firing the ball into the net. "My heart sank as I realised that it could have been me receiving the celebrations at scoring such a wonder goal," he recalled. "Instead, I was lying on the floor feeling sorry for myself."

Ignored by Revie afterwards, Johanneson wrote his manager a letter to apologise for his behaviour but was placed on the transfer list instead. He eventually signed for York at the end of the season but made just 26 appearances before being released in 1972, his career over at the age of just 32. "I wasn't fit enough, my weight was getting worse and my drinking habits were getting me into trouble," he told Harrison. "I wasn't what you would call a pleasant drunk. My life became a blur and because I was a bastard in so many ways, the one outstanding love I had in my life, my wife and my children, I drove them away. I can never forgive myself for that; my beautiful wife and children were gone."

Finally having had enough of his drinking, Norma decided to return to Jamaica in 1974 with Yvonne and her youngest daughter Alicia, ending almost ten years of marriage.

"It was an interesting dynamic because I think it was a decision my mother had to make for the well-being of the family at the time," says Yvonne, who now lives in Atlanta in the United States. "Evidently it is one that over the years I have had to reconcile with. I had the good fortune of seeing him when I studied in France, although my sister didn't get to see him before he died. We maintained sporadic contact and I would share pictures with him but there was very little feedback. I had the opportunity to speak with him after he went into rehab. He shared his thoughts with regards to our sister and with regards to not having been in our lives and it was very sad. It was difficult on both sides."

***

In 2007, more than a decade after Johanneson's death, *Nationality: Wog, The Hounding of David Oluwale* by historian Kester Aspden was published. It told the story of the Nigerian immigrant living on the streets of Leeds who had drowned in the River Aire in 1968 in mysterious circumstances. Three years later, two police officers were jailed for a series of assaults on Oluwale but cleared of his manslaughter despite evidence of several witnesses who had seen them chasing him near the river on the day in question. The story was largely forgotten outside the growing black communities of Leeds until Aspden, who had worked at the local university, came across it.

Described as "the physical and psychological destruction of a homeless, black man whose brutal, systematic harassment was orchestrated by the Leeds city police force" by the *British Journal of Criminology*, the book laid bare the racist attitudes that existed during the 1960s, drawing parallels with the negative experiences Johanneson encountered as two of an estimated 450 black men living in the city at the time. "At the start, their lives couldn't have been more different, and yet both men's lives ended tragically and needlessly early," wrote Leeds historian Sam Gibbard.

Like Wharton and Mokone before him, the unravelling of Johanneson's life began almost as soon as his playing days were over. After an unsuccessful season back in South Africa, he returned to Leeds determined to get one more chance but ended up washing dishes in a Chinese restaurant to make some cash. Without his family, who had subsequently moved to Florida, he quickly slipped into alcoholism and became a regular sight in Leeds drinking establishments. Typically, that was where Harrison first encountered the man who had been his hero as a child.

"I know this sounds stupid but I regarded him as a friend," he says. "When I met him in the pub and I saw him sitting in the corner, my heart went out to him. I just thought, 'Poor guy. I can help him.' He was really open and there was a guy called David Robinson who was his agent who said that if anyone wanted to do something they had to go through him. This guy was controlling Albert. The more I looked into it, the more seedy it became. He was clearly part of the underworld in Leeds."

Over the next few years, Harrison would meet up with Johanneson regularly to discuss his memories. It was at that point he began to think about writing a book.

"I remember telling him about it in the pub [Johanneson was only permitted to drink orange juice by Paul] and he said, 'Nobody will buy it. Nobody will be interested.' And I said, 'Albert, there are a lot of people who are interested but it's not about standing in the pub and having a drink with you' – and there were a lot of people in Leeds who could say they had done that – 'it's a book about what you've done. It's an incredible life.' And he went, 'Well, I'll tell you but I need to think about it.'

"I asked him whether he knew that he was held in high esteem in some quarters, and he said, 'No. People just think I'm a bum and I'm black.' He had gone so far into that dark place that I wanted to try and pull him out. He was a big bloated fella when I met him and I used to think sometimes, 'This isn't the same bloke.' It's almost like someone had blown air into him like a Michelin man."

Like Oluwale, who had stowed away in a British cargo ship sailing from Lagos to Hull in 1949, Johanneson also became a regular target for the local police. His exploits on the wing for Leeds long forgotten, they would often chase him down the road and physically assault him if he was seen out in the city centre. "The police are not my friends," he told Harrison. "It's not a crime for people to stand and speak in the street, but if you are a black ex-footballer called Albert and in Leeds, then you are targeted by the police as some sort of criminal." On one occasion in 1981, he remembered being dragged to his feet by an officer and told to "go back to Africa with all the other darkies". An attempt to make a complaint was met with derision by the local sergeant. "What I suffered and saw in South Africa in my youth was no different to the hurtful torment and pain I suffer here. The police are corrupt and society doesn't really want to know the truth."

Disgusted by the treatment of the man who had made football history, Harrison resolved to finish the book as soon as possible. "I wanted people to realise that this was a human being as well. Not just an icon."

The Black Flash was eventually published in 2012, nearly 50 years after Johanneson had made his debut for Leeds. But while Johanneson's daughters dispute some of the details in Harrison's book, their own fight to have their father's name honoured proved to be just as long a process.

"We noticed that the UK and America and other countries that have had high immigrant populations have tended not to highlight the contribution made by people of colour," Yvonne says. "But increasingly we saw how people like Jackie Robinson and others have got credit for what they have done here so we were always conscious that one day Dad would be remembered in some way. We started reaching out to people for many years before. If you go back you can see emails going back as far as 2004 when we started expressing our opinion and trying to gather interest."

With the initial help of Lord Herman Ouseley from anti-racism organisation Kick It Out and then Danny Lynch at the Football Association, their persistence was eventually rewarded when they were invited to attend the 2015 FA Cup final between Arsenal and Aston Villa as special guests. Alicia was unable to accompany Yvonne on the trip due to illness but half a century since their father had made history at Wembley, it was long overdue recognition.

***

A few weeks after Arsenal's 4-0 victory, Johanneson's losers' medal from the 1965 final went on display at the National Football Museum in Manchester alongside various other memorabilia from his career, including a letter from a Leeds fan that described him as their hero. Yet while there are plans to make that a permanent feature of the museum, Johanneson's legacy continues to live on in other ways as well. Paul Eubanks, a teacher from Leeds who grew up watching him from the terraces at Elland Road, has presented several talks on his hero in local schools over the years while the Football Unites, Racism Divides project in Sheffield also produced a comic entitled *Albert Johanneson: The First Black Superstar* to mark the 50th anniversary of his cup final appearance. It has since been read by thousands of children in various schools across the country.

"For me that is the kind of legacy that I would like to see," says Yvonne. "You can have a statue but something that is part of an educational process that can be used for years to come – that creates the ongoing awareness. I feel very proud. The progress African players have made on the field is proof of everything that I've told my children: follow your path and don't be discouraged. If you're the first that's great. Be a pioneer. That's what Albert was. He may not have gone down the happy-ever-after story route. But I tell people all the time that as hard as it is to think of his ending, his legacy has not ended. So many people would love to leave a legacy to the world and he did. I don't even think he knew that was going to happen – during his lifetime it wasn't there."

After years of effort from his daughters, a blue plaque marking the club's second black player was unveiled outside the East

Stand reception at Elland Road in January 2019. "Born and raised in South Africa, he made a new life in England," reads the inscription. "A mesmerising left winger, he made 200 appearances for Leeds United from 1961 to 1969, scoring 67 goals, playing an integral part in helping the club win promotion to the First Division in 1964. In 1965, he became the first black African to play in the FA Cup final."

Harrison says he would also like to continue spreading the word about his hero's impact on English football and admits he finds it increasingly hard to see others head down the same road of despair.

"It's a lesson that needs to be broadcasted," he stresses. "If you make the wrong decisions, then you let the racists win and you can end up like Albert easily. When I used to ask him where it all went wrong, he always said it was the cup final that broke him."

Buried in the idyllic surroundings of Lawnswood Cemetery – six miles from Elland Road up the Otley Road – at least he is at peace now. Johanneson's gravestone bears an inscription from the Maya Angelou poem 'Still I Rise' that required permission from the celebrated American author's estate before it could be erected in 1995:

Out of the huts of history's shame, I rise
Up from a past that's rooted in pain. I rise
I'm a black ocean, leaping and wide. Welling and swelling I
bear in the tide
Bringing the gifts that my ancestors gave I am the dream and
the hope of the slave
I rise. I rise. I rise.

"It speaks about the affliction of black people – despite everything we have gone through, we're still here fighting and achieving," explains Yvonne. "Albert grew up in apartheid but was still able to have a successful career as a footballer. He was kicked every week and had his leg broken when referees were not looking out for him and yet he still would show up for every match. He's not here today and maybe he could have done more with his talent but he still made the pioneering step to open up the doors for others. He made the next generation think, 'If this guy can do it, so can I.'"

SIX

THE PRIDE OF ANFIELD

Whatever happens next in his career, Naby Keïta will never forget his first visit to Melwood in August 2017. "It was an incredible day for me," reflected the Guinea midfielder ten months later when his move to Liverpool was finally completed for a club record £53 million.

Dressed in a pinstripe suit and crimson tie and accompanied by his father Sekou, Keïta's welcome meeting with Jürgen Klopp at the club's suburban training ground after an agreement had been struck with RB Leipzig for him to join the following summer was just coming to an end in the manager's office when there was a knock at the door. In walked a certain Steven Gerrard – at that stage working as the club's Under-18 manager – brandishing a Liverpool home shirt.

"He gave me the No. 8 jersey," added Keïta fondly. "When he came in, I looked at him and said, 'Wow,' because he is a legend. He is somebody who always showed respect, who gave his all on the pitch, somebody who is loved here. If somebody like that gives you his shirt number, it's not to play around with, it is to try and do as much as he did – that's my motivation."

Since Gerrard's departure for LA Galaxy more than two years

earlier, the famous shirt worn by the club's former captain for more than a decade had yet to be reallocated. Now, hot on the heels of Mohamed Salah's purchase from Roma, another African player had been chosen to replace one of the club's most iconic players. The man who lifted the 2005 Champions League trophy after the most famous of all comebacks against AC Milan in Istanbul had anointed his successor.

"Eight is a number I've always liked," admitted Keïta. "It's also the number my dad wore when he played so it's special to me. When we played, because I'm a midfielder and Steven Gerrard was always the boss of the team, I had to be him. I couldn't be anyone else but Steven Gerrard when I played. I wanted to be like him."

Sekou Keïta had grown up watching Kenny Dalglish, Ian Rush and the famous Liverpool side of the 1980s, sneaking into the local shebeen in the Guinean capital of Conakry as a teenager to catch a glimpse of his heroes. "As far back as I can remember, he has been talking about them," said his son. "Before I even knew what Liverpool was as a kid, he was mad about them."

The arrival of Aboubacar Sidiki 'Titi' Camara at Anfield in 1999 had only cemented the club's popularity in Guinea. Born just up the road from the Keïtas in a suburb of Conakry, Camara had moved to France as a teenager and forged a successful career at St Etienne, Lens and Marseille – reaching the UEFA Cup final in his final season – before joining Liverpool for £2.6 million and becoming the first Guinean to move to English football. At the time, still only a handful of African players could be found on the books of Premier League sides such as Leeds captain Lucas Radebe from South Africa or Cameroon midfielder Marc-Vivien Foé at West Ham.

But at the club where Jamaican-born John Barnes had blazed a trail for black players almost two decades earlier and Zimbabwe international goalkeeper Bruce Grobbelaar became a hero of the Kop, Camara's outpouring of emotion when he scored against West Ham in October 1999 only endeared him more to the Anfield faithful. Less than 24 hours after the death of his father and with manager Gérard Houllier unable to call on injured strikers Robbie Fowler and Michael Owen, Camara insisted on playing and dropped to his knees in tears when his winning goal went in. "There was no way I could play after something like that," reflected former captain Jamie Carragher in the documentary *100 Players Who Shook the Kop*. "But for him to score the winning goal as well . . ."

Also watching on was a young Naby Keïta, who had already shown his ability with the ball at home. "It's a gift he was born with," acknowledged Sekou. "Even when he was a little boy, I knew he was going to be a great footballer one day."

***

More than 4,000 miles away from the plush surroundings of Liverpool's training ground, a group of teenagers are playing football in the streets of Koleya in the shadow of Conakry's Grande Mosquée. "At the moment he's Africa's best player," says Ibrahima, 17, as he demonstrates some jaw-dropping skills with a patched-up yellow ball. "This is street football. Everybody has to go through this first to become a professional player. Naby had to as well."

Dodging the constant stream of cars, mopeds, cyclists and pedestrians during their five-a-side match using makeshift goals made from wood and string, Ibrahima and his friends display skills that would not look out of place on a Saturday afternoon at Anfield. But for these young men, this is probably as good as it will ever get. While Keïta's impending multi-million pound transfer illustrated that African players had never been more in demand at the start of the 2017/18 season, the chances of making it all the way from the backstreets of a city like Conakry to the perfect pitches of the Premier League remain an unlikely dream that only a select few get to realise. Seven years since he first left Koleya to pursue his fortune in France as a teenager, Keïta makes regular trips back to his old neighbourhood whenever possible.

"I always buy boots when I'm back for as many kids as I can because I know how much it can mean to have something so simple," he explained to Goal.com journalist Melissa Reddy in 2018. "I wanted to be Deco, Titi Camara or [Guinea's record goalscorer] Pascal Feindouno when I was young, and now there are kids with my name on the back of their shirts! That is such a big motivation for me and I hope I continue to show them that with courage and determination, they can achieve anything.

"When I go home, my friends organise small tournaments and people come to watch us play," Keïta added. "I also enjoy that as I get to play with people, but it's not as important to me as it is to my friends. It makes them very happy, even if I do just a couple of minutes, because the pitch is quite dangerous so I have to be careful I don't injure my feet or legs. To learn football in Guinea the street is the best school. I believe that all boys in Africa, at least in Guinea, play on the streets and learn it there. You play football between all the cars."

With his father struggling to make ends meet working as a motorcycle mechanic, the young Naby would accompany his mother to the market every day to help sell bottles of ice-cold water to parched workers in a city where the average temperature rarely drops below 28 °C. Guinea is known as the 'water tower of Africa' due to the large number of rivers that originate inside its borders, including the River Niger that runs for more than 3,000 miles in a crescent through West Africa and the oil-rich Niger Delta before emptying its waters into the Atlantic Ocean. Built on Kaloum Peninsula, a 22-mile long stretch of land poking out of the mainland, Conakry was a sleepy port town with fewer than 500 inhabitants until the late 1880s when Britain ceded it to France.

But far from being an inconsequential outpost, Guinea had once been the centre of one of the most formidable African empires in history. In a clash that brings to mind a Premier League skirmish between Liverpool's and Chelsea's key midfielders in the 21st century, Sundiata Keïta defeated Sosso ruler Sumanguru Kanté at the Battle of Kirina in around 1235, beginning the transition that would establish the Mali Empire as the region's most powerful force for more than 400 years. Born in Niani on the border of modern-day Guinea and Mali, Keïta – whose name means 'inheritor' (heir-apparent) in the Mandinka language – overcame childhood disability to become leader of a liberating army which overthrew Kanté's rule and eventually encompassed large swathes of modern-day Mali, Guinea, Guinea-Bissau and Senegal over nearly 500,000 square miles.

Sundiata Keïta's grandson Mansa Musa was responsible for much of the expansion and also the introduction of Islam to the region following his pilgrimage to Mecca in around 1324. Today, approximately 85 per cent of the country are Muslims. But when the Europeans arrived in the late 15th century, they found a territory that had become beset by tribal rivalries and divided into several kingdoms that made conquest a relatively straightforward process. Neighbouring Sierra Leone had become an early outpost for the burgeoning slave trade and it is estimated that around 500,000 people in the region were taken from their homeland to various destinations around the world over the next 300 years.

It was only in the late 1890s that Guinea became a French colony after Samori Touré's Wassoulou Empire was defeated in battle, ending Islamic rule. It became part of French West Africa – administered from more than 1,000 kilometres away in Dakar, Senegal – until the collapse of the Fourth Republic government in 1958 offered an opportunity to ambitious young political leader Ahmed Sékou Touré. In a referendum of all eight colonies that made up the region, Guinea was the only one to vote for independence and it was granted immediately, with Touré named as the president.

France promptly withdrew all economic aid and, after a brief flirtation with the Soviet Union, Guinea became a one-party socialist state that relied heavily on foreign aid from several sources to feed its people. After more than 30 years in office, Touré's death in 1984 left a country that had been devastated by his oppressive policies. Around 50,000 people are believed to have been killed in concentration camps, with thousands more fleeing across the borders to escape what had become one of the poorest places in the world.

Lansana Conté – a former solider in the French army who had fought in the Algerian War of Independence – seized power in a coup but proved to be a reformer at first, restoring democratic elections and civilian rule. More than 200,000 displaced Guineans are estimated to have returned home in the decade after he took power, with the population of Conakry growing from fewer than 40,000 in the late 1960s to more than one million in 1995. By the time Naby Keïta was ten years old, it was approaching two million.

But with Chinese investment in the country's vast resources of aluminium and bauxite still a few years away, the country's GDP had shrunk by 16 per cent by the turn of the century, leading to mass unemployment in what was already one of the poorest economies in West Africa. It was in this environment that Sekou Keïta tried to raise his family, making a few precious extra francs turning out for his local amateur side as a central midfielder. The young Naby would often watch his father from the sidelines and then disappear for hours afterwards with his friends as they tried to replicate what they had seen.

"We played with whatever we could and I would have nothing on my feet, or sometimes play with old, damaged shoes," he remembered. "I didn't have boots and treasured football shirts that were given to me. All that has helped me be better prepared for anything now as a professional and I'm also not scared of anything on the pitch. I was quite small and so I had to fight for everything: the chance to play, for the ball, to get respect and that's why not even cars could stop me. It's where the aggression in my game, which is so important for my position, comes from."

According to his father, Naby had fallen in love with football before he could even talk. "My dad told me that as a baby, I loved the ball – to look at it, to touch it. I always wanted it around me. I always looked forward to going to the supermarket with my mother. There were a lot of round things to play football with. Unfortunately, there were also things like lampshades, which got broken. My mum always says that shopping with me was very expensive!"

Four years later, Sekou was watching the Champions League final between Porto and Monaco when he noticed the skilful No. 10 for the Portuguese side. Deco ended up scoring the second goal as José Mourinho's side won their second European title in style, with young Naby adopting a new nickname from that day forward due to his similarity to the Brazilian-born midfielder, who went on to win another Champions League at Barcelona in 2006. So when it came to choosing replica shirts for his junior side to play in, there was only one choice. "I wanted us to get the Barcelona strip – they were my favourite," said Keïta. "All my friends were Liverpool supporters, though, and I really liked the club too so we decided on them."

As word about Naby's outstanding ability spread, at the age of just 12 he was encouraged to follow his fortune in the promised land for African footballers: Europe. Yet with concerns that their son was not big enough to make the grade, Sekou and his mother Mariam urged him to concentrate on his education instead.

"They wanted me to study," Keïta recalled. "They felt education was the most important and more stable, but there was nothing else for me but football. They tried and tried, but they could see where my head and my heart was. Everyone in the community would say to them that I'm the best player in Conakry and, eventually, my parents told me they know I've got a special gift so they will fully support my dream."

While most would have jumped at the chance to try their luck in Europe as quickly as possible, Keïta rejected the opportunity to leave home at 14 despite offers from various agents keen to cash in on the child prodigy. "I was not mentally ready yet for such a big step," he admitted. "About two years later, I would watch a lot of Ligue 1, Champions League and Premier League games on TV and I knew I wanted to be playing at that level. It was impossible to do that at home, so it was clear that I would have to test myself in Europe. I was determined to become a footballer, not only because I loved the game, but so I could provide for my family. My parents had nothing, and they put all hope on me. Whenever I played well, I received some cash which I could pass on to my family."

The offers were soon flooding in. Having started at a local side called FC Bouba, he progressed through a series of amateur teams until one day he was greeted by an agent called Malick Kebé.

"Our first meeting took place in Koleya near the Total station, and he played for the club FC Alia," Kebé recalls. "I told him that I had heard he has a superb technique with the ball at his feet. Naby told me that he dreams of playing one day for Barcelona. It was really ambitious and he knew what he wanted. In return, I asked him to give me the African Golden Ball. But the thing that really touched me and made me believe in him was when he told me to go and see his mother to arrange the collaboration agreement. I realised that this young man was under parental supervision and that he was blessed. The love he has for his family and especially the love he has for his mother is the secret to his success."

By the age of 15, Keïta was already starring for Santoba FC's first team in the second tier of Guinea's domestic league and the scouts were circling. "Everyone thought that Naby was going to play for the biggest clubs in Europe," said former Santoba teammate Fodé Kebé.

When Guinea legend Feindouno – who remains the country's all-time top scorer with 30 goals having spent the majority of his career in France's Ligue 1 – recommended his former club Lorient should take a look at the exciting teenager, he finally took the plunge. "My parents were terrified. They didn't want me to go so far away and they were worried about how I would adapt to these new surroundings," Keïta admitted. "It was more difficult than I could have imagined as everything except the language was different. I was used to playing football with my friends, but now I was with strangers that wanted to mostly keep to themselves."

Like so many young African players had found before him, life in Europe was more difficult than he could have ever imagined. Rejected by Lorient – where he lodged with future international teammate Guy-Michel Landel – he then saw a potential move to Le Mans collapse in 2011 after the club ran into financial difficulties. "Naby had inconclusive negotiations with a few clubs and each time had to come back to Guinea," Kebé adds. "But he has always been a fighter."

"I was never exposed to the professional side of the game," Keïta explained. "I didn't grow up in an academy; everything I knew was from the street. I would get the ball, I would run with it, show some skill to beat a player and score. During these trials, coaches were asking me to do things I'd never heard of! They were using football terms that I couldn't understand and giving instructions that I had no clue about. I didn't know about tactics and when I was rejected that is what I was told."

Keïta eventually returned two years later when Kebé and former Guinea defender Abdoul Karim Bangoura arranged for him to attend a tournament in Marseille for prospective players that had been organised by former Celtic defender Bobo Baldé. Watching on was former Hibernian midfielder Frédéric Arpinon, who had become sporting director at Istres – a tiny club based 50 kilometres up the Côte d'Azur that had spent just one season in its 90-year history in the French top flight, finishing bottom. Keïta was offered a three-year deal following a successful trial in 2013, joining the established second tier outfit who played in the 17,000 capacity Stade Parsemain. It wasn't long before he was thrown into the deep end against Nimes – four times runners-up in the French league during the 1960s – for the home fixture on 22 November 2013.

"I had waited so long, had so many setbacks and when I got my first chance, I wanted to prove I belonged in Europe," Keïta remembered.

In what was to become something of a habit, it took him only 36 minutes to make an impression with a goal on his debut as Istres went on to win 4-2, with their teenage midfielder also adding an assist. The journey to Anfield had begun, even if Sekou and Mariam couldn't quite believe what their son had achieved. "My parents were still very worried about me. I had to call them six times a day and tell them everything that was happening . . ."

***

Alongside former Paris Saint-Germain midfielder Jerome Leroy – by then approaching his 40th birthday – Keïta went on to make 23 appearances that season in Ligue 2, scoring four goals in total and making his full international debut for Guinea against Mali. Having himself played alongside the great George Weah in his first year as a professional and in his 20th season as a professional, Leroy was the perfect role model for his young teammate. "Jerome gave me a lot of advice and taught me that it is necessary to work hard in order to fulfil my potential. I often think about that," Keïta recalled when he moved to Red Bull Salzburg at the end of the season after Istres were relegated following a 6-1 home thrashing by Lens.

Despite the disappointment of his first season in Europe ending in failure, it was a recommendation from Houllier – the man who had brought Camara to Anfield 15 years earlier and also played a role in Sadio Mané's move to Austria – that prompted Red Bull to take a risk on him. By the time Keïta first came to the attention of Benoît Thans – a former player from Belgium who now works for Red Bull Global Soccer as a scout in France – during Istres' surprise away victory at Lens in December 2013, Salzburg's sister club RB Leipzig were already on their way to the Bundesliga having finally achieved promotion to the third tier and hired Ralf Rangnick, a career coach who had previously taken charge of Schalke and Stuttgart among others.

"I followed him a few times," Thans told ESPN. "It was an away match and Istres were not in a good situation, but in this match he was the best on the field. For me, it was very important because it told me that he wanted to continue to have good progression, to play for the team, to win. He was the best on the pitch in this match. I followed him for three or four matches and he was always the best player on the pitch."

The previous year, Houllier had become Red Bull's head of global football after leaving Aston Villa in what turned out to be his last post in management. Acting on the recommendation from Thans, at the end of May 2014 he went to watch Keïta play a friendly against Mali in France with Rangnick, who was to become a key figure in his career and at that stage acted as sporting director for both Red Bull Salzburg and RB Leipzig. A five-year deal was swiftly agreed, with Keïta moving to the Austrian champions for just €1.6 million in the face of late competition from some French clubs.

In Salzburg, he joined a squad boasting several established international stars including Mané. Having scored 31 times in fewer than 60 appearances since joining from Metz in 2012, the Senegal star was sent off in the first half of the away game against Wiener Neustadt in July 2014, with Keïta making his debut off the bench as Salzburg extended their 1-0 half-time lead to win 5-0. He made his first start the following week but had to wait until the 8-0 thrashing of Grödig to play in the same side as his future Liverpool teammate due to Mané's suspension. They played together once more before Salzburg eventually decided to let Mané join Southampton but, with both now also sharing agents in the form of Björn Bezemer's arena11 company, the pair had struck up a strong friendship in their short time together.

"At first, I wasn't starting and it was very frustrating," Keïta admitted. "I didn't like it and it made the settling-in period harder. But Sadio said: 'My little brother, stay calm. Your chance will come and when it does, you will make the most of it.' He helped me with everything – the language, making friends, understanding the club and the city. And, of course, he was right."

Keïta followed in the slipstream of his big brother and won back-to-back league and cup doubles in 2015 and 2016, capping it with the award for Austria's best player in the latter. By then, he had already been on Liverpool's radar for two years after scout Mads Jørgensen watched him during the Champions League qualifier against Malmo. Keïta was hauled off at half-time after being booked as Salzburg slumped to a 3-0 defeat to exit the competition but Jørgensen continued to keep tabs on him as he settled into his new club. When it became clear he had outgrown the Austrian league, Liverpool enquired whether he could be available but were informed a proposed move to RB Leipzig was already predetermined.

Keïta signed a four-year contract in Germany just as Leipzig had achieved promotion to the Bundesliga two years ahead of the schedule predicted when the club was formed in 2009. This time, he slotted seamlessly into the side assembled by Rangnick – now described as a father figure despite the frequent invasions of his private space during their four years together.

"He told me I was like a koala that you want to hug. He often hugs me," admitted Keïta in an interview in 2016. "I don't know exactly what a koala looks like. In fact, I often fear animals because in Guinea a lot of them are dangerous."

A former amateur midfielder who turned out for non-league side Southwick when he spent a year at the University of Sussex, Rangnick proved to be far more successful as a manager. Starting with the youth team at VfB Stuttgart in the mid-1980s, he earned a reputation as one of Germany's most innovative coaches and later helped establish Hoffenheim – a team from a town with a population of just 35,000 bankrolled by software millionaire Dietmar Hopp – as a force in Germany's top flight. It was that success that prompted Red Bull to entrust him with doing the same with their latest project and Rangnick turned to well-regarded Austrian manager Ralph Hasenhüttl, nicknamed the 'Alpine Klopp' for his all-action approach to the game.

Having finished as runners-up behind Bayern Munich in their debut Bundesliga season to qualify for the Champions League, Rangnick had insisted that none of his best players would leave the club that summer. Keïta was an obvious target given that he had just been voted as the second-best player in the league having scored eight goals and contributed almost twice as many assists. Always keen to snap up their domestic rivals' best players,

Bayern Munich immediately made no secret of their interest. Just like he had with Liverpool's sporting director Michael Edwards, however, Rangnick told them that not even an offer of €100 million would be enough.

A former trainee at Peterborough, Edwards went to university to study business management and informatics before becoming an expert in the emerging field of football analytics. He joined Liverpool in 2011 as head of analytics before progressing through the ranks to become technical director, impressing owners Fenway Sports Group with his negotiating skills and eye for a bargain. Having already instigated Sadio Mané's move from Southampton, it was his relationship with arena11 which proved to be key in persuading Keïta to follow him to Anfield.

Talks over a potential £35 million move for Alex Oxlade-Chamberlain from Arsenal and Liverpool's determination not to sell Philippe Coutinho to Barcelona meant Edwards and Jürgen Klopp had to be patient. But, they pondered, why not try to strike a deal for next summer instead? Edwards went back to Rangnick and eventually agreed a £52.75 million fee – almost £5 million more than his release clause. While disappointed to have to wait to complete his dream move, Keïta was relieved to have resolved his future and had just about come to terms with the prospect of another year in Germany when Rangnick spoke out at a coaching conference in Bochum.

"There should be someone who points them into the right direction," he said in clear reference to Keïta. "The boys themselves are not the problem here. It is their surroundings. A whole village in Guinea or somebody from their entourage tells the players why they must do something right away. I can't blame the players."

Rangnick's comments caused uproar, not least in Conakry. But asked to clarify them a few days later, the 60-year-old seemed to dig himself an even bigger hole.

"I know Naby from the very first day when he came to Salzburg," he said. "We therefore have a very close relationship, also to his adviser. We are in a trusting exchange. That is exactly what I said in my lecture in Bochum. Behind many players with an African background, and I've met a lot of them, there is a clan and sometimes a whole village that lives from the help of one football player. And it's the case that there are people behind Naby, that demand his transfer. Believe me, my knowledge in geography is good enough to differentiate between Guinea and Africa."

At first, Keïta vowed to never play for Rangnick again. He eventually relented but struggled to replicate his form from the previous campaign and was accused by some pundits in Germany of having one eye on his next destination. The ripple effect of Neymar's world record £198 million move to Paris Saint-Germain a few months earlier would also put that to the test when Barcelona's pursuit of Coutinho finally came to fruition as the Brazilian moved to the Camp Nou for an astronomical fee worth a possible £142 million.

Sensing an opportunity, Klopp immediately raised the prospect of bringing forward Keïta's transfer to fill the gap but once again found RB Leipzig standing in their way. A cheeky request to include emerging teenage star Trent Alexander-Arnold as part of the deal was politely rebuffed, with Rangnick adamant that it would cost another £17 million to prise him away six months early.

"Keïta would only be available for the final chunk of the season, would require a bedding-in period and had already played in the Champions League and so was cup-tied for the competition," wrote Paul Joyce in *The Times*. "They had waited four years; another four months would not represent too much hardship."

SEVEN

CREATING A DYNASTY

As the clock ticked into the 89th minute of the 1988 Littlewoods Cup Final at Wembley, Luton Town's Mark Stein picked up the ball midway inside the Arsenal half and deftly pushed it around the onrushing Tony Adams. A clattering challenge from the England defender sent the diminutive forward sprawling on to the turf as referee Joe Worrall awarded the foul. With the scores level at 2-2 after a mistake from Gus Caesar – later cruelly satirised in Nick Hornby's book *Fever Pitch* – had allowed Danny Wilson to equalise from Stein's cross, the team from Bedfordshire had an opportunity to win their first senior trophy in 104 years of existence.

Captain Steve Foster, wearing his trademark white headband, trundled forward into the Arsenal penalty area as Wilson prepared to take the free kick. It was headed away as far as substitute Ashley Grimes, who nodded the ball past Kevin Richardson to take him to the byline and then delivered a cross into the box with the outside of his left boot. Within an instant, Stein's elder brother Brian was on to it, beating Nigel Winterburn to despatch the ball past the despairing dive of goalkeeper John Lukic.

"Luton Town, the little club that plays on a wall-to-wall carpet and refuses to accommodate visiting supporters, yesterday won the Littlewoods Cup in a match as unpredictably dramatic as the FA Cup final of 1979," wrote Stuart Jones in *The Times* the next day. That afternoon, the Stein brothers accompanied manager Ray Harford and the rest of Luton's victorious team as they descended from their open-top bus to walk the final stretch of their journey from their plastic pitch at Kenilworth Road to the town hall. "This time we did ourselves justice," said Brian in a TV interview as he clutched the trophy, which had earlier been snapped in two during the celebrations. "It's a dream come true."

***

Almost exactly 20 years earlier, a former boxer, known as 'Boston Tababy' in his fighting days, and his family arrived at Cape Town's docks to board the ship that would take them to their new lives. Isaiah Stein had been hounded by the police for his political activities with the fledgling ANC movement in his homeland and finally decided it was time to get out.

"We were all very excited," recalls Edwin Stein, the eldest of three brothers born in South Africa who would go on to play professional football in England. "There were some other families that we knew who were going to Canada and others who were coming with us to the UK. It was all very organised because they knew we needed to get out of the country to try and create some pressure through the international community."

Stein's father had worked for a Jewish family as a teenager growing up in Cape Town and later adopted their surname, as was common at the time for members of the black community. He later became a prominent member of the growing anti-apartheid movement as chief organiser for the Coloured People's Congress and facilitated meetings, protests and marches from his home in Cape Town's 'coloured' suburbs. Stein had been one of the first people to be forcibly removed from District Six – a

thriving black and coloured community in the heart of the city –
by the government's Group Areas Act in 1950. He took over his
father's property business and married Lillian Jacobs, who had
also been evicted from her home. They would eventually have
eight children of their own and adopt a daughter.

Both spent time behind bars due to their political activities and
suffered the indignity of being dragged naked from their home
in the middle of the night by police during one raid in 1964.
"They chucked her in the van and took her to the police station,"
remembers Edwin. "My dad went on hunger strike to protest
against it and I remember him telling us after that was over that
he had already made plans for us to leave. I was aware of what was
going on because I saw it with my own eyes – they didn't have to
tell me. People were watching us all the time. My father was under
house arrest but he used to find ways of getting away to take charge
of meetings. He was a mover and a shaker. We had an open-door
policy in our house – anyone who needed food, a place to stay or
help with the police, my parents would try to look after them. My
father was a fearless guy – you could sense that even as a kid. There
were times that we never saw him because he was in hiding."

Stein senior spent 18 days on hunger strike before the police
finally relented and released his wife. He was subsequently
placed under 24-hour house arrest as part of the nationwide
crackdown that sent Nelson Mandela to Robben Island. Enough
was enough. Accompanied by 11-year-old Edwin, nine-year-old
Brian and youngest child Mark, who had only been born 18
months earlier, the Stein family boarded the *Southern Cross* on 7
February 1968.

"It wasn't in secret – people knew he was leaving," says Edwin.
"He knew he had to go. The government encouraged it. I
remember there were four tugboats surrounding the ship as it
sailed out of the port to make sure we didn't try to come back.
That showed they didn't want him there."

Their voyage from Cape Town to Southampton took two weeks. They were met by the Bishop of Stepney, Sir Trevor Huddleston, who had become a prominent member of the anti-apartheid movement having published his book *Naught for Your Comfort* in 1956. He arranged temporary accommodation for the Steins and even provided furniture, with Isaiah always treasuring the wooden dining table that stayed in the family until after his death.

"When we arrived it was probably the coldest I have ever felt in my entire life. My brothers' hands had turned blue," laughs Edwin. "It took us a while to get used to that. We stayed in Bayswater for a few weeks and then we were moved to Westbourne Park and then Paddington. My parents had to leave with nothing – we're still trying to find out what happened to all of their properties."

They eventually moved to Willesden Green, with Isaiah starting work as a distribution manager for Heinemann, the leading publisher of African authors – a job that was provided by another anti-apartheid supporter Canon John Collins of St Paul's Cathedral. Life in London was not easy for his children, with Enoch Powell's infamous 'Rivers of Blood' speech a few weeks after their arrival reminding them that a new country did not necessarily mean an escape from racism.

"It took a while to settle," admits Edwin. "My father took me to a few schools and it didn't work. Eventually I ended up at Hampstead School and found out later on that it was a place where a lot of the exiles from South Africa went. At the time we didn't know that they were all there as well but obviously we all had the same problems."

Isaiah soon became involved in the sporting boycott campaigns of the late 1960s and early 70s, becoming a key member of the South African Non-Racial Olympic Committee (SANROC), which was based in London. They ensured South Africa was removed from the Olympic movement in 1970 and Stein would later represent SANROC at meetings with the United Nations' Special Committee Against Apartheid, the Supreme Council for Sport in Africa and International Sports Federations, also attending the 1976 Olympic Games in Montreal.

"Isaiah was much more astute politically than the others, who were mainly sports exiles," says Sam Ramsamy, who went on to become chairman of SANROC and met Stein in 1972. "He was very good to me and we became very good friends."

Leading figures in the boycott movement like Ramsamy were regular visitors to the family home as Edwin, Brian and Mark grew up. Dennis Brutus, who had met Ramsamy in a chance encounter on a ship sailing from Madeira to London, was the driving force in establishing SANROC as a powerful organisation that eventually ensured South Africa's almost complete sporting isolation. It was the work of activists like Stein, whom Edwin later remembered would attempt to disrupt rugby matches using any means possible.

"My dad used to take us to Twickenham. Moles," he says with a smirk. "He slung the moles over the wall and went in there. If you put moles anywhere there is grass, then they dig. It was to show us all what he did and the reason why all this was happening. It was simple but so effective. I found out recently that my dad had organised terrorist cells. No one knew who was in the group because it was all so secretive. His main aim was to disrupt the sporting landscape as much as he could."

Following in the footsteps of Steve Mokone, who was part of the delegation that travelled to Mexico City in 1968 to formally ask for South Africa to be expelled by the International Olympic Committee, Stein's work for SANROC was responsible for ensuring the political pressure on apartheid grew throughout the 1970s.

"But activism on the world stage never prevented him from achieving the grass-roots connectedness by which he had become such an irritant to the apartheid regime and a well-loved figure to the comrades of the struggle," wrote Canon Chris Chivers in Stein's biography for *The Independent* in 2014. "He drilled into his children – all of whom achieved much in sporting, educational and youth-work contexts – that justice was the foundation of everything. This invariably meant sleeping with blankets on the floor as visiting South African struggle figures took their beds."

"The most important thing for my parents was that they had someone to make sure that my brothers were looked after," Edwin confirms. "For me it was always about making sure everyone was OK – even now, if there's any issues with the family, I get phone calls. They're welcome phone calls because we've always been close as a family.

"But it was a massive strain on the family," he adds ruefully. "I trusted my parents so I wouldn't use the word resent. It was more like admiration – we knew they were doing something for the common good. We were always brought up to believe that we always have trials and tribulations in life. His fight wasn't our fight. He reminded us of that all the time. He didn't want us to get involved in it. This was his life's body of work and he wanted people to know about that."

***

As South Africa's exiled community were using sport to fight the establishment during the late 1970s, however, there had hardly been a flurry of players to follow in the footsteps of Albert Johanneson. Zambians Freddie Mwila and Emment Kapengwe were spotted playing for American side Atlanta Chiefs by Aston Villa manager Tommy Docherty in the summer of 1969 and invited to the Midlands for a trial. Mwila had scored the winning goal in Atlanta's 3-2 victory over Manchester City and he and Kapengwe impressed enough to earn two-year contracts. Pathé

News announced their arrival with a special news report that showed Mwila training with his new teammates at Villa Park and described him as "likely to become the first East African to play league football in England".

That prediction did not quite come true as Kapengwe beat him to it by one week, starring in the 1-0 win over Carlisle on 12 November 1969 with a performance that made quite an impression on the *Birmingham Mail's* correspondent Dennis Shaw. "In nearly 30 years of watching football I have never seen a player make such an impact in his first Football League appearance," he wrote. "He showed more natural talent than any other player on the field and remember he was in the company of Bruce Rioch who cost a six-figure fee."

His success prompted Docherty to select both Zambians for the next match against Blackpool but, just like for Johanneson and Francis in their historic selection against Stoke almost eight years earlier for Leeds, the match ended in a disappointing 0-0 draw. That proved to be Mwila's only appearance for the first team, while Kapengwe made just one more.

"We didn't have too many chances to play because the team was struggling when we got there and the environment was totally different," recalls Mwila, who now lives on a farm near Lusaka having gone on to manage Zambia's national side during the 1990s. "It was OK but we were used to playing where it was sunny all the time and suddenly it was very cold and raining every week. It was a bit of a shock for us both."

Even sharing digs with his compatriot, Mwila admits that he found it hard to adapt to life in England. "I felt boxed in – it wasn't easy," he adds. "When we travelled to training we were always having to go to facilities in Sutton Coldfield and come back again. I would have to get up every day at 6 a.m. to be there on time and by the time I came back it was already dark. But it was fun."

Docherty, Rioch and club secretary Eric Woodward also tried their best to make them feel at home, often inviting the Zambian duo for dinner with their respective families after training. Even in a big city like Birmingham that had experienced a large wave of immigration from the British Commonwealth over the previous decade, however, the pervading feeling that they did not belong was hard to shift.

"Do you remember the bovver boys? They scared us a lot," admits Mwila. "There were several instances where we were made to feel uncomfortable. We had lots of near-misses. In the end we were happy to leave England and go home. I am proud because at the time there were not many black players in England. It was unfortunate that I did not get the opportunity to play many games but it meant a lot to be one of the first to make the move."

The sons of the Windrush generation who had arrived in the UK from the Caribbean during the early 1950s slowly began to make their breakthrough in English football over the next decade, with West Brom's 'Three Degrees' of Cyrille Regis, Laurie Cunningham and Brendan Batson becoming pioneers for the next generation. Viv Anderson's landmark appearance for England's senior side against Czechoslovakia in November 1978 was overdue recognition that black players were among the best in the country.

Yet even by the start of the 1980s, you could still almost count the number of players with African heritage to have played in English football on one hand. Ade Coker – a winger who had moved to London with his family from Nigeria when he was 11 – was part of the West Ham side that fielded three black players against Tottenham in a First Division match in April 1973 but made just ten appearances in total before moving to the United States. He was followed by John Chiedozie, who came through the youth ranks at Leyton Orient just as Cunningham was sold to West Brom in 1977. Chiedozie was also born in Nigeria but raised in London and went on to join Tottenham for £375,000 in August 1984 after excelling at Notts County.

Then there was Justin Fashanu. Born in London to a Guyanese mother and Nigerian father, he and his younger brother John grew up in a Barnardo's home before being adopted by a couple from Norfolk when Justin was only six. He was signed from Norwich by Brian Clough's Nottingham Forest for £1 million in April 1980 after winning the 'Goal of the Season' for his spectacular volley against Liverpool and became the first player with African heritage to play for England's Under-21 side two years later.

Fashanu's life ended in tragedy in 1998 when he hanged himself in a deserted lock-up garage in Shoreditch, east London amid allegations that he had sexually assaulted a teenage boy in the United States. Plagued by personal problems and struggling with his homosexuality at a time when life as a gay man was fraught with discrimination, particularly within football, his public disownment by his younger brother after he came out in the press in 1990 was the beginning of his sad downward spiral. Fashanu was inducted into the National Football Museum's Hall of Fame alongside Arthur Wharton and Johanneson in February 2020.

***

Four years after Fashanu's famous goal for Norwich, Brian Stein made history by becoming the first black African-born player to represent England's senior side in a friendly against Michel Platini's France. It capped a remarkable rise from non-league football to the international stage in just over six years.

With the anti-apartheid movement in full swing, Isaiah's political career continued to take up all of his time, leaving his sons free to pursue their own interests. "My parents weren't really coming along with us because they were so busy," remembers Edwin. "I had to look after my younger brothers and we would be out all of the time. If we weren't playing football, we'd be playing tennis. If we weren't playing tennis, we'd play table tennis. We were champions of Middlesex and I was London champion at tennis. We just wanted to be active because there was always the three of us. Mark would act as the ballboy because he was so much younger!"

Having started out at local non-league club Edgware Town, Edwin – a speedy right-winger – and Brian both joined Luton in November 1977.

"Harry Haslam was the manager at the time, with David Pleat in charge of the reserves," recalls Edwin. "He was very influential in our football careers. He and Graham Taylor both came to watch us at Edgware and wanted to sign both of us. David persuaded us that Luton was the best option and Brian made his debut within a month of going there. He went from the Athenian League to the Second Division in one big step."

While the Football Association made a mistake at the start of the 1978/79 season by accidentally publishing his surname as 'Steyn', Brian thrived under the tutelage of Pleat when he succeeded Haslam as manager, moving him from the wing to a more central role. But his elder brother's stay was already over, with Edwin moving to Dagenham and then on to Barnet in 1982, beginning a long association with the club based in the leafy suburbs of north London.

"I was at Luton for about seven months but left because I wasn't getting a game. David tried to stop me but I wanted to go and earn some money. There were one or two other clubs who wanted to sign me but they wouldn't let me go so I just left to go and play non-league. I got myself a job working for the Liberal Party in the mailroom. Then I got involved in collecting all the information from all the constituencies. It was a big coincidence because I met [former anti-apartheid campaigner and MP] Peter Hain when I was working there. He knew about my dad."

Brian's goals helped Luton achieve promotion to the First Division as champions in 1982, beating Taylor's Watford by eight points. The following season, he announced himself in the big time with two goals at Anfield in a thrilling 3-3 draw with Liverpool but ended up being out for several weeks after breaking his foot against Watford. Stein famously returned for the last game of the season that saw Luton needing victory over Manchester City to survive. He supplied the cross for future Atlético Madrid manager Raddy Antic to score the crucial winning goal, prompting Pleat's hilarious jig across the Kenilworth Road turf that was later immortalised by Baddiel and Skinner's *Fantasy Football* sketch 'Phoenix from the Flames'. But while his father continued to risk his life in his quest to end apartheid in his homeland, Isaiah warned Brian to concentrate on his football career rather than risk taking a public stand in aid of the cause.

"I advised him at the time that getting involved in activities like that would make his form suffer," says Ramsamy, who eventually led South Africa's readmittance to the IOC in 1992 under the new Rainbow flag. "To us, Brian was more important playing top-class football because that created an image for us. He had come from a suppressed society and this was not happening to all black South Africans. That was important. He demonstrated that by playing so we did not want him to get involved in the political arena. I personally mentioned that to Brian."

The anti-apartheid movement had grown from strength to strength in the early 1980s as global pressure grew on South Africa's ruling National Party to abandon its racist policies. Yet with British Prime Minister Margaret Thatcher having described the ANC as "a typical terrorist organisation" and being fiercely opposed to imposing sanctions against the apartheid regime as late as 1987, Ramsamy remembers the importance of the younger Stein's role in enlisting some of the other high-profile black players of the day.

"Brian was very good because he helped get other footballers involved," he adds. "Chris Hughton came to have a chat with us and since then I got to know him very well. I also got to know Garth Crooks and John Fashanu at that stage. They were very sympathetic to what I was doing because it also related to what was happening in the UK at the time. The UK still isn't a totally non-racist country. They were important in doing their bit for the anti-apartheid struggle by being at the top of their game."

On 20 September 1983, Brian Stein made history when he became the first African-born player to represent England's Under-21 side in a friendly against Denmark at Carrow Road. Playing alongside former Luton strike partner Paul Walsh, he scored twice in a 4-3 win and followed that up with another goal in a 2-0 victory over Hungary a month later.

His performances for club and country could not fail to attract the attention of England manager Bobby Robson, who was already clinging on to his job after failing to qualify for the European Championships and had become desperate to find new talent for his ageing squad. Stein was selected to face France at the Parc des Princes in Paris on 10 February 1984 on another historic night for African football. Except it didn't quite go as planned.

Once again, he was partnered with Walsh but struggled against the team who would go on to become European champions a few months later. Stein was described as "lacking the pace to succeed as a striker at the top level" by the *Daily Mirror*'s Frank McGhee after Platini scored twice in the second half to record a 2-0 win. Stuart Jones of *The Times* was not much kinder, saying he had been "a huge disappointment" and had "looked overawed by the occasion". Yet the significance of his appearance had not gone unnoticed at SANROC, where his first cap was hailed as evidence that black Africans could be accepted into English culture.

"What Brian was doing was part of our overall campaign, although the flag was shrouded," admits Ramsamy. "Everyone knew that he was a black South African and the opportunity Luton gave him wasn't available to black South Africans in South Africa. That was very important. They were all born in South Africa and the only reason they became UK citizens was because of political circumstances. That was good because there is no way Brian would have played at that level in South Africa. They would have been part of the system that saw people just get swept under a carpet."

Undeterred by his disappointing full debut, Stein returned to the Under-21 squad for the second leg of their European Championship semi-final against Italy and played in the 1-0 defeat that ensured they went through to face Spain in the final on aggregate. But, for whatever reason, the game against Italy in Florence in May 1984 was to be the last international appearance of his career as he was not selected in the side which won the tournament for the first time.

Back at Luton, the emergence of his younger brother Mark and close friend Paul Elliott helped soften the disappointment of his experiences with England as Luton's fortunes continued to improve. Meeting their father certainly had a profound effect on Elliott, who moved to Aston Villa in 1985 before spells in Italy, Scotland and at Chelsea.

"I met Brian Stein at Luton and I got to know Isaiah very well," Elliott remembered in an interview in 2014. "We had many conversations about his life, his upbringing and the challenges he faced in South Africa. I couldn't believe the suffering he experienced – what he stood up and fought for in South Africa at the time of the apartheid movement. It was a story that I found fascinating. It really moved me and what he and his children must have experienced had a profound effect on me. I knew then – coupled with the experiences that I'd had – that we had to campaign for equal rights and opportunities. It all started from the age of 18."

Elliott was forced to retire due to a knee injury in 1994 that had been caused by a challenge with Liverpool's Dean Saunders two years earlier, but he became heavily involved in anti-racism movements in football and was awarded a CBE in 2009 for his charity work. Meanwhile, Pleat's largely homegrown Luton team had served notice of their rapid progress by coming within minutes of reaching the FA Cup final in 1985, losing in the semi-final against Everton after extra time. They finished ninth in 1986, prompting Pleat's departure for Tottenham in the summer but Stein remained loyal to Luton despite interest from several bigger clubs.

He was rewarded when new manager Ray Harford guided them to seventh place in his first season before they finally made it to Wembley in the Littlewoods Cup in 1988 after beating fierce rivals Oxford United in the semi-finals. Nobody had given Luton a chance of overcoming George Graham's Arsenal in their first major final but Brian's winning goal – instigated by his younger brother and with his parents watching on proudly from the stands – capped the most famous day in the club's history.

"It was the only game my mother ever went to," admits Edwin. "Brian scored twice. She wanted us to enjoy it."

Within three months, however, both brothers had left Kenilworth Road, with Brian opting for a new start with French side Caen and Mark joining Queens Park Rangers. It seemed a sad way for it all to have ended, although within two years Brian was back in time to be part of the most recent Luton side to have played in the top flight. Their relegation in 1992 ensured he would never grace the newly established Premier League and he ended up winding down his career at Barnet under the management of Barry Fry.

Edwin had already been working as Fry's assistant for almost a decade when Southend lured him away from the club where he had endured a testing relationship with chairman Stan Flashman to say the least. The amiable cockney had been sacked eight times and reinstated each time but finally decided he had had enough in April 1993. Edwin was appointed as caretaker until the end of the season, overseeing their promotion to the third tier for the first time in their history.

"When Barry left, I got promoted and that made me the first black manager in the UK," says Edwin. "Keith Alexander came two weeks after me. We were good friends. Keith rang me when he was appointed and said, 'You lucky bastard! I've just been given the job two weeks later!' I went to his funeral and his wife said to me, 'Sorry, they've made a mistake. He wasn't the first, you were.' I said, 'It doesn't matter.'"

I ask if he felt his achievement had been overlooked.

"No, I don't think it has been overlooked," he says adamantly, before changing his mind. "It has been overlooked . . . ! But it's not for me to rectify that. We ended up getting promotion and that's the highest they have ever been: in the Third Division. I'm not one of these guys who wants my name up in lights because it's just about achieving and going through that experience."

But Edwin admits both he and his brothers always preferred it when they could express themselves on the pitch.

"I'm very much like my old man and just want to get on with things and let other people talk," he says. "I felt conscious of it when I went to the managers' meeting at The Savoy at the end of the season. I felt very uncomfortable in that kind of company. It wasn't for me. You had people going around with false pretences. The worst thing now is that the chairman of Barnet is trying to rewrite history. He has got nothing on the walls about any of the old teams. It's almost like we have been forgotten."

While Edwin followed Fry to Southend and Birmingham, Brian later stepped in as Luton's caretaker in 2007 having spent several years there as a coach under former teammate Mike Newell but left to join Grimsby after the arrival of a new manager. Mark had already been retired for three years having returned to Luton in 2001 following spells at Stoke, Chelsea and Bournemouth. His 21 goals in 50 Premier League appearances for Chelsea between 1993 and 1998 made him the first black African-born player to appear for the club, beating the likes of Didier Drogba and Michael Essien to that accolade by several years. All three had certainly come a long way since Edwin – a Chelsea fan to Brian's Manchester United when they were growing up in west London – had stood at The Shed End with his younger brother to watch their local team.

"I would have people pissing down the back of my legs," he remembered. "When you tried to tell them to stop, they said, 'Shut the fuck up.' I took Brian there with me a few times but Mark was too young to come with us. But the racism never bothered me. It just went over my head. I knew it was a tactic that was just trying to take my focus away, in football and in the rest of life."

Yet even in 2003, Mark had come face to face with the ugly side of the game when he tore up his contract with Dagenham and Redbridge after the club refused to investigate alleged racist comments made by manager Garry Hill against teammate Fitzroy Simpson.

"I still love playing but I don't know if I'll get another club," he said at the time. "I sometimes think I might get tarnished, but this is so important to me that I can't worry about the consequences. With something like this I'll put my neck on the line. My dad was a political activist who fought against racism in South Africa all his life. So why should I have to put up with it here?"

***

On a cold, crisp January morning in 2011, more than 200 people gathered at a cemetery in Golders Green in north London to pay their respects to Isaiah Stein. Almost 80 years after his birth in South Africa, the man credited with playing a major role in bringing an end to apartheid was laid to rest at a service led by Canon Chris Chivers. Brought up in Bristol, Chivers first became aware of events 8,000 miles away in South Africa when his mother gave him a copy of *Naught for Your Comfort* as a child.

"I couldn't really understand it all," he admits. "But I could get some of the stories and thought, 'That's what I want to be.' That's really how I came to be a priest. We also grew up near the cricketer Mike Proctor in Bristol and I was very much aware of the issue of apartheid when I grew up."

As the country moved towards independence in the early 1990s, Chivers worked closely with young people giving evidence at the Truth and Reconciliation Committee designed to help black South Africans recover from the traumas of apartheid. He recalls meeting Isaiah briefly a few years earlier and was honoured to be approached when the Bishop of Edmonton was not available for the funeral.

"He was a guy called Peter Wheatley who had chaired one of the anti-apartheid committees," says Chivers. "Because he knew me and my South African connection he passed it on to me. It was really when I came to write the address for the funeral that the idea for the obituary came. I just thought, 'This isn't supposed to just disappear. It deserves to have a wider audience.'"

As well as then Birmingham manager Hughton – the son of a former postman from Ghana who went on to manage Newcastle,

Norwich and Brighton in the Premier League – and a host of anti-apartheid heroes, all three of his sons were present to hear Chivers pay tribute to the man that had made it all possible.

"It was an amazing turnout," he says. "There were a lot of the organisations represented, a tremendous number of them. He was held in a lot of affection by a lot of people. It was packed with people."

Yet just as Edwin feels the significant achievements of his children have never really been fully recognised, so too his father was never satisfied that their struggle was over. "If he were to write an autobiography it would be called *All for Nothing*," wrote Chivers in his obituary. "But to that title a question mark would certainly have been appended – and the widely read Stein was meticulous about such things. For he knew that only by critiquing the new South Africa and its governing class would another generation be encouraged to find new energy for the ongoing struggle for justice, equality and freedom. Isaiah Stein gave his life for that struggle."

I asked Chivers why he had been so despondent.

"He said it to all his children," he explains. "He was very depressed about the new South Africa and where it was going at the end of his life. A lot of people who were involved in the struggle feel like that. I too can get depressed when I look at how awful some of the stuff that is happening is. It isn't quite what people thought would happen."

Edwin does admit he felt at times that his father had disapproved of their choice of career given his own background. Eventually, though, he also came to recognise how their presence on the pitch during the late 1970s and 1980s made things easier for future generations of African players.

"My dad wouldn't encourage us to go and play football because for him the most important thing was education," he reflects. "He was wary of it. There were times that I felt a little bit ashamed that I took the football route because my brothers followed because of what I was doing. For a long, long time, I felt I had let my parents down. I knew how important education was to them."

After the funeral, Edwin, Brian, Mark and another brother, Karl, travelled to Cape Town with their father's ashes. It was then that they decided to establish the Stein Foundation in honour of their parents "driven partly by their own experiences of feeling empowered with education through sport". Founded in 2012, it has since helped disadvantaged communities in South Africa and the UK and is aiming to build a sports and community facility in Cape Town that will bear Isaiah Stein's name. It would be a fitting memorial to the father of a footballing dynasty.

"My dad didn't do it for a pat on the back," says Edwin. "He did it because he knew it was the right thing to do. There's plenty of people similar to my parents who didn't get any credit either. But I just want to show that ordinary people can do extraordinary things."

EIGHT

UNDER THE SPOTLIGHT

"My dad was always behind me; he wanted me to be a footballer," remembered Riyad Mahrez in an interview with *The Guardian*'s Paul Doyle in September 2015. "He was always with me. He came to every game with me to give me help. He played before for small teams in Algeria and France so he knew what he was saying, so I listened to him. [His death] maybe was the kick-start. I don't know if I started to be more serious but after the death of my dad things started to go for me. Maybe in my head I wanted it more."

By then, it had been almost a decade since Ahmed Mahrez – a former midfielder who was born in Beni Snous, not far from Algeria's border with Morocco – had passed away due to a long-standing heart condition. Mahrez senior was fitted with a pacemaker at the age of 23 after moving to France in the early 1970s for treatment that ended up prolonging his life for almost three decades. It enabled him to fall in love with his Moroccan-born wife Saliha in the Parisian suburb of Sarcelles and produce two sons, one of whom would go on to make history for Africa in May 2016 when he was voted the PFA Players' Player of the Year.

Accepting the award after yet another goal – his 17th of a spectacular season – had helped Leicester move to within touching distance of a scarcely believable fairy-tale Premier League title by thrashing Swansea 4-0, Mahrez dedicated it to his father. A few days later, Tottenham's bad-tempered 2-2 draw with Chelsea in a match that became known as the Battle of Stamford Bridge handed the crown to Claudio Ranieri's side. The 5,000-1 shots had achieved the impossible.

Mahrez became the first Algerian international to receive a Premier League winners' medal and the first African to win the prestigious PFA award. Suddenly his unlikely meteoric rise was big news. The tabloids were filled with stories of his childhood in Sarcelles on the outskirts of the French capital, where a year before Ahmed's death riots had swept through the *banlieue* on a tide of disaffected youth of largely African descent. "They didn't get involved in any of the rioting," one friend of the family told the *Daily Mail*. "Ahmed also taught his sons to respect their religion, to pray and go to the mosque. He told them: 'Be afraid before God because he is always with you.'"

His father's job as an electrical engineer meant Mahrez actually had a relatively comfortable childhood despite growing up in an area of Paris where opportunities are few and far between. But the divorce of his parents when he was eight meant more responsibility for raising Mahrez fell to his mother, even if regular visits to Algeria during the school holidays ensured there was only one option when it came to international football. "I lived in France and grew up there and my mum still lives there but my heart is more Algerian," he later admitted.

Mahrez made his debut for *Les Fennecs* against Armenia a few months after he had joined Leicester for just £400,000 from Le Havre in January 2014. His inclusion in their World Cup squad for Brazil 2014 was criticised by Algerian supporters, some of whom had even claimed that he had paid manager Vahid

Halilhodžić for his place. Having helped Leicester to promotion with a series of impressive cameos after arriving in January, his selection seemed warranted. But the tournament ended with just one appearance in the opening defeat to Belgium as Algeria recovered to reach the second round. It remains the last time an African side have managed the feat, with none reaching the knockout stages in 2018 for the first time since 1982 as Sadio Mané's Senegal cruelly missed out to Japan only because of an inferior disciplinary record.

Individual African players had continued to attract big-money fees in the meantime, however, and Parisian-born Gabon forward Pierre Emerick-Aubameyang usurped Naby Keïta as the most expensive in history when he signed for Arsenal from Borussia Dortmund in January 2018 for £56 million. That also proved to be a short-lived reign when, two years after inspiring Leicester to their historic title, Mahrez was finally granted the move he craved when he joined Manchester City in the summer for a cool £60 million. A series of disagreements with Leicester over his future that culminated in Mahrez refusing to play had somewhat soured his relationship with their supporters. But City's determination to secure him after being rebuffed in the January transfer window was eventually rewarded as Pep Guardiola strengthened the formidable squad which had amassed a record number of points (100), victories (32) and goals (106) as they cantered to the title a few months earlier. If anyone was going to stop them this time, it would certainly take some doing.

***

The sun was already up but Jürgen Klopp still wasn't ready to go to bed. In the hours after Liverpool's Champions League final defeat to Real Madrid in Kiev, the manager and his trusted lieutenant Peter Krawietz drowned their sorrows back at the team hotel with their friends Campino – the lead singer of German punk rock band Die Toten Hosen (The Dead Trousers) – and journalist Johannes B. Kerner. Like most drinking sessions involving Klopp, it wasn't long before things started getting out of hand and someone had the bright idea of recording a video that would soon go viral around the globe.

"We saw the European Cup," began Klopp, clutching what seemed to be a picture of injured midfielder Alex Oxlade-Chamberlain as he sang with his friends. "But Madrid had all the f****** luck. We swear we'll keep on being cool. We'll bring it back to Liverpool."

After what had just transpired inside the Olympic Stadium, his choice of language could perhaps be forgiven. Mohamed Salah's departure in tears during the first half and the two howlers from Loris Karius that had gifted Real Madrid the victory was the kind of bad luck no manager could have ever planned for.

"In Kiev, the dressing room was like a sick bay," Krawietz, who first met Klopp when he worked as chief scout at Mainz in 2005, later revealed in an interview with the Athletic website. "Imagine that you get in there and one guy has already been to the hospital and is now back, in pain and crying. And then you hear your opponents celebrating. And in the dressing room next door, the referees are celebrating as well.

"I don't know why, but they were singing and partying, with a case of beer," he continued. "For us, it was awful. Finding the right reaction is tough. But that's all part of it. You have to show strength and greatness in defeat. And the right reaction. Yes, they really hurt us, but they haven't knocked us out. We're down, but it's not over."

On the other side of town at Shevchenko Park, there had been a similar feeling of defiance. An estimated 20,000 Liverpool supporters – easily outnumbering the 16,000 who had been lucky enough to purchase a ticket for the match – had watched on big screens in the picturesque park 15 minutes' walk from the stadium having endured nightmare journeys, most encompassing a combination of planes, trains and automobiles. But rather than wallow in self-pity, South African-born journalist and Liverpool fan Melissa Reddy remembers the overriding feeling was one of positivity.

"That experience was so overwhelming that it superseded the game itself," she admits. "That sounds like a weird thing to say but it felt like there was a definite divide between people who were at Shevchenko Park and those that weren't. A lot of the guys that covered the game at the stadium were completely devastated after the final whistle, whereas there was a sense of defiance among those who were at the fan park. It felt like this was just the beginning.

"Jürgen is very good at turning defeat into a positive and motivating factor," adds Reddy. "If you go back to the Europa League final in 2016, there was a party scheduled for afterwards that he refused to cancel so everyone went to it. He got up on stage and said, 'We will be in more finals so don't let this get you down. When we eventually win something we will remember moments like this because it is what is going to help us get over the line.'"

The signing of Brazil midfielder Fabinho for £40 million from Monaco within 48 hours of their defeat in Kiev was further evidence that Liverpool meant business for the new season. When he and Naby Keïta were followed by compatriot Alisson Becker – the world's most expensive goalkeeper at a cool £67 million from Roma – two months later, it became clear that Klopp was assembling a formidable squad capable of challenging Manchester City.

"That was a message that said, 'Listen, we're not content with what we have done,'" says Reddy. "Alisson was what Liverpool called 'the transformer'. They have needed a top goalkeeper for several years and they had tried several half-measures before that didn't really work. Alisson was the one they really wanted. They had been working on him since 2013 and were finally in a position to bring him in. Liverpool got to that final in Kiev because of their attacking might but were still a little bit defensively suspect. Virgil van Dijk (who had joined halfway through the previous season from Southampton for £75 million – a world record for a defender at the time) cured half of that problem but the addition of Alisson made them a real unit."

A week after his signing was confirmed, Liverpool flew to the picturesque Alpine town of Évian-les-Bains to begin pre-season training. Under a baking sun with temperatures exceeding 35 °C at times, Klopp put his players to work over five days of intense training. Double sessions starting at 7 a.m. and ending at 6 p.m. were intended to produce the fittest side he had ever produced. There was no doubt about the target this time.

Even as Liverpool surprised everyone by reaching the final of Europe's most important cup competition, the club's supporters yearned for one trophy above all others. Having won their last league title in 1990 when the competition was still known as the First Division, four years on from Steven Gerrard's infamous slip against Chelsea handed the title to Manchester City and broke Liverpool's hearts, could Klopp's vibrant attacking side finally put the hoodoo to bed and win the Premier League title for the first time in their illustrious history?

At the end of the week in Évian, the players gathered on their hotel patio for the moment they had been waiting for all week: the initiation songs. Speculation had been rife about which numbers new signings Fabinho, Xherdan Shaqiri, Alisson and Keïta would select, while Van Dijk had also been told he had to take part after missing out on the tradition when he joined in January. The big Dutch defender kicked off proceedings with Tamia's 1998 R&B hit 'So Into You' before a timid Fabinho mumbled his way through a Brazilian number. He gave way

This photo was taken in around 1896, when Arthur Wharton
was 31 and playing in goal for Stalybridge Rovers. *Getty Images*

The statue of Arthur Wharton was unveiled at St George's Park in 2014 almost 130 years after he arrived in England from the Gold Coast. *Getty Images*

Steve Mokone joins American sports stars including New York Yankees pitcher Jim Bouton (far right) in supporting a boycott of the 1968 Olympic Games after South Africa was readmitted.

Albert Johanneson in September 1964. His performances that season helped
Leeds almost win the First Division title and reach the FA Cup final. *Getty Images*

Zambia's Freddie Mwila and Emment Kapengwe in the only league match they played together for Aston Villa against Blackpool in November 1969. *Credit unknown*

Peter Ndlovu leaves Manchester United's Gary Pallister in his slipstream at Old Trafford in May 1994. The Zimbabwean ended the season as Coventry's top scorer with 11 goals. *Getty Images*

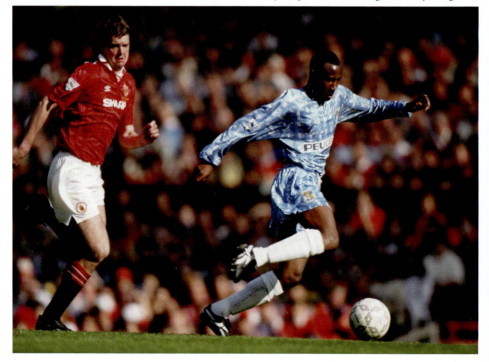

Brian Stein embraces his younger brother Mark after scoring Luton's winning goal in the Littlewoods Cup final in February 1988. Their family had been forced to leave South Africa almost 20 years earlier. *Getty Images*

Daniel Amokachi celebrates Everton's 1995 FA Cup victory with Graham Stuart.
He became the first Nigerian to win English football's most famous trophy. *Getty Images*

Tony Yeboah joined Leeds from Eintracht Frankfurt in January 1995
and the Ghanaian soon became known for his spectacular goals. *Getty Images*

Lucas Radebe and Phil Masinga relax in the Victoria pub in Leeds. The South African duo followed in the footsteps of Gerry Francis and Albert Johanneson at Elland Road.. *Getty Images*

Morocco's Youssef Chippo and Mustapha Hadji point the way for Coventry during a Premier League game against Leicester. *Getty Images*

Christopher Wreh of Liberia – the first African player to win the English league title – savours his historic achievement with Arsenal in May 1998. *Getty Images*

Michael Essien, Salomon Kalou, Florent Malouda and Didier Drogba toast
Chelsea's 2012 Champions League final triumph against Bayern Munich. *Getty Images*

Kolo Touré presents Yaya Touré with a commemorative shirt before his last game for Manchester City. The brothers from the Ivory Coast won four titles and three FA Cups between them. *Getty Images*

Mohamed Salah of Egypt exorcises the demons of the 2018 Champions League final with his penalty against Tottenham in Madrid a year later. *Getty Images*

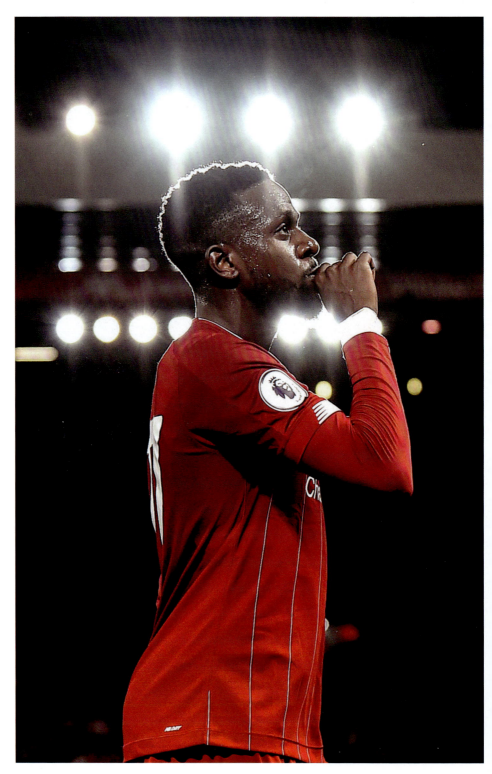

Divock Origi celebrates scoring in the victory over Everton in December 2018. He went to become Liverpool's hero of the remarkable comeback against Barcelona at Anfield. *Getty Images*

Sadio Mané – the boy from Bambali in Senegal's deep south – shows what it means to become a European champion after running away from home to pursue his dream. *Getty Images*

Naby Keïta celebrates scoring against Bournemouth in December 2020. It was the
Guinea midfielder's first goal of another frustrating season at Liverpool. *Getty Images*

to compatriot Alisson, who perhaps unaware of their links to City, chose the Oasis classic 'Don't Look Back in Anger' before launching into his own guitar solo.

Shaqiri, who had been signed for a cut-price fee from relegated Stoke to provide some support for the attacking triumvirate of Salah, Mané and Roberto Firmino, opted for Kop favourite Bob Marley's 'Three Little Birds'. His singing voice left Daniel Sturridge less than impressed judging by his expression on an Instagram post. The England striker also filmed Keïta as he prepared for his rendition of Guinean hip-hop star Soul Bang's latest hit, asking if he was ready. "Yeah I'm ready," Keïta chuckles into the camera. "Everything will be OK," replies Sturridge as the message "he ain't ready" filters across the screen. The England striker admits he "had to join him still", performing his trademark robot dance as Keïta raps his way through the song as his teammates cheer them on.

"There was a great atmosphere at Évian – I have to say I enjoyed it a lot," Keïta later admitted. "There were a lot of new players there obviously and we had this rite of passage where everybody had to get up and sing, and I did my bit. I really did enjoy it – I was quite nervous, but I did enjoy it! I'm someone who loves music myself. A trip like that is, for me, very good for the team, to go somewhere together. It does create a lot of cohesion among the players."

Asked who had been the best performer, he replied: "Me!"

As expected despite a late neck injury that had hampered his pre-season, Keïta was named alongside Mané and Salah in Liverpool's team to face West Ham in the first match of the 2018/19 Premier League season on 12 August. It was the first time three African players had started for the club in its 127-year history, Keïta's presence taking the tally to 17 in total in the Premier League era – starting with Bruce Grobbelaar in 1992. The Durban-born former soldier in the Rhodesian Army, who made 440 appearances for Liverpool and was part of the last team to win the title in 1990, watched on with pride as the new signing wearing the No. 8 shirt pulled the strings in midfield during a comfortable 4-0 victory.

Less than 20 minutes had gone at Anfield when Keïta showed exactly what all the fuss had been about. Finding himself in space 15 yards inside West Ham's half after a pinpoint pass from teenage right-back Trent Alexander-Arnold, he set off. Two opponents in claret-and-blue shirts attempted to make a tackle but Keïta shrugged them aside before delivering a swaggering pass with the outside of his right boot into the path of the other onrushing full-back, Andrew Robertson. The ball was in the net less than a second later, touched home by Salah at the far post for the easiest goal of his Liverpool career.

Two more either side of half-time from Mané – the first a superb reaction to James Milner's cutback – ensured he became the first Liverpool player to score in three successive opening league fixtures since John Barnes in 1992 as the hosts made a flying start to the campaign. *The Times* featured Keïta on the front page of their football pull-out 'The Game' with the headline: 'Worth the Wait'.

"This was the reason Jürgen Klopp was willing to sanction a £52.75 million deal and then wait a year," wrote Ian Doyle in the *Liverpool Echo*. "Keïta's dynamism has already brought something different to Liverpool's midfield, along with his willingness to run at the opposing defence from deep."

A long preview in the *Sunday Times* ahead of the next match against Crystal Palace also focused on the new signing, with Jonathan Northcroft comparing him favourably to Gerrard's league debut when the future legend's second touch was a cross overhit so badly "it almost sailed over the Centenary Stand. Incey [Paul Ince] looked like he wanted to murder me."

"Twenty years on from Gerrard's debut against Blackburn," Northcroft wrote, "Naby Keïta took his Liverpool bow last weekend against West Ham, and Keïta's first action also involved a steady piece of possession play. His second? An exuberant pass, played with the inside of his heel, to Andy Robertson. Anfield was smitten quicker than you could say '£52.75 million'."

***

On reflection, it probably wasn't even his fault. Yet a whole season can sometimes change in the most fleeting of instances. For Naby Keïta that moment came in the 85th minute of Liverpool's Carabao Cup meeting with Chelsea at the end of September 2018.

Klopp's side had gone into the match on the back of seven straight victories since the start of the season for the first time ever, with their new signing once again impressing in the win over Crystal Palace at Selhurst Park. Not for the first or last time, it had been Salah who had created the opening goal when he went down in the area under a challenge from Mamadou Sakho and was awarded a penalty, although replays suggested minimal contact. James Milner made no mistake from the spot and Mané's third of the season – a brilliant breakaway strike in tandem with Salah – wrapped things up late on after Aaron Wan-Bissaka had been shown a red card. Once again, though, it was Keïta who was the subject of most interest when Klopp spoke to Sky TV's Gary Neville and Jamie Carragher after the match.

"He's a shy person so he's not very extroverted," admitted the Liverpool manager. "On the pitch you don't see that. He needs to settle still a little bit. He's very next to Sadio all the time. Everybody loves Naby but we don't know exactly if he loves us. This is because he doesn't speak a lot. Football-wise the potential is outstanding. But we have to give him time. I don't know exactly where that leads to. Just an awesome football player. Tactically he can improve and has to improve."

Keïta played 67 minutes of the next game against Brighton as Salah's goal ensured they went top of the table for the first time, although he found himself on the bench for the trip to Leicester a few days later. It was to become a recurring theme. A 2-1 victory courtesy of Roberto Firmino and Mané's fourth of the season meant Liverpool went into the international break leading the way, having conceded just once from their first four matches. Keïta returned home to Conakry to link up with his international teammates and paid a visit to his old neighbourhood.

"I think it's fair to say that the Premier League is a tough league," he admitted to local journalists. "I'm very motivated to be playing in it – it's an attractive proposition – but I've been told by many people that a lot of overseas players come into the Premier League and they take time to integrate, depending on the circumstances."

On his return, Keïta was relieved to see he was in the side to face Mauricio Pochettino's Tottenham side at Wembley as Liverpool made it five wins in a row thanks to goals from Georginio Wijnaldum and Firmino. That meant for the first time that season, no African player had found the net for Klopp's side, although Mané had certainly played his part in the Brazilian's second, slicing through the right side of the Spurs defence and presenting the ball on a plate for his teammate to bundle home. The only downside had been that Keïta had failed to take an opportunity to score his first goal for the club after a quick breakaway with Mané and Salah ended with a weak shot and he was substituted in the 83rd minute. It was to be his last Premier League start until December.

Keïta was left on the bench throughout the thrilling victory over Paris Saint-Germain in the Champions League that saw the expensively assembled French side come back from 2-0 down, only to be undone by a last-minute goal from Firmino. Former England defender Rio Ferdinand felt that a lack of experience was working against their new signing as Jordan Henderson was preferred once again for the win over Southampton at Anfield, with Salah scoring the third goal before half-time as the hosts ran riot to stay top of the nascent table.

A 20-minute substitute appearance meant that Keïta was certain to start against Maurizio Sarri's Chelsea a few days later in the Carabao Cup, with the visitors having also made a blistering start under their new chain-smoking Italian manager, even if they had dropped their first points of the season in a 0-0 draw with West Ham that weekend. Everything seemed in order when Sturridge – making the most of a rare start – scored with a volley just before the hour mark. But after Emerson equalised, the match seemed to be drifting towards penalties when Eden Hazard took possession of the ball on the right-hand side of Liverpool's penalty area.

Drifting past Keïta for the first time with a deft change of direction, the Belgian headed back infield to evade the challenge of Alberto Moreno before leaving both players in his slipstream as he headed into the box. Split seconds later, his shot flew into the net despite the tight angle as Liverpool's 100 per cent start to the season in all competitions was shattered.

As is the norm in this era of trial by social media, there had to be a scapegoat. And, scrolling through Twitter that evening, it appeared to be Keïta who was singled out as most to blame by frustrated Liverpool supporters. Moreno also took his fair share of criticism, even if the reserve left-back must have been used to it by then with two difficult seasons at Anfield already behind him. To see the player bought to replace Gerrard singled out for criticism – even after a defeat in a competition that held little importance to their season – was another matter entirely.

**

The meeting of Klopp's red juggernaut and Pep Guardiola's blue machine at Anfield on 7 October 2018 had been one of the most eagerly anticipated matches in the illustrious history of the Premier League. Separated by just goal difference after seven matches, it was billed as an early indicator of where – if not quite decisively – the title could be heading come May. "It felt like the longest title race ever," reflects Melissa Reddy almost a year later. "Even in September everyone knew it was going to be between Liverpool and City."

Going into the match, Liverpool had been indebted to substitute Sturridge for his late equaliser in the league game against Chelsea following the international break – a result that saw them drop points for the first time that season to fall behind City at the top. Defeat in the Champions League match against Napoli a few days later had also come at a cost. Keïta was restored to the starting line-up in the Stadio San Paolo, with Klopp citing his desire to have his new signing's "specific skills in between the lines" against Carlo Ancelotti's side. He ended up lasting just 19 minutes after colliding with José Callejón and was kept in hospital overnight as a precaution, with tests revealing he had suffered a back spasm but not suffered any spinal damage. Keïta returned to Merseyside on a private jet on Thursday and was miraculously passed fit to face City three days later, although Klopp opted to start with him only on the bench.

Meanwhile, City's victory over Hoffenheim, which saw Mahrez come off the bench as they recorded a 2-1 victory in Germany, had settled a few nerves among Pep Guardiola's squad following defeat in their opening group stage match of the Champions League at home to Lyon. Other than a draw at newly promoted Wolves in their third league match, their record was otherwise unblemished when they made the short journey to Anfield for the Sunday afternoon fixture.

Mahrez was named in the City starting line-up in the Premier

League for only the third time having followed up his first goal against Cardiff with another against Oxford in the Carabao Cup a week earlier, while France international Benjamin Mendy – the son of immigrants from Côte d'Ivoire – was selected at left-back. His presence brought into question comments made by Yaya Touré, who had left City a few months earlier after eight years that yielded three Premier League titles and saw him crowned African Footballer of the Year for four successive seasons between 2011 and 2014.

"He [Guardiola] insists he has no problems with black players, because he is too intelligent to be caught out," Touré said in an interview with *France Football* a few days after his departure in June. "But when you realise that he has problems with Africans, wherever he goes, I ask myself questions. He will never admit it. But the day he will line up a team in which we find five Africans, not naturalised, I promise I will send him a cake."

Guardiola later dismissed his accusations as "a lie", with several of his players publicly adding their support for the manager. Nonetheless, it represented a regretful ending to the City career of one of the club's most influential stars, even if the former Barcelona and Bayern Munich manager had other things to worry about by the time his side stepped out at Anfield.

Guardiola's previous visit seven months earlier had not ended well, with Mané and Salah both scoring as Liverpool swept to a 3-0 half-time lead in the first leg of the Champions League quarter-final. For a brief moment in the second leg, it looked as though City might have a chance of an astonishing comeback, only for a linesman's flag to rule out Leroy Sané's goal that would have made it 3-2 on aggregate just before half-time. Another goal from Salah and Roberto Firmino's winner ensured Liverpool ended up winning the match and convinced Guardiola he must take a different approach. Opting to leave Sané – whose father Souleyman settled in Germany after his playing career, marrying a former German Olympic gymnast – on the bench, Guardiola employed Mahrez on the right-hand side of his attacking three alongside David Silva and Raheem Sterling, with Sergio Agüero as the lone striker.

By the time Keïta had been summoned to replace James Milner when he limped off with a hamstring injury in the 29th minute, it was clear that, in an unusual approach for a side that had already scored 18 goals from their seven league matches, City had come to frustrate their hosts. The plan worked. Liverpool's front three were nullified as Guardiola's players shut off their supply line by simply not allowing them the ball. It looked as though the game was meandering towards a stalemate when Van Dijk misjudged his challenge on substitute Sané in the 84th minute and referee Martin Atkinson immediately pointed to the spot.

With usual penalty taker Agüero having been substituted, next in line was Brazilian striker Gabriel Jesus. But Mahrez had other ideas, grabbing the ball before anyone could notice and getting the nod to proceed from his manager when Jesus complained. It was to prove a costly decision. Mahrez struck it well enough but the ball kept rising as it cleared Alisson's crossbar, sending the Liverpool fans at the Kop end behind the goal into delirium.

"During the training sessions every day I see Mahrez taking the penalties and it gave me a lot of confidence," Guardiola reflected afterwards, perhaps not realising that he had actually missed four of his last seven spot kicks. "It will be good experience for him, next time it will go in. Jesus wanted to [take it]. I apologise. It was my decision."

A relieved Klopp was happy to escape with a share of the points, admitting that his team had ridden their luck in a tight game. But with just eight games played and nothing to separate the two title rivals, he knew the battle had only just begun.

NINE

BRAVE NEW WORLD

Even for the most famous player on the planet, it was a bold statement. By 1977, Edson Arantes do Nascimento – better known, of course, as Pelé – was approaching the final match of his illustrious career that had seen him win three World Cups and score more than a century of goals for Brazil. Like most of the descendants of the three million slaves it is estimated arrived in South America from Africa between the mid-1500s and 1850, he had been born into poverty in a remote town in São Paulo state but risen to the pinnacle of the game against all the odds.

Pelé had been persuaded to come out of retirement by Henry Kissinger and was earning a reported $7 million from a three-year contract with New York Cosmos in the glitzy but ultimately short-lived North American Soccer League. At the age of 37, he wanted to give something back to the continent he considered to be his spiritual home. A few years earlier, he had even been credited with causing a brief ceasefire during the Nigerian Civil War after his Santos side arrived to play an exhibition match, although that may have been stretching the truth somewhat. This time, however, Pelé had something else up his sleeve: a prediction.

"An African nation will win the World Cup before the year 2000," he confidently told a reporter ahead of his final match in New York in October 1977, which was attended by his father and Muhammad Ali among others.

Given that Africa's most recent representatives Zaire had conceded 14 goals and scored none at the 1974 World Cup finals, there were more than a few eyebrows raised at the time. Mwepu Ilunga's infamous dash out of the wall to boot away a free kick against Brazil in their 9-0 defeat – which had actually been intended as a protest against the decision of President Joseph Mobutu's government not to pay the players their bonuses as promised – remains ridiculed by the rest of the world to this day.

Yet when Tunisia earned a creditable draw with reigning champions West Germany in 1978 and Cameroon exited the tournament four years later despite having drawn all three group stage matches, suddenly Pelé seemed to be on to something. Algeria were also denied a place in the knockout stages in 1982 by a collaboration between Germany and Austria that ensured the North Africans' victory over the former in the opening match was not enough to send them through – an incident that became known as the 'Disgrace of Gijón'.

Morocco did make it through in 1986, topping a group containing England before losing to the Germans in the last 16. But when a Roger Milla-inspired Cameroon smashed through the glass ceiling in 1990, reaching the quarter-finals having defeated reigning champions Argentina in the opening match before losing to England after extra time, it represented a watershed moment for the continent's footballers. Over the next five years the number of African players plying their trade in Europe's biggest leagues grew steadily, although there were none present in the starting line-ups on the inaugural day of the Premier League in August 1992. In stark comparison to today's competition, only 13 non-British players were selected by the

22 teams, with Ipswich's Canadian goalkeeper Craig Forrest the only representative from outside Europe.

That statistic changed a week later, however, when a skinny teenager from Bulawayo came off the bench in Coventry's 2-0 win over Tottenham at White Hart Lane to become the first African player to feature in the Premier League. Bobby Gould's side went on to win five of the next six games in which Peter Ndlovu featured, with a victory over Sheffield Wednesday briefly taking them second in the table.

"His balance is as perfect as Trevor Brooking's and he's quicker . . . he gets your knees wobbling with his skill," admitted the Coventry manager, who had been in the crowd at Highfield Road nearly 40 years earlier to see Steve Mokone's debut. "I've never seen a man with quicker feet. Some of his tricks are astounding."

In more ways than one, English football had entered a new era.

***

Winston Makamure still enjoys telling the story even two decades later. "I hired a car from St Albans for £15. I put £10 of petrol in it and went up to Coventry," he remembers with a broad smile. "I stayed with a relative on Sunday in Tamworth and went to the training ground the next day but the laundry lady outside told me that they weren't training that day. I was supposed to drop off the car later on but I phoned the company and arranged to have it for another day. Then I went to a service station on the M1 and slept in my car. I was so determined to win that bet."

As he made his way to Coventry's training ground on a cold December day in 1992, what Makamure didn't know was his wager with university friends would end up changing his life forever. It had been 18 months since Peter Ndlovu had moved to the Midlands as a teenager having been first spotted by 1987

FA Cup-winning manager John Sillett playing in the same team as his elder brother Adam.

"We went on a pre-season tour to Zimbabwe in 1990 and played against their national side. Both Adam and Peter were playing for them," Sillett recalled in an interview in 2012 after Adam's untimely death in a car crash that also left Peter in hospital with life-threatening injuries.

"Afterwards I said: 'What chance have we got of getting the two of them to England?' We were allowed to bring both of them over. Eight months later I signed Peter – I wanted to sign both of them, but the board would only let me sign one of them. Adam went off to Switzerland and had a good career but Peter was the most talented player I have ever seen. They were both cracking lads, and were very, very close as brothers."

The youngest Ndlovu brother eventually arrived at Coventry – by then managed by former England defender Terry Butcher – in the summer of 1991 from Highlanders for just £10,000 having turned down a move to the United States. Still only 18, he made his debut in August 1991 as a substitute for goalscorer Micky Gynn in the 1-1 draw against Queens Park Rangers, becoming the second Zimbabwean to appear in England's top flight after Bruce Grobbelaar. He ensured instant hero status a few weeks later when he scored the second goal against Arsenal at Highbury in a famous 2-1 victory over the reigning champions that also featured Lee Dixon's comical own goal lob over David Seaman. It was the first time George Graham's side had lost at home in the league for 18 months.

Ndlovu was soon promoted to the starting XI, scoring a brilliant individual goal against local rivals Aston Villa in a 1-0 victory at the end of September. It was his last goal of the season as injury intervened, while an awful run of form that saw Coventry lose eight matches out of nine in October and November eventually led to Butcher's dismissal. Former Arsenal manager Don Howe stepped in to prevent relegation by just two points at the expense of Brian Stein's Luton despite winning just one of their final nine league fixtures. Even so, it had been a solid first season for the spindly teenager who had fondly been christened 'Nuddy' by his teammates and supporters.

"When I used to watch English football on TV I would think, 'Oh, that's a big league', but I never thought I would have the chance to play there," Ndlovu admitted in 2014. "When I got there, I asked myself, 'Am I good enough to be here?' because I quickly realised I had to start taking it seriously."

The emergence of stars like David Rocastle, Ian Wright and John Barnes – the son of a military officer from Trinidad and Tobago and a Jamaican mother who became the first black winner of the prestigious PFA Player of the Year award in 1988 – during the previous decade meant that black players were firmly established in English football's top flight by the time Ndlovu arrived at Coventry. Yet he still remembers being targeted by some supporters in those early days.

"There was a lot of racism coming from the fans but the other players helped me settle," he recalled. "It was a surprise because I had never experienced that before."

As Coventry prepared for the inaugural Premier League season following the appointment of Bobby Gould, the former Sky Blues striker who had led unfancied Wimbledon to their unlikely FA Cup triumph in 1988 since his first spell in charge a decade earlier, their new manager had certainly been impressed by Ndlovu's performances in pre-season.

"I didn't know much about him at all when I first got there. He was as quiet as a field mouse," admits Gould. "But all of a sudden when I saw him in training I thought, 'My goodness, what have we got here?' He came under the radar really. Looking back now, the nearest person I can compare him with today is Eden Hazard. There is no shadow of a doubt about that. He's the nearest of today's players that I can equate to the way Nuddy played. He was best on the wing because he wanted to be running on to the ball rather than off the frontman. He was so hard to stop when he had that momentum."

With victories in their first three matches of the new season against Middlesbrough, Tottenham and Wimbledon, the same applied to Coventry as they briefly went top of the Premier League table for a few days before being brought down to earth with successive defeats against QPR and Blackburn at the end of August. But having been dogged by inconsistency in his opening season, Ndlovu's historic appearance against Spurs earned him a regular starting spot for the first time.

"He was living in digs, which is never easy. When you leave Zimbabwe it's hard to adapt," admits Gould. "It's always a bit difficult for African players to come and settle in but I think it was the way everyone loved him. It was a real love affair between him and the fans. He was a lovely young man who had come over with no airs and graces but just wanted to be successful. After a while he just blossomed. There was a hostel that he went in for the first year but we felt he needed to come out of it to grow in stature. The hostel was a bunch of young lads who were well looked after but we thought he had to go out into the big wide world. Having come over from Zimbabwe he had to express himself and learn how to look after himself."

Ndlovu's diving header in the win over Sheffield Wednesday at Hillsborough was Coventry's third away victory in succession and they made history a few days later by beating Oldham at Boundary Park to equal their best-ever run in the top flight. Suddenly, they were fighting it out with Norwich at the top of the table.

"We were a flying machine," laughs Gould. "Every good team has balance and blend, although sometimes it can take a while to get the players in the right positions. But the lads grew to love Nuddy and appreciate how much natural ability he had. All the great players I played with like Trevor Brooking or George Best had this natural balance and the same could be said about him. He could run with the ball, get knocked but go with sway the other way and he'd still be standing on two feet. Nuddy's ability to control the ball and run with the ball – that's where he was light years ahead of the rest."

Another narrow win over Tottenham – their second in the space of just 25 days in a bizarre quirk of the fixture list – in front of the Sky television cameras moved Coventry into second spot. Despite a draw against Nottingham Forest at the City Ground a few days later, Gould's side went into their fixture against Norwich at Highfield Road on 26 September 1992 knowing that victory would see them climb above their opponents to the summit of the Premier League. It all seemed to be going wrong, however, when Ian Crook scored for the visitors in the 13th minute. Ndlovu had other ideas. Racing on to a through ball from veteran defender Kenny Sansom after a clever dummy from Kevin Gallacher, the 19-year-old beat his marker to the ball and sped towards the penalty area. Two Norwich players tried to stop him but Ndlovu seemed to glide past them before wrong-footing goalkeeper Bryan Gunn with a wonderful shimmy and sending the ball into the bottom corner.

"That is a lovely goal by the Zimbabwean," exclaimed BBC commentator Barry Davies. "Wonderful balance. Smooth as silk."

On the touchline, Gould celebrated with vigour.

"The reaction from everybody – there wasn't a cheer immediately but then everyone realised what he had done. It was a brilliant goal virtually from the halfway line," he remembers with a large slice of embellishment. "The balance and the finish were amazing."

After the match had finished with a 1-1 draw that meant Coventry slipped to third behind Blackburn, Gould claimed that

Ndlovu ranked with Manchester United's emerging star Ryan Giggs – whose grandfather was born in Sierra Leone – "just behind Best" in terms of ability, much to the amusement of many of the assembled press. Yet having scored a third goal in six appearances following his goal against Scarborough in the League Cup a few days earlier, *The Independent's* Phil Shaw was certainly impressed.

"The sun may have set on the Empire, but the stunning equaliser by Peter Ndlovu that earned Coventry a point proved there are still rich pickings in transfer imperialism," he wrote. "The 19-year-old Zimbabwean, whose name is pronounced 'Un-love', first came to Highfield Road from the Highlanders club during John Sillett's reign as manager. When Sillett boasted that Coventry would be 'shopping at Harrods', he obviously meant 'shopping in Harare'."

***

After the early promise, however, a series of draws turned into defeats as Coventry plummeted down the table. Ndlovu had continued his knack of scoring at some of England's most famous grounds with goals in the draws against Everton and struggling champions Leeds on Halloween. Yet by the time Makamure was preparing to travel to England in December to begin studying for a degree in IT at Hatfield Polytechnic in his latest posting for the Zimbabwean army, Coventry were without a win for nearly three months.

"My friends and I were having a drink one night and talking about football," he explains. "One guy said to me, 'There is a very good youngster who is now at Coventry who is good enough for any team in England.' Having been there before a few times already, I said it wasn't possible, that it was 'drink talk'. I said that he wouldn't make it in England. We then had a bet of 20 Zimbabwe dollars that I could get a photo with him."

Having returned to the training ground the next day after a rough night in his car, Makamure adopted a novel approach to gain access to his hero.

"I told them that I was from the same village in Zimbabwe as Peter and I had come to meet him. I had never even seen him play! Luckily they let me in and I waited for the players to finish training. When he came out, he had already been told that someone from Zimbabwe was there to see him. Unfortunately, I couldn't speak Ndebele and he was terrible at Shona! So we started speaking in English. One of the players said, 'If you're from the same village then why are you speaking in English?' Peter said, 'It's for the benefit of everyone else and we don't want to be rude!' He brought me some sandwiches and I said to Peter, 'Here is a bet I did with my friends back home, so can I please have a photo with you.' He called the entire team and I had pictures with them."

Gould wandered over and asked what was going on and for some reason Ndlovu said, "Gaffer, this is my agent."

"I had no idea what he was talking about," admits Makamure. "I had just gone there to take pictures! But that is how it started."

As he prepared to leave, Ndlovu offered him tickets for the game against Ipswich at Highfield Road that weekend.

"I knew that I didn't really have any money to come back up but agreed to anyway," Makamure laughs. "We exchanged numbers and I went straight to a place to get my pictures developed. Then I went to a phone box to call my friends and tell them I had won the bet! I said, 'Guys, I've got the pictures. Just make sure you've got my money!'"

Ndlovu was voted man of the match as Coventry were denied an elusive win by a late penalty, with Makamure watching on as his guest from the stands having given his seat in the directors' box to his cab driver because he wasn't wearing a suit and tie.

"Afterwards we went for a meal at KFC and we were just chatting. He told me how much he earned a week from playing for Coventry and it wasn't a lot. He told me that he needed some help getting a new contract so I said I would talk to a friend of mine at university who might be able to give us some advice. Then he asked me if I would be able to do it and I said that I could try. We shook hands and that was the start of our business relationship."

With little more than six months until his original two-year contract was due to expire, there was plenty of work to do.

"Before I went, I told Peter to tell Coventry that I was going home but we should talk about it when I returned," says Makamure. "At first, they were not very keen to talk to anyone else and just wanted to do it with Peter on their own. A friend of mine said to me, 'They don't want anyone else to be there because they know they will end up paying more money.' Not that I had a clue what to do in negotiating."

Makamure returned home to Harare and immediately received a call from Coventry's secretary summoning him back to the UK.

"They gave me a bit of a bollocking saying, 'You've messed up our player' and all this stuff. They asked to meet with me on Thursday so I told them that I had just arrived back home so it may be a problem. They told me not to worry and told me just to get myself to the airport and there would be a ticket waiting for me. I went to see my parents for one night and then went back to England. At Gatwick there was a guy waiting for me and he took me to speak to Peter. When I got there I was just wearing my jeans and T-shirt again so he took me to Marks & Spencer to get some smarter clothes."

He was then driven to Highfield Road and met chairman Derrick Robins to discuss the terms of Ndlovu's new contract, with Gould also making an appearance.

"They were ever so nice to me. They had absolutely no idea about how I had come to be Peter's agent. We chatted and I said, 'OK, I need some time to talk to Peter about everything' and asked them to put their offer in writing. We went away together to discuss things and did a disappearing act. They were trying to find us to get us to come back the following day but we stayed away. Eventually we came back and went to meet them."

Incredibly, Ndlovu had been earning just £495 a week since joining from Highlanders and his new offer was double that. But Makamure, who would go on to represent Ndlovu until his retirement in 2011 and several other Zimbabweans including Benjani Mwaruwari, had been doing his homework.

"I'd been asking around to see what other people were earning so we knew what he was worth," he says. "What they had offered I multiplied by four and they agreed immediately. Peter signed the contract and was also paid a signing-on fee for the first time. He increased his wages fourfold. I have no idea whether I took my ten per cent. All I was interested in was winning my bet and I could now go and watch Premier League games. I wasn't in it for business or anything. He signed the contract and I ended up going back to college. I think he gave me about £100 to say thanks."

Ndlovu missed the 5-1 thrashing of Liverpool on 19 December due to injury as Coventry's search for a victory finally ended after 11 matches to ease the pressure on Gould. Another win in their next fixture against Aston Villa raised hopes of a strong second half to the season, with their star forward's goals in the wins over Oldham and Middlesbrough lifting Gould's side up to fifth place with just ten games remaining. But as Ndlovu celebrated his 20th birthday and supporters started to dream of a first European campaign since the 1970/71 Inter-City Fairs Cup, the sale of strikers Kevin Gallacher to Blackburn and Robert Rosario to struggling Nottingham Forest in March saw them lose three successive matches to slip down the table once more.

Coventry ended the season in 15th place – the lowest position they had been all season – after a thrilling 3-3 draw with Leeds on the final day that saw Ndlovu score his seventh league goal of the campaign. That summer, director Bryan Richardson assumed control of the club and, much to the delight of their manager, Coventry began the second Premier League season by beating Arsenal 3-0 at Highbury thanks to Micky Quinn's hat-trick – their second successive win in north London.

"George Graham said to me at the end of the last season, 'Gouldy you always play 4-4-2.' So I went away on holiday and I was sitting on the beach in Portugal with 11 stones in the sand making pretty patterns. In the end I decided to play with a sweeper. We went up to Rotherham for a pre-season game and George had sent a scout to watch us play. We played four different systems so I f***** him right up! They couldn't handle it at Highbury and Peter was an important part of that win."

Yet despite starting the season nine matches unbeaten with Ndlovu scoring again in a 3-3 draw with Oldham, Gould's relationship with the new chairman deteriorated quickly. After the 5-1 hammering against QPR at Loftus Road that saw the Zimbabwe forward grab a consolation goal, the manager surprised everyone by resigning via a short statement at the post-match press conference. *The Daily Telegraph* reported at the time that not even Gould's son Jonathan, who had just let in five goals, had an inkling.

"When my dad came into the dressing room and told us the news I was as surprised as anyone else," he said. "I had no idea that this was going to happen."

"I got a bit tired," admits Gould. "There was a changeover in chairman and that affected me greatly. The relationship I had with the previous chairman was phenomenal and all of a sudden that was going to be taken away from me and replaced with a chairman I didn't have any respect for."

Gould was succeeded by Phil Neal, the former Liverpool defender who had been working as Graham Taylor's assistant during his calamitous spell as England manager. He guided Coventry to 11th place at the end of the season as Ndlovu finished top scorer with 11 goals despite missing much of the season through a cruciate ligament knee injury – a fantastic return for a player of such tender years. Suddenly, Makamure was fielding calls from some of England's biggest clubs enquiring how much it would cost to purchase the talented forward, with Liverpool's Roy Evans showing most interest.

"Phil Babb had just gone there for a lot of money and I got wind that there may be some interest from them in Peter as well," he recalls. "I headed up to Coventry to talk to the club but one of the doctors from the Zimbabwe team warned them to be very careful with his recovery because there could be a danger he wouldn't pass the medical. Obviously Coventry came back and said they wanted to review his contract and they offered a big rise. All that was done very quickly so he chose to stay."

***

Almost a century after Arthur Wharton had blazed his trail with Preston, the success of Coventry's flying Zimbabwean in the first two seasons of the Premier League's existence finally opened the door for other African players in English football. By the time Ndlovu returned to pre-season training in July 1994, Aston Villa's signing of exciting Ghana forward Nii Lamptey from PSV Eindhoven was the talk of the transfer market.

Once described as his "natural successor" by Pelé after his performances at the Under-16 World Championship in Scotland a few years earlier, he had been subjected to repeated physical abuse from his father as a child and was forced to escape without a passport to fulfil his dream of becoming a professional player. Posing as the son of Stephen Keshi – the Nigeria defender then playing for Anderlecht who would go on to become an inspirational coach of the Super Eagles – Lamptey reached Belgium and broke into the first team immediately alongside his adopted mentor, scoring in five successive matches having forced the league to lower its minimum age limit to allow the 16-year-old to play senior football.

He quickly became one of the most sought-after young players in Europe and headed to the Netherlands, where his performances for PSV Eindhoven persuaded Villa manager Ron Atkinson to take the plunge ahead of the 1994/95 campaign. Atkinson – who had been in charge of West Brom almost 20 years earlier when Cyrille Regis, Brendon Batson and Laurie Cunningham, the 'Three Degrees', had led the way for black British players – kept faith with Lamptey after a disappointing season at Villa and took him with him to Coventry. Once more, however, he failed to live up to the hype and departed having made only six appearances alongside Ndlovu.

"To get such high praise from him [Pelé] was wonderful but it had its negative side – everywhere I went I was supposed to live up to very high standards," Lamptey later admitted. "Once I couldn't meet people's expectations I was considered a failure."

In contrast, South African Phil Masinga started well for Leeds following his move from Mamelodi Sundowns, scoring two hat-tricks in pre-season and then finding the net three minutes into the 3-2 defeat by Chelsea on 27 August 1994. His compatriot Lucas Radebe took a little longer to settle after joining from Kaizer Chiefs three weeks after Masinga, with both players having been recommended by Leeds' chief scout, Geoff Sleight. The defender who would go on to become one of the club's most iconic captains was mysteriously deployed on the left wing by manager Howard Wilkinson as both he and Masinga started the game against Sheffield Wednesday.

"The English game was so quick compared to what I was used to, and it was pretty difficult for me," Radebe later remembered. "But the atmosphere was fantastic and I knew I was going to enjoy playing in England – as long as I could play in my proper position . . ."

It had been almost 35 years since Gerry Francis and Albert Johanneson were selected by Don Revie in the fixture against Stoke in April 1961, although that was news to their successors at the time.

"When I first got there, I had no idea there had been this South African playing for Leeds 30 years before me," Masinga told me in 2015. "We were told all about him when we arrived and we watched some of the old videos of Albert. It was really interesting to know that we weren't the first from our country to experience this club. He was a great ambassador for the country because he left when there were a lot of problems at home and made people aware that there was a lot of talent in South Africa."

Like Francis and Johanneson, Masinga and Radebe had been recruited directly from South Africa and at first found the transition to English football almost as hard as they had. But it was Ndlovu's success at Coventry that persuaded them to believe they could thrive thousands of miles from home.

"We knew about English football because we used to follow it on TV but our chances of making it there seemed a long way away," remembered Masinga, who died in January 2019 of cancer at the age of just 49 following a troubled retirement that at one point saw him declared bankrupt. "At that stage there were hardly any African players in England – I can only remember Peter and before him Bruce Grobbelaar at Liverpool. We all knew about Peter from playing against Zimbabwe and it was exciting to see him doing well in the Premier League. Every player was hoping to emulate him. He was a real inspiration for the entire continent."

Living in digs for the first six months, the two new arrivals struggled with the Yorkshire weather but found the transition was made much smoother by the influence of landlady Susanne Humphrey.

"It wasn't easy. But not just going to England – any country," said Masinga. "Going out of your own comfort zone from somewhere where there is a lot of sunshine like in South Africa and coming to Europe – everything is different. It's a massive culture shock because you have to learn how to do things differently. Living in digs was helpful because I was used to my mum doing everything for me at home – cooking, cleaning. So I was really grateful to have someone there who could look after us. They were really nice people who made us feel at home.

"I remember them saying to us how exciting it was to have two African players in Leeds," he added. "We would always ask them questions about what things were like in England and how to go about certain things. Our landlady was a brilliant woman. When I went to live in Italy I was always asking Lucas how she was because we became very close."

Masinga's early performances quickly won over the crowd at Elland Road but it would take a while longer for Radebe to establish himself as a key player for Leeds. Yet having scored a hat-trick in extra time against Walsall in the FA Cup, the arrival of Ghana striker Tony Yeboah in January 1995 for £3.4 million from German club Eintracht Frankfurt ensured that Masinga would spend the majority of the next year on the bench before leaving to join Swiss side St Gallen and then Serie A side Bari. Having become one of the first black players to appear in the Bundesliga, Yeboah had suffered terrible racist abuse in Germany but won over the majority of fans with his barnstorming performances that saw him end as the league's top scorer for two successive seasons. He carried on that form in England, scoring 12 goals in just half a season – including a brilliant hat-trick on

4 April in a 4-0 thumping of Ipswich – as Leeds ended up in fifth place.

Not to be outdone, Ndlovu – despite enduring his worst season so far as Neal was sacked in February with the team under threat of relegation – had become the first opposition player to score a hat-trick at Anfield since 1961 in Coventry's 3-2 win over Liverpool three weeks earlier. Thriving under new manager Atkinson, who had been shown the door by Villa in November, Ndlovu scored in the wins over West Ham and Leicester but had gone three games without a goal when they travelled to Merseyside on 14 March.

It took him just 21 minutes to open the scoring at Anfield as he pounced on teammate Dion Dublin's miskick to slam the ball past David James. Ndlovu doubled his tally from the penalty spot ten minutes later when former Liverpool player Mike Marsh was brought down in the area but it was his third goal that lived longest in the memory. After a stray pass from a hopelessly overweight Jan Mølby, the ball was played forward to the Zimbabwean 40 yards from goal. Taking a gentle touch with his left foot, Ndlovu picked up speed as he closed in on the penalty area and Neil Ruddock desperately back-pedalled. Then, with one swift touch that took the ball on to his right foot, he smashed a shot that flew past James and into the bottom corner of the net.

"I still have the pictures from after the game," admits Makamure fondly. "It was quite an achievement, although I didn't really realise at the time what it meant but looking back, it was something else."

***

Even though Ndlovu's heroics saw him reach double figures once again as Coventry avoided relegation with relative ease, however, the biggest feat by an African player in English football that season was still to come. And from an unlikely source. Daniel Amokachi had starred in Nigeria's run to the second round at the 1994 World Cup, scoring two goals before they were controversially eliminated by a Roberto Baggio-inspired Italy after extra time but earning plaudits for their performances under Dutchman Clemens Westerhof.

"The naivety of our African mentality meant we were knocked out when we could have gone further," he reflects more than 20 years on. "In those days, all of the 20 teams in the Nigerian Premier League could practically represent the country because there was talent left, right and centre. I remember Westerhof taking us on a tour to Holland before the tournament and we played Utrecht and beat them 8-1. Afterwards, he said it was a fluke. I think he knew the players he had but he didn't believe in our quality. In the next two games we beat Ajax (who would be crowned European champions 12 months later) 2-1 and then PSV 2-0, playing against all the stars like Aron Winter and Frank Rijkaard. That was when he knew he had something special. And we showed the world that we were a team to be reckoned with."

Four brilliant seasons at Belgium side Club Brugge saw Amokachi awarded the inaugural *Soulier d'Ébène* (Ebony Shoe) award for the league's best player of African origin as well as scoring the first-ever Champions League goal against CSKA Moscow. Coupled with his performances at the World Cup, Everton manager Mike Walker was persuaded to pay £3 million to sign him in August 1994.

"The first offer I had was from Juventus but Brugge asked for a lot more money," adds Amokachi. "Then Everton came with an offer of £3 million, which was good for the club and they let me go. But it wasn't just me – I think 90 per cent of that Nigeria team ended up moving after the World Cup. Pretty soon, we were scattered all over the European continent."

At a club where only two players with black heritage – Mike Trebilcock and Cliff Marshall – had ever worn the famous royal blue shirt, Amokachi admitted settling into his new surroundings was far smoother than some of his friends had predicted.

"I had played in Europe already for four seasons so it was just a change of scenery for me. The only thing I really was focusing on was playing football. But I do remember going out to buy myself a nice blue-and-white blazer because I knew the fans would like that when I went out. I wanted to show them that I was a true blue. I'm an African but I became a Scouser. People were very friendly in Liverpool."

Amokachi's debut against Blackburn a few weeks after he joined didn't exactly go to plan, however, as Everton went down to a fourth successive defeat to leave them bottom of the table.

"When I arrived, they called me 'The Bull' but I knew I had a lot of work to do. In my first game against Blackburn I remember being marked by Colin Hendry and he gave me hell. I had about three chances that on a normal day I would have buried but he showed me that I needed to be quicker to make it in the Premier League. I was just about to pull the trigger but he would take the ball away."

His first appearance at Goodison Park proved to be a much more memorable occasion. Handed a starting spot alongside Paul Rideout, Amokachi equalised Les Ferdinand's opening goal in the tenth minute before playing a major role in Everton's second, only for Ferdinand to earn a point late on as Everton were cut further adrift at the bottom.

"When I went on to the field for the first time, the fans gave me a good reception," he recalls. "But I put my hands to my ears as if to say, 'I can't hear you', so they would shout it louder. I think they enjoyed that."

"The Nigerian's home debut was the source of rich encouragement for Everton," wrote Dave Hadfield in *The*

Independent the next day. "His speed, strength and willingness to chase lost causes will make him an important asset, provided he has players of comparable effectiveness around him."

Yet it would be another six months before 'The Bull' would hit the mark again. Everton's freefall under Walker had seen them only escape the club's first relegation since 1951 the previous season thanks to a dramatic final day win over Wimbledon. A poor start to the new campaign saw the former Wales international shown the door at the start of November having only just achieved their first win of the new season. He left Goodison Park with the worst record of any post-war Everton manager and was replaced by former striker Joe Royle, who had scored over 100 goals for his boyhood club before moving to Manchester City.

Royle's return transformed Everton's fortunes almost overnight. They beat Liverpool in the Merseyside derby in his first match before following it up with another two victories to move well clear of relegation trouble. But a combination of injury and his own insecurities meant Amokachi had made only 12 league appearances by the time they faced Tottenham in the FA Cup semi-finals at Elland Road on 9 April.

"The injuries made it difficult but it was more about getting used to what was required in England," he insists. "Training was always 100 miles an hour, whereas in Europe it was more working on technical stuff. It also didn't help that we were struggling under Mike. When Joe Royle came in he had a plan for survival and it was route one football. I think Mike was a bit soft on the players but Joe was a tough cookie. He made it clear that this was how he wanted to play. If you weren't ready to do that then you would be out of the team. I was the type of player that if you give me five minutes, I will show what I have. That's why the Evertonians appreciated me because I always tried to give 100 per cent."

The warm welcome didn't extend to everyone, however. While he can't recall being subjected to any racist abuse during matches, Amokachi does remember some of the hate mail he was sent during his first season in England in the days before social media.

"Directly in my face, I didn't see any," he says. "But I received a lot of racist letters. I still have those letters because my wife kept them. They were from fans but definitely not anyone who was an Evertonian. They were threatening me with this and that. Once, I came down and the Porsche I had brought from Belgium had the bumper pulled off it and it was scratched all over. It's all a part of life so you just have to get on with it. We live in a world of ignorance."

Anyone who resented his presence at one of England's most famous clubs would not have enjoyed the game against Spurs. Having successfully overturned a 12-point deduction and FA Cup ban imposed for financial irregularities under the previous board, Tottenham had signed German World Cup winner Jürgen Klinsmann but dispensed with the services of manager Ossie Ardiles a week before Walker was sacked by Everton, replacing him with QPR's Gerry Francis. They were hot favourites to reach Wembley and face Manchester United in what some sections of the media had dubbed "the dream final" but Everton and Royle in particular had other plans.

Yet even their manager could not have predicted how events would unfold on that spring day in Yorkshire. Everything seemed to be going to plan for Royle's side when Graham Stuart scored in the 55th minute to put Everton 2-0 up after Matt Jackson's goal in the first half but a controversial penalty from Klinsmann soon after gave Spurs hope of mounting a late comeback. An injury to Paul Rideout – who had just returned from seven matches out with injured knee ligaments – then saw the striker go down for treatment, with the doctor and physio both signalling that he should be substituted.

"Joe insisted that we should give him an extra five minutes but

I was already out warming up," says Amokachi, enthusiastically taking up the story. "So I went up to the fourth official and told him that we would be making a substitution. I gave him my number and Rideout's number and then took my tracksuit off. By the time Joe realised what had happened I was on the field and it was too late!"

Given that Rideout had just indicated he was able to continue, Royle flew into a rage on the touchline when he realised but there was nothing he could do as the game continued. His anger at his striker's act of selfishness soon turned to joy, however, when Stuart's floated cross picked out Amokachi at the far post to head home the third goal in the 82nd minute. A precise side-footed finish into the roof of the net from Gary Ablett's pass in the dying moments of the match capped a spectacular afternoon for the man from Kaduna state and saved him from the bollocking of a lifetime from his manager.

"I wanted them to hold on for a few seconds but Daniel wandered on to the pitch, the fourth official held up the board, and that was it," reflected Royle after the match. "He was desperate to play but he should not have been on. What a good mistake it was."

"In the end I think he was quite pleased, even if it was something that I definitely shouldn't have done," admits Amokachi. "But I just got caught up in the moment."

Suddenly, everything seemed to fall into place for the first Nigerian international to have played in the English top flight since John Chiedozie a decade earlier. Amokachi started the next game against Newcastle and scored both goals in a 2-0 victory before also finding the net against Chelsea in a thrilling 3-3 draw. But he ended up being left out of the starting line-up in the final against Manchester United as Royle preferred Rideout as his lone striker against Alex Ferguson's side, who had been pipped to the league title by Blackburn a week earlier after failing to beat West Ham on the final day. His decision was vindicated as Rideout scored the only goal of the game with a header from a corner, with Amokachi introduced in the 69th minute for Anders Limpar and leading the celebrations at the final whistle by donning a blue beret.

"The final capped it all off," he says. "To beat Manchester United to win the FA Cup at Wembley was something huge in Nigeria and for me to be part of it was amazing. Being the first Nigerian to do that is something to be very proud of."

Given that Blackpool's Bill Perry, who was born in Johannesburg to parents of mixed heritage, scored the winning goal for Blackpool in their 4-3 victory against Bolton Wanderers in the 1953 final that also featured a 38-year-old Stanley Matthews, Amokachi certainly wasn't the first player of African heritage to pick up a winners' medal. Yet after Bruce Grobbelaar's three titles with Liverpool between 1986 and 1992, the significance of a black player from the continent succeeding in the world's oldest knockout competition was not lost on millions of fans back in Lagos, Dakar and Accra. Africa had finally made its mark on English football's biggest stage. There was no turning back now.

TEN

LIKE FATHER, LIKE SON

Anyone who watched Channel 4's sitcom *Desmond's* in the early 1990s will remember Matthew. One of the regulars who seemed to spend the majority of his time in the Peckham barber shop along with lovable rogue Porkpie, he was a student from The Gambia who was fond of offering advice prefaced with the phrase "there is an old African saying".

Matthew surely would have approved of the ancient Ghanaian proverb that states "when you follow the path of your father, you learn to walk like him". That prediction has applied to several African footballers, with Manchester City's Leroy Sané and Timothy Weah of Lille just two of the latest to have followed in their famous fathers' footsteps on the field. For Mike Origi, watching his son Divock play for Belgium at the 2014 World Cup was the culmination of a journey that began in 1992 when he became the first Kenyan to play professional football in Europe at KV Oostende.

"It was a very proud moment to see my son play and above all score in Brazil," he told Kenyan journalist Claudia Ekai for *The Guardian* in 2014, a few weeks after his son had moved to Liverpool for £10 million. "I was there and as a former player, I know that is the tournament every player wants to play in. I did not get the chance – Kenya never has – but Divock did. For all the sacrifices he made, it was a reward for the hard work."

Born in Nairobi in 1967, Origi's father was known as Mike Okoth in his playing days and started his career as a goalkeeper before being converted to a striker. A distant relative of former US President Barack Obama through their Luo heritage, he was one of four brothers who went on to play for the national side, the Harambee Stars, appearing in three successive Africa Cup of Nations finals and earning his move to Europe as a result.

"Mike ended up going because he played later than me," explains his eldest brother Austin Oduor, who captained Kenya during the 1980s and also has a son – Arnold – who played international football. "We had not qualified for the Africa Cup of Nations for a long time but we managed it in 1988 and then again in 1990 and 1992. Mike played in the AFCON for all three and he did well. The scouts were there and that's how he drew their attention. That's when they started looking at Kenya."

Originally a swashbuckling midfielder who later became a central defender, Oduor helped create Kenya's most famous football dynasty while also working part-time as a civil servant. At just 25 – following the death of their father and eldest brother – he became the family's main breadwinner and also established himself as a national hero thanks to his exploits for club side Gor Mahia and the national team. Yet while Oduor and his contemporaries had grown up dreaming of playing professionally in Europe, they soon realised their ultimate destination was still out of reach.

"We used to watch English football all the time," he recalls. "But in those days the door wasn't open. I would have wished to play there but by the time players started moving to Europe from Africa at the end of the 1980s, my career was almost over."

While clubs in the French and Portuguese top flights had continued to import players from their former colonies, their

English counterparts were much slower on the uptake. New regulations imposed on the Football Association by the European Community in February 1978 that permitted each club to sign two foreign players after decades of restrictions saw Tottenham bring in Argentina's World Cup-winning pair Ossie Ardiles and Ricky Villa to great success, with Ipswich's Dutch duo Arnold Mühren and Frans Thijssen clearing the pathway for players from mainland Europe. But the idea of signing a player directly from Africa never really crossed anyone's minds until Peter Ndlovu arrived in 1991.

"The scouts hadn't explored East Africa and there was this issue of colonisation," says Oduor. "Most of East Africa was colonised by the British whereas West Africa was mainly French. The French opened the pathway to their country to their colonised areas much earlier so accessing the league was easier for Francophone Africa. For us, it wasn't easy because the British didn't open the gates for many years. That's why Mike ended up going to Belgium."

A dramatic late goal – a motif that was to become something of a family trait – against Sudan which sealed his country's spot at the 1992 AFCON helped convince Oostende to take a risk on Origi senior, although Oduor admits his brother found the transition extremely testing at first.

"It was very difficult because he was going from amateur football to the professional game," he says. "The kind of training he had to adapt to was very hard but he had to persevere to prove he was good enough to be there. The climate was also harsh for him because we don't have winter in Kenya. Experiencing that for the first time was a bit of a struggle for him. With all those changes, it was very hard to stay there. Lots of players would go to Europe and come back very quickly because they couldn't adapt."

Thrown in at the deep end in an alien environment and forced to adapt quickly or be shown the door, it's no surprise that so many of the early African pioneers failed to make the same kind of impact as Ndlovu or Tony Yeboah.

"It is a massive culture shock when you come over and life is completely different," says Jürgen Klopp. "There was a story about a Brazilian player who had three colds in the first three months he was there. The team manager went to his flat and realised that he hadn't realised he needed to turn the heating on! We believe the whole world is the same but it's not. It's not in 2019 and it wasn't in 1990."

Liverpool's manager remembers how one of his coaches in Germany quickly ran out of patience with a new African player after he failed to follow his instructions.

"The coach thinks, 'I have so much other work to do so let me just get another player.' That was how it was. In football you need to be confident on the pitch. But they were often so respectful of everything that it can be a challenge in terms of culture. It's sometimes difficult. I had more teammates like this when I was playing because the quality of my teammates was unfortunately not the same as the players I am managing! But it was like that. Some had a body like this [makes a well-built shape with his hands] and skills like crazy but the mentality was not quite ready. It wasn't an African mentality: it was just the culture. They were so respectful with authority – the coach and the older players – that they could never be themselves. They always wanted to be the player that we wanted them to be rather than being able to express themselves."

Origi proved to be one of the few who lasted the course. His persistence in those early months soon paid off with a regular starting spot for Oostende, becoming an instant legend when another late goal saved them from relegation in 1995 – the same year that his son Divock was born in Belgium. Having moved to Genk three years later, Origi went on to win the title before eventually retiring at the age of 39 in 2006 having earned more than 120 caps. By then, Divock was a star of Genk's burgeoning youth academy which had produced the likes of Thibaut Courtois, Kevin De Bruyne and Christian Benteke, turning down a move to Manchester United in 2010 in favour of Lille.

"I came back from school and my father and mother sat down and I saw them discussing and I knew they had a way that they wanted things to go but they told me I could choose," Origi junior recalled. "For my parents to say this to a child at 15 . . . I had a day of thinking and for me the most logical option was Lille. It was a good choice. I think it was just the decision of my heart. I saw Eden Hazard come through and these other players there like Gervinho and Joe Cole. I thought I'd have the chance to go through there. I didn't have anything against Manchester United or any team. My dream was to play in the Premier League one day but my heart said that I had to go through at Lille."

Five years on, his dream came true when Origi came off the bench at Old Trafford a few months after his exploits in Brazil, even if he ended up on the losing side in Liverpool's 3-1 defeat. But while there were some highlights among his first two years at Anfield including two goals against Everton and the priceless away strike against Klopp's former club Borussia Dortmund in the Europa League quarter-final in 2016, it was no surprise when he was loaned to Wolfsburg for the 2017/18 season having made just one Premier League appearance in the previous campaign. He returned to Merseyside the next summer with two years of his contract remaining as Liverpool let it be known that they were prepared to sell the 23-year-old if anyone matched their £24 million valuation. Despite interest from Dortmund and Valencia, however, no deal could be agreed.

"Divock is still a Liverpool player," Mike Origi confirmed in August 2018. "The coach is already happy with what he's seeing with Divock in training and it's up to the young man to now fight for a place in the team."

***

Naby Keïta could not hide his disappointment. It was a few minutes before half-time of Guinea's Africa Cup of Nations qualifier against Rwanda in Kigali on 16 October when he felt it, the dreaded pain of a hamstring tweak that means at least a couple of weeks on the sidelines, if you're lucky. As his teammates surrendered their 1-0 lead on the artificial surface at the Stade Regional Nyamirambo, Keïta received treatment on his injury before returning to Merseyside the next morning. His worst fears were realised when Liverpool's doctors confirmed the hamstring would rule their summer signing out of action until at least the start of November at a particularly busy period of the season. A few days later, Mohamed Salah scored the only goal – his 50th in English football – as Liverpool kept up their promising start in a scrappy victory at Huddersfield. "It is the first period in my life that we can win average matches," admitted Jürgen Klopp afterwards.

While the rest of his squad prepared for the visit of Serbian champions Red Star Belgrade in the Champions League, Keïta began his recovery under the watchful eye of Liverpool's physiotherapist Christopher Rohrbeck – a recruit from Klopp's old club Mainz in the summer of 2017. He would prove to be a regular companion over the course of the next few weeks as Liverpool's new No. 8 struggled to regain his fitness, not returning to Liverpool's starting line-up for a Premier League game until the start of December.

"Naby just needed normal time to adapt first and foremost but in that time he got injured twice," reflects Klopp. "He's a fantastic player – the other two boys came in and spoke the language already and that's a massive difference. Sadio was ready immediately. Mo was ready immediately. Naby was an investment in the future. It meant we could give him time – if we had to buy this player in two years we couldn't have got him any more. There's no chance. So we buy him now and give him the time and we all grow together.

"I don't read a book about how to be with African players – that's not how it works," he adds. "I usually learn the rest from the boys. You try to be as normal as possible and talk with them and you realise step by step that some information helps and some doesn't. But that's one of the parts that I really love in my job – to have these challenges. It's never the same. Always having to adapt to the next development level of the person that you are working with. Because we all deal with things in a different way. Our lives change really every day – the awareness of people on the outside and how we respond to that."

Liverpool's manager is also convinced that the expectation that came with being anointed as Gerrard's successor had nothing to do with Keïta's early struggles.

"The shirt was never an issue," he insists. "RB Leipzig is a good club in Germany but it's a big step to go to Liverpool. The only really positive thing in the first moment is to earn more money. All the rest is much more pressure – from being by far the best player and way ahead of everyone else to having to be at your best every week to make sure that you play in the team from the beginning. Adapting to that takes time and you don't have to be from Africa to feel that problem. It's enough if you come from Scotland."

***

Everyone in France can be forgiven for thinking it was a *fait accompli*. Marseille – led by goal machine Jean-Pierre Papin and ably supported by Chris Waddle and Abedi 'Pelé' Ayew – would steamroller the team from an eastern European country on the brink of civil war and finally end Ligue 1's never-ending wait to produce Europe's best team.

Pelé, one of 18 siblings and the father of future Premier League stars André and Jordan Ayew, had earned his illustrious nickname back in Ghana before moving to France in 1986. A short spell in Switzerland with FC Zurich had prepared the attacking midfielder for the challenge which awaited him but could not have been ready for the initial reception when he signed for Marseille 12 months later. "I started playing with them and three weeks later I called my manager and said: 'Look, I would like to change club because I wasn't accepted by the players,'" he said in 2013. "Any time they see me passing, they spit on the ground . . . [and say things like] 'go back to where you come from, go back to the bush.'"

A brilliant spell on loan with Lille – where Divock Origi would later emerge – saw Pelé force his way back into Marseille's plans as he was convinced by his wife to "go and prove to them that you are the best". Having helped Marseille move to within touching distance of a third successive league title, he opened the scoring in the first leg of the 1991 European Cup semi-final against Spartak Moscow before repeating the feat in the second leg to book a showdown with Red Star in Bari. After winning the first leg in Germany, Ljupko Petrovic's side went through in the last minute in front of a raucous home crowd of more than 100,000 in Belgrade when Bayern Munich captain Klaus Augenthaler put through his own net in the last minute.

Marseille had started the season under Germany's 1990 World Cup-winning coach Franz Beckenbauer but his replacement, Dutchman Raymond Goethals, moulded a team that had dispatched Arrigo Sacchi's double reigning champions AC Milan in the quarter-finals. There surely could only be one winner. Yet, to everyone's surprise, the last-ever Yugoslavian champions boasting the attacking talents of Robert Prosinečki, Dejan

Savićević and Darko Pančev killed the game before eventually winning 5-3 on penalties.

Pelé would have to wait another two years to become the first black African international to win the European Cup when Marseille defeated Milan in the final, although the French club were found to have engaged in match-fixing, were stripped of their domestic titles and relegated to Ligue 2. The decline was even sharper for Red Star, however, with Yugoslavia being thrown out of the 1992 European Championships as the country plunged into civil war.

By November 2018, when Liverpool faced Red Star at the Marakana stadium which had hosted the famous semi-final against Bayern at the start of November 2018, the Serbian champions had reached the group stage of the Champions League for the first time since they defended their title 26 years earlier. The draw hadn't been kind: not only did Vladan Milojević's side have to contend with beaten finalists Liverpool and Serie A runners-up Napoli, big-spending Paris Saint-Germain featuring Neymar and Kylian Mbappé – costing more than £350 million combined – also lay in wait. But a stalemate with the Italians in their opening match as Liverpool defeated PSG at Anfield showed they would be no pushovers on home soil, even if 6-1 and 4-0 thumpings in their next two matches in France and England showed qualification may be beyond them.

Salah and Sadio Mané had starred in Liverpool's win at Anfield which took them top of Group C following the 2-2 draw between Napoli and PSG but both were powerless to stop them slumping to a 2-0 defeat in Serbia two weeks later in a lackadaisical display. Milan Pavkov scored twice in the space of seven minutes in the first half, with Origi making his first appearance since May 2017 11 minutes from time as Klopp desperately attempted to salvage something from their trip to Serbia.

The defeat left Liverpool's hopes of repeating the success of the previous campaign in the Champions League resting on the final two matches against PSG and Napoli. A crushing 2-1 loss in France after a brilliant performance from Neymar meant they needed to beat Carlo Ancelotti's side in their final match to reach the knockout stages. Once more it was Salah's goal that proved decisive, tricking Napoli goalkeeper David Ospina into thinking he was about to cross the ball from the byline before sliding it through his legs in the first half.

"It was a significant moment in Salah's own drama too," wrote Barney Ronay in *The Guardian*. "His focus has narrowed in recent weeks, his edge returned; although it turns out even a jaded second-season Salah is good enough to be the Premier League's top scorer in mid-December."

Yet it could all have been so different had Arkadiusz Milik taken the opportunity that came his way in the second minute of injury time. Only a brilliant save from Alisson that saw the Brazilian somehow block the Poland striker's point-blank effort with his knees ensured Liverpool reached the last 16, leading Klopp to describe his £67 million goalkeeper as "a lifesaver". "If I knew Alisson was this good I would have paid double," he admitted afterwards.

***

Liverpool's progress in the Champions League may have gone down to the wire but their league form had continued to impress during the autumn as Salah and Mané continued where they had left off before the stalemate with City. A 4-1 victory over Cardiff at the end of November thanks to Mané's two second-half goals maintained the statistic that Liverpool had won all 19 of the home matches in which he had found the net for them. Cardiff manager Neil Warnock's honest assessment beforehand that it would be "impossible" for his newly promoted side to win against such illustrious opponents proved to be true, although they became the first opposition side since February to score a league goal at Anfield.

Nonetheless, with 26 points from their opening ten fixtures, Liverpool returned to the top of the table for 48 hours at least as Manchester City prepared to travel to Wembley to face Tottenham on Monday evening. After his penalty issues at Anfield three weeks earlier, it was a happier night for Riyad Mahrez as the Algerian's early goal was enough to seal a critical victory for Pep Guardiola's side on a pitch that had been left in tatters by an NFL fixture between the Jacksonville Jaguars and the Philadelphia Eagles the previous evening.

Liverpool arrived in north London a week later to face an Arsenal side who had gone 12 games unbeaten under new manager Unai Emery. With the game judged to have come slightly too early for Keïta, Klopp opted to select James Milner, Fabinho and Georginio Wijnaldum as his midfield three and saw Mané's perfectly legitimate effort in the first half disallowed for offside. Milner's goal on the hour mark appeared to have earned the points for the visitors until a small lapse in concentration eight minutes from time allowed Alex Iwobi – nephew of former Bolton and Nigeria star Jay Jay Okocha – to play in Alexandre Lacazette, who finished brilliantly from a tight angle to earn a share of the points.

"Our workhorses in midfield, we put too much on their shoulders. And it was one time we didn't close Alex Iwobi and he plays the pass for the goal," admitted a rueful Klopp.

City's 6-1 thrashing of Southampton the next day no doubt added to his frustration as Pep Guardiola's side established a two-point lead at the top before hammering six past Shakhtar Donetsk in their Champions League tie three days later. Yet while a 2-0 victory over Fulham ensured Liverpool remained on City's coat-tails going into the final international break of the year, their chances of ending the season on top were rated slim by most pundits. They had needed the intervention of referee Paul Tierney to see off the bottom side at Anfield after he controversially disallowed Aleksandar Mitrovic's goal for offside, with Salah's sixth league goal of the season coming just 14 seconds later following a quick restart from Alisson. Xherdan Shaqiri made the points safe in the second half as Keïta made his first appearance since the draw against City more than a month earlier, replacing Fabinho in injury time.

Despite Jordan Henderson's red card in the 3-0 win over Watford at Vicarage Road, though, he remained on the bench after Salah had set Liverpool on course for a tenth win from their 13 matches, with their tally of 33 points more than they had ever amassed in a Premier League season. But it was their defensive statistics that really caught the eye, with just five goals conceded compared to 18 at the same stage in the previous campaign.

The Merseyside derby at the start of December would provide another stern test of their title credentials, with Marco Silva's Everton side also well placed with more than a third of the season completed. The blue half of the city had not tasted victory at Anfield since the turn of the century, it was Klopp's side who justifiably went into the match as heavy favourites on the 232nd meeting of the two famous clubs. Liverpool v Everton is never a fixture for the faint-hearted and when Origi was introduced from the bench in the 84th minute for his first Premier League appearance for almost 18 months, tensions were at boiling point in the stands. As the game went into time added on with the score still 0-0, there was an enormous roar of encouragement from the Kop when the fourth official's board showed four added minutes. An injury to Everton's Senegal midfielder Idrissa Gueye that required treatment meant almost six had been played when Trent Alexander-Arnold launched one last hopeful long ball into the Everton penalty area straight on to the head of Yerry Mina, whose clearance only found Virgil van Dijk on the edge of the box. The Dutchman normally has an unusually deft touch for a central defender but on this occasion his volley came off the side of his right boot and spiralled high up into the dark winter sky. Turning away in disgust as supporters groaned their disapproval, Van Dijk immediately started running back to the halfway line to get in position for a potential counter-attack.

Even the Everton defenders had assumed that the ball was going to sail over Jordan Pickford's crossbar and out for a goal kick. But not Origi. Sensing where it was about to drop, the substitute moved into position and waited as the England goalkeeper jumped up, only for the ball's flight to deceive him at the last minute and bounce off the crossbar. Incredibly, it came down on to the woodwork again before falling perfectly into Origi's path, allowing him to nod home the unlikeliest of winners. Exploding with joy, Klopp sprinted onto the pitch and embraced Alisson with a jumping bear hug. He later apologised to Silva, admitting that he hadn't meant to be disrespectful. A slow-motion replay of the manager's re-enactment of David Pleat's sprint onto the pitch almost 40 years earlier quickly went viral, with Klopp admitting afterwards that he had been overcome with emotion.

"The goal was lucky of course but our idea was clear: we wanted to win until the last second," he said. "We wanted to show that by bringing strikers on. It was a long and open game. I think we deserved the three points."

"I'm enjoying the moment, it's a special win for the club and the city," added Origi. "The goal was just instinct, I knew there would be some open balls like this, so had to be nice and sharp. In the end Virgil gave me a nice assist! I just have to focus on shining my light. If I do that then I can help the team and the rest will follow. I always believed in myself and I have good people around me so I just thank God for the moments I get."

Incredibly, it was the third time in four appearances that he had found the net against Everton and, according to his uncle, just reward for the patience and self-belief he had shown in the summer.

"We felt for him," admits Oduor. "It's really hard if you are not playing regularly because you become rusty very quickly. But Divock has a unique character – if you talked to him back then he would never be complaining and always focusing on what was coming next. We knew that he was capable but he just needed a chance to show what he could do. But with those other forwards like Salah and Mané the competition is very tough.

"Divock is just like his father was – he's still only 24 but he has already been through a lot," he adds. "If you look at the way he plays, he does it with a lot of personality. Divock has always been very mature but that is something that runs in the family. All of us are very mature – I started playing football when I was 12 at school and was always captain of my teams throughout my career. We all have that leadership quality within us."

As Mané had found two years earlier with his last-minute goal against Everton at Goodison Park, scoring the winner in the Merseyside derby ensured Origi achieved instant iconic status among those of a red persuasion. The best was yet to come.

ELEVEN

STRIKING GOLD

In May 1990 – just as Kenny Dalglish's Liverpool side were wrapping up the old First Division title for the 18th time – a teenager born in one of Monrovia's poorest slums took the first step on a journey that would end up with him making history for African football. It was almost a year since the start of Liberia's bloody civil war and fighting between government troops and Charles Taylor's National Patriotic Front of Liberia had intensified, leaving thousands on both sides dead.

"We got to the airport and were told that only one more flight would be leaving that night," remembers Christopher Wreh, who had just turned 15 and was heading for trials with Ligue 1 side Monaco on the recommendation of his second cousin, George Weah. "The guards said there was no way we could get on because it was full."

Using his best diplomacy skills and aided with a handful of US dollars, Wreh somehow persuaded them to let him through security and on to the plane to Paris. It was the last commercial flight to leave Roberts International Airport for almost five years. A few weeks later, a direct missile strike caused most of the main terminal building to collapse.

"As soon as we got to France, the situation back home got a lot worse," Wreh adds. "If we hadn't been allowed on, who knows what might have happened to us? We could have been killed or something like that. I was very lucky."

By then, Weah was already established as a key player for Monaco under manager Arsène Wenger having been recommended to the future Arsenal manager by his old friend, Claude Le Roy. A former player for a succession of mid-ranking clubs in France, Le Roy had just embarked on the first of ten posts as manager of an African nation when he spotted the powerful striker playing for Cameroonian club Tonnerre Yaoundé in 1988. "When I arrived, I was very, very young," he said in an interview in 2015. "Some players were the same age as me, like Roger Milla and Théophile Abega. George came to Cameroon national squad training even though he was a Liberian. I was dazzled by his talent and called Arsène."

After cutting his managerial teeth with Nancy, Wenger had been appointed Monaco's manager in 1987 and won the Ligue 1 title in his first season thanks partly to the signings of England internationals Glenn Hoddle and Mark Hateley. Acting on Le Roy's recommendation, he flew to Yaoundé to watch Weah in the flesh and was suitably impressed to negotiate a £12,000 fee with his club. But the powerful striker struggled initially to find his feet as he attempted to settle into life in Europe.

"When I moved to Monte Carlo I didn't play for the first six months," Weah recalled in an interview with *The Guardian* in December 2017, a few weeks before he became Liberia's president following years of campaigning. "But I was determined to showcase my talent, to prove to those back home, who thought that my coming to Europe was a waste of time, that I was a good player."

At the end of that first season, he had been voted African Player of the Year for the first time having scored 14 goals for a Monaco side that finished third and also reached the last eight of the European Cup. Weah celebrated by returning to Monrovia and inspiring Liberia to victory over Egypt to keep alive their hopes of qualifying for the 1990 World Cup. Those were dashed by a 0-0 draw in Malawi in August 1989 but another solid season back at Monaco helped Wenger's side reach the semi-finals of the Cup Winners' Cup and win the Coupe de France. As he prepared to return home that summer, Weah went to see his manager to ask if he would be interested in handing trials to several of his international teammates and a couple of rising stars.

"Liberian players were unknown; agents didn't come to Liberia," he remembered in 2000. "It's a very small country. It's not a footballing country. We used to play basketball but after the revolution we started promoting sports like football. I told Wenger that I have a lot of friends, who are good players, and was it possible to help bring them to Europe? Arsène said: 'No problem. Bring them one at a time. If they are good, we will keep them. If not, they go back.' I brought seven players over, like Christopher Wreh."

Along with midfielder Kelvin Sebwe and striker James Debbah, Wreh joined Monaco's youth sides and immediately impressed, even if he found the language barrier difficult to overcome at first.

"At the start, I couldn't speak a word of French," he recalls. "The club had put me up in a hotel where every night I was supposed to let the chef know what I would like to eat. But the problem was I didn't know any words for food and there was no dictionary to explain myself! It was very difficult at times. To go from Liberia to Monaco, to discover the luxury, the 'bling-bling' as we say today, it was a shock."

"George was a superstar when I got to Monaco," Wreh continues. "He was in the first team and I was at the academy so it was good to have someone that I could look up to. There were five of us there at the time and we were like family. We would encourage each other every day to work hard so that we could achieve our dream of following George."

Back home, however, news of Wreh's immediate family was scarce. One of 16 siblings – seven girls and nine boys – it became impossible to make contact in the first two years he was in France as the conflict escalated. A two-month siege of Monrovia in 1992 by Taylor's soldiers saw thousands of deaths and resulted in refugees streaming across the border into neighbouring countries.

"I knew there was no turning back. There was a war in Liberia so I had to be strong to become a professional footballer otherwise it would have been impossible. I didn't hear from my family for two years . . . the war had really intensified and there was no way of communicating. I was looking for my brothers and sisters for a long time before I found out that some of them had moved to Guinea and a few others had gone to Ghana to escape. Eventually I was able to visit them but we were apart for several years. Fortunately there was James and George by my side. I remember, Jürgen Klinsmann took me to training, with Sonny Anderson. I was with Thierry Henry, they would pick us up. 'Titi' was one of my best friends at the training centre. We made jokes, we ate together, we did everything together."

As well as his teammates in Monaco, Wreh found much of his emotional support came from Wenger. Then in his early forties, the man who would go on to spend two decades at Arsenal was already renowned for his thorough approach and took a keen interest in Monaco's youth sides.

"I met him when I was playing for the Under-17 team," Wreh recalls. "He used to come to most of our matches to watch us and I remember speaking to him after one of them. He told me to keep working hard because I was a good player and not to worry about everything going on at home because he would look after me. He was like a dad to me. We would speak about my family back in Liberia and he would tell me that things would get better."

In 1992, Weah was sold to Paris Saint-Germain after Monaco lost to Werder Bremen in the Cup Winners' Cup final and finished runners-up in the league. Still only 18, Wreh made his debut the following season and scored three times in ten appearances in Ligue 1. He came on as a substitute in the one-legged semi-final of the Champions League against Fabio Capello's Milan at the San Siro as Wenger's side went down 3-0 in what turned out to be the manager's last season due to him taking up a lucrative offer to move to Japan. It wasn't long before they would be reunited.

***

Without his mentor's guidance, Wreh struggled to match his initial impact at Monaco and was eventually allowed to join lowly Guingamp on loan in 1996, just as the war in Liberia was coming to an end. In seven years it is estimated that one out of every 17 people in the country had been killed as the economy of Africa's oldest republic had been destroyed. That made Weah's success even more remarkable as he became the first African (and non-European) player to win the coveted Ballon d'Or after finishing top scorer in PSG's run to the Champions League semi-finals and moving to Milan – at the time Europe's most successful club – in 1995. He remains the only African to have been honoured with football's most prestigious individual award.

Having won two Serie A titles in four seasons, Weah was later voted the African player of the century by sport journalists from around the world and would later enjoy brief spells at Chelsea and Manchester City before embarking on his political career. Yet it was Wreh who became the first Liberian to play in

English football in September 1997 when he came off the bench in Arsenal's UEFA Cup tie against PAOK Salonika, replacing Nicolas Anelka in a 1-0 defeat.

Having moved to Highbury in September 1996, Wenger had already installed Senegal-born Patrick Vieira at the heart of his midfield weeks before he took over and set about building a new side that he hoped could challenge Manchester United's domestic dominance. A third-placed finish in his first season had persuaded the Frenchman that more recruits were required and the purchase of Gilles Grimandi and Emmanuel Petit from Monaco reunited Wenger with two of his former players. Marc Overmars also arrived from Ajax for £7 million two years after helping the Dutch side win the Champions League, linking up with compatriot Dennis Bergkamp in a potentially thrilling attack that also boasted Ian Wright and teenage prodigy Anelka.

It's fair to say not many people paid much attention when Arsenal paid £300,000 for Wreh only two days before their first match of the season against Leeds on 9 August 1997. Nonetheless, the new arrival was confident he could force his way into Wenger's plans having helped Guingamp reach the cup final after a successful loan spell that also yielded ten league goals.

"When Arsenal first tried to sign me, people at Monaco told me not to come here because they had Bergkamp and Ian Wright, but it never bothered me," Wreh told the newspapers at the time. "I never thought I had anything to prove to people. In Liberia I'm a star and I trust in my own ability."

That kind of self-belief had persuaded Wenger to take a risk on the 22-year-old, although Wreh would have to wait until the League Cup victory over Birmingham in October for his first start. Living at Arsenal's temporary training base at Sopwell House hotel in St Albans, he found it difficult to adapt to his new surroundings at first but found the presence of familiar faces like Petit and Grimandi to be a welcome distraction.

"It made things a bit easier for me because we used to speak French together and would sometimes go out for lunch and things like that. They helped me a lot," he remembers. "I was at the hotel for four or five months before I moved into my own house. It was hard because in England if you don't know anyone, you can't do anything . . . Mentally you have to be strong – I didn't play as much at the start because it took me some time to settle in. Wenger knew I had been playing well because he told me he had been watching a lot of my games for Guingamp. I knew that I was a good player and that I could fit in there. The manager told me that I needed to work hard and I could get a place in the first team."

But it wasn't until March 1998 when a hamstring injury to Ian Wright, which proved to be the end of his record-breaking Arsenal career, saw Wreh finally handed an opportunity to start a Premier League match after five previous appearances as a substitute. Arsenal found themselves trailing United by 12 points when they faced Wimbledon at Selhurst Park, albeit having played three games fewer than Sir Alex Ferguson's side, who were attempting to win a third successive title. After West Ham took an early lead against United at Upton Park, a delayed start due to a bomb scare meant Wenger's side knew a victory could keep alive their faint hopes of winning the league.

Wreh's early effort was ruled out for offside after he followed up Bergkamp's shot but, a few minutes later, his big moment arrived. Seizing on a cutback from Overmars, he slammed the ball past Neil Sullivan to give Arsenal a priceless lead that they just about held on to following a late onslaught. "Ambitious Arsenal's Wreh of hope," read *The Independent*'s headline the next morning.

Meanwhile, United had rescued a priceless point at West Ham but faced a crucial showdown with Wenger's resurgent side at Old Trafford three days later. Wreh was selected in attack alongside

Bergkamp once more but it was Overmars who scored the vital goal 15 minutes from time. Suddenly, despite one bookmaker in Manchester having already paid out on United, Arsenal were in a title race.

Yet another 1-0 win a week later – their third in succession, this time over Sheffield Wednesday – set up another important away fixture on Tuesday, 31 March at Bolton, who boasted South African defender Mark Fish in their ranks. In the absence of Dennis Bergkamp, suspended for three matches after elbowing West Ham's Steve Lomas during the FA Cup quarter-final replay, Wreh was paired with Anelka up front. Knowing that victory would move them to within three points of United at the top with two games in hand, Arsenal lost Overmars to an ankle injury in only the second minute at the Reebok Stadium and were frustrated by a stubborn Bolton side battling to avoid the drop as they went in at half-time with the scores level.

Three minutes into the second half, however, a moment of magic from Wreh suddenly changed the complexion of the title race once and for all. Controlling a pass from Stephen Hughes ten yards outside Bolton's area, he took one touch to set himself before unleashing an unstoppable shot with his right foot that flew into the net with incredible velocity. Wreh celebrated by performing a spectacular double somersault as his teammates rushed to congratulate him, with Wenger also showing his emotions on the touchline. Despite the dismissal of Martin Keown soon afterwards for two yellow cards, the visitors held on for a vital victory with supporters singing "We'll win away with Christopher Wreh" as they made their way back to London.

"It was definitely my best goal for Arsenal," admits Wreh, 21 years on. "That was such a critical moment – we had to win the game because United were six points ahead but had played three games more than us. That win was so important for us to go on and do the double."

Already brimming with confidence thanks to his extended run in the first team, he was named in the side to face Wolves – then bankrolled by property developer Sir Jack Hayward – in the FA Cup semi-final at Villa Park five days later. Wreh took just 12 minutes to open the scoring after goalkeeper Hans Segers had scuffed a clearance straight to Vieira, whose surging run laid the ball on a plate for his teammate.

"With a single shot as true as a sniper's bullet, young Wreh had become the first refugee from war to score such an important goal in the 126-year history of the cup and had extinguished Old Jack's lifelong dream of taking his team, Wolverhampton Wanderers, to Wembley," wrote Rob Hughes in the *New York Times*. "One imagines that scoring goals, hitting them crisply and cleanly and spontaneously with his right foot, is not a problem to a young man – he is 22 – who might otherwise have had to fight for survival with a sub-machine gun."

Another dogged defensive display saw Arsenal secure a fifth 1-0 win in succession to reach the final against Newcastle, scheduled to be the last match of the domestic season on 16 May. In the meantime, Arsenal had to face Kenny Dalglish's side in the league and followed up their Cup success with a 3-1 win to move within four points of United. The return of Bergkamp meant Wreh was rested for the victory over Blackburn but he returned to come off the bench and score the fifth goal as Wimbledon were despatched at Highbury 5-0. That victory – their eighth in a row in all competitions since beating the same opponents at the start of March – completed an incredible turnaround in the league table as Wenger's side went top.

Yet Wreh's goal proved to be the last he scored in a competitive fixture, not counting his strike against United in the Community Shield a few months later. By then, Arsenal had won a famous double thanks to three more victories over Barnsley, Derby and Everton which secured the title with two games to spare, while Wreh played 62 minutes of the FA Cup final triumph at Wembley before being replaced by David Platt.

A fortnight after he had made history as the first African to win the English league title, the player who had only arrived in Europe eight years earlier had also become the first to win the domestic double that had eluded Arthur Wharton with Preston more than a century earlier. Not that Wreh quite appreciated the significance of his achievement at the time.

"To be honest I didn't realise until later on when I read about it on the internet," he admits with a smile. "I have also seen that I was the first African player to score at Wembley so that's a pretty good record! In Liberia they are very proud of this fact – people are always saying to me, 'The first African man to score at Wembley is from Liberia.' That's always there."

But there is also another memory that still sticks in Wreh's mind. Ian Wright was an unused substitute in the final against Newcastle and would end up leaving that summer after seeing his chances of adding to his club record 185 goals limited by the emergence of Anelka. After the match at Wembley, Wreh recalls having to comfort the emotional England striker in the changing room.

"He was crying so much so I asked him, 'Wrighty, what is going on?' He said, 'I'm so happy and proud to win the double. But now I've got to leave Arsenal.' It was a sad moment."

A week later, Wenger – who had become the first overseas manager in history to win the English league title – Wreh and Wright took part in Arsenal's open-top bus parade from Highbury to Islington Town Hall. An estimated crowd of 300,000 people thronging the streets meant that the bus took more than 90 minutes to cover the two-mile route, with the evergreen Wright leading the celebrations dressed in a dark blue shirt and wearing black shades. "I came here to win medals and I can't believe how many I've got now," he told supporters. "Just enjoy it and have a great time because we are the champions."

***

When Wright – by then aged 35 – moved to West Ham in July 1998, it appeared to clear the way for Wreh to enjoy a long and successful career in north London. Yet despite his goal in the Community Shield as Arsenal cantered to a 3-0 win over United, he struggled to recapture the scoring run that had ignited the title-winning campaign, making 18 appearances mainly as a substitute before moving to AEK Athens on loan in January. By the time he returned for the new season, a familiar face was already settling in. Wenger paid £11 million to bring Henry to north London in August 1999 as he attempted to gain the upper hand on a United side which had won the treble a few months earlier and Wreh was deemed surplus to requirements, joining Championship side Birmingham on loan.

"I wasn't playing so I made the decision I wanted to leave," he explains. "The manager understood why so I went to Birmingham. It was very hard to leave Arsenal but I had to try something different."

Once again Wreh hit the ground running, scoring just 34 minutes into his debut against Grimsby in a 1-1 draw but ended up making only six appearances for Trevor Francis' side in the second tier. Another loan spell in the Netherlands with Den Bosch proved to be his last, however, as Wenger decided to cut his losses in the summer by allowing him to join Saudi Arabian side Al Hilal to begin a steady decline in his career. When Wreh arrived at St Mirren a year later, he had already been rejected by Bournemouth for being overweight and ended up playing just 57 minutes for the Scottish First Division side in a disastrous spell that saw him end up being without a club for nearly 18 months. His final international appearance came in a warm-up match for the 2002 Africa Cup of Nations finals in Mali against

Niger, when Wreh was criticised by the Liberian press for his less than impressive display that saw him left out of the squad.

"Lone Star's odd man out was a complete disparagement of spectators," wrote one. "Chris Wreh's lethargy on and off the ball robbed the Lone Star of many scoring chances. The over-weight former Arsenal poster boy must either shape up or ship out."

Wreh certainly didn't help himself by later suggesting that the presence of Weah – by then playing for Al Jazira in the United Arab Emirates – was detrimental to the team's unity.

"We became a one-man show," he told the BBC at the time. "Weah always had his favourite group of players that he used in the team even if they were unattached to any clubs. He ignored others and I was one of his victims. Weah made everyone believe that he was the one and only person supporting the team financially, which was untrue. All the players used to pay for their air tickets to play for Liberia."

Seventeen years on, his opinion over his second cousin and now president has softened somewhat. Wreh returned to Liberia in 2018 to manage the Lone Stars' Under-20 side and local club Nimba United and admitted that he and the 1995 World Player of the Year are still fond of the odd game when time permits.

"We still meet up sometimes for a kickabout," he laughs. "When I'm in Liberia we always meet up. We're very close these days. He has shown what is possible if you put your mind to something."

Wreh is justifiably proud of his own career, even if there is a tinge of sadness in his voice when we discuss life after Arsenal. After a short spell in Iran with Persepolis, he went on trial at Northampton Town but departed after just seven weeks with manager Terry Fenwick describing him as "very heavy". At the age of 28, Wreh's professional career was effectively over when he joined sixth-tier side Bishop's Stortford in August 2003 – just five years after winning the double.

"I had two kids and a home in Milton Keynes so even though I ended up playing abroad, it was always where I came back to," he says.

Most of Wreh's family still live in the area, with his son Chris having turned out for non-league club Dunstable Town as a striker in recent years. Wreh made just one appearance for Bishop's Stortford and finally ended his career playing in Indonesia. But, as his achievements have faded with time, Wreh's status as a cult figure among Arsenal supporters has grown. He appears in various articles featuring football's strangest signings while in 2013, one supporter tracked down "the player so good that Arsène Wenger signed him twice" in a film entitled *Finding Wreh.*

Two years later in an interview with *France Football,* Wreh addressed a number of the urban myths that had sprung up about him, including one that he was the singer for a band called Soul Rebels which turned out to be untrue. Surprisingly, however, the story about him once outrunning a lion was accurate.

"Yes, yes it is true," he said. "When I was young, I ran faster than a lion. It was in a stadium in Monrovia. But beware, it was not a big lion, a real lion, and I started before him. But he did not catch me, I was too strong."

To trivialise Wreh's career in such a way does not do justice to his impact on English football, albeit brief. While John Salako, Peter Ndlovu and Nii Lamptey had briefly appeared in the same Coventry side under Ron Atkinson in the 1995/96 season and Tony Yeboah and Lucas Radebe prospered at Leeds, with the Ghanaian awarded 'Goal of the Season' for his brilliant volley against Wimbledon, the Liberian's success under Wenger at one of the country's most successful clubs helped transform the horizons for African players.

Over the next two decades until the Frenchman's departure in 2018, 16 were signed by Arsenal – with the arrival of Ivory Coast forward Nicolas Pépé in August 2019 as the most expensive in history when he moved from Lille for £72 million continuing the tradition post-Wenger. Nwankwo Kanu and Lauren were part of the side which emulated Arsenal's class of '98 by winning the double in 2002, with Nigeria star Kanu having established himself as an instant hero following his hat-trick in 15 minutes in a comeback win over Chelsea in October 1999.

After helping Arsenal to the FA Cup once more in 2003, he also played a bit-part role in the Invincibles season before leaving for West Brom and then Portsmouth, where the striker won his third cup winners' medal. Cameroon's Lauren, who had been an integral member of the Invicibles' defence along with Ivorian youngster Kolo Touré having been converted from a midfielder to a right-back by Wenger, was also in Harry Redknapp's side that beat Cardiff in the final. The likes of Emmanuel Adebayor, Emmanuel Eboué, Marouane Chamakh and Gervinho didn't quite hit the heights of those earliest pioneers as Wenger's era came to an end, yet their influence on the club was plain to see in the number of Arsenal shirts you now see on any given day in Dakar, Lagos or Johannesburg.

"When I meet people like Eboué, Kolo Touré and Adebayor they always say, 'Hey brother, how you doing? We are happy to see you. You are one of the players who helped us to come to England.' It's something that makes me very proud," admits Wreh.

"My time at Arsenal went very quickly but sometimes when you are blessed, you are blessed. To have achieved what I achieved . . . there are some football players who play for 20 years and don't get near to that so I'm very proud. It's amazing to think that I made some people happy."

TWELVE

KEEPING THE FAITH

There were still nine days until Christmas but Liverpool fans couldn't hide their excitement. Two goals from substitute Xherdan Shaqiri had just condemned eternal rivals Manchester United to a humiliating 3-1 defeat at Anfield that saw Jürgen Klopp's side record 37 shots – their most in any league match for more than two years – and return to the top of the table.

"Maybe it was appropriate that José Mourinho and his players stayed at a hotel named after the *Titanic*," wrote Daniel Taylor in *The Guardian*. "Fill in your own jokes here."

World Cup winner Paul Pogba – the son of a former telecommunications engineer turned high school teacher from Nzérékoré, Guinea's second biggest city, who had moved to France in the 1960s – found himself on the bench for the third successive league match after being stripped of the vice-captaincy by Mourinho earlier in the season. But despite Sadio Mané's brilliant volley from Fabinho's cross opening the scoring in the first half, a rare error from Alisson when he spilled Romelu Lukaku's speculative shot into the path of Jesse Lingard gifted the visitors an equaliser.

With 20 minutes to go, the scores remained level as Liverpool bombarded United's goal. Enter Shaqiri. Pogba watched on from the bench in the pouring rain as two deflected shots condemned Mourinho to his fate. The Frenchman later caused controversy when an Instagram post featuring a smirking Pogba with the message "Caption this" appeared within an hour of United's announcement the next day that the Special One had been shown the door. "'Caption this' . . . you do one as well!" responded Gary Neville, to the delight of many on Merseyside.

Two days later on 18 December at around 8 a.m., the unshaven, beleaguered United manager left the more familiar surroundings of the Lowry Hotel in Salford for the last time as he made his way to the club's training ground in Carrington, a ten-mile journey that can sometimes take as long as an hour depending on traffic. Ed Woodward, United's vice-president, was there to meet him. He delivered the news that Mourinho had surely expected after a run of only one win in six matches had left them 19 points behind the leaders despite the season having yet to reach its halfway point.

The man who had proved such a thorn in the side of previous Liverpool managers eventually emerged a few hours later clean-shaven and looking refreshed in a white T-shirt and jacket as he no doubt contemplated his rumoured £24 million pay-off. While supporters at Anfield, who had ironically chanted "Don't sack Mourinho", were denied their wish, the travails of the club who usurped them as English football's most successful under Sir Alex Ferguson had been a long time coming as far as they were concerned.

Yet everyone knew it was the team from the other side of Manchester who were the real threat now, even if there were signs that Pep Guardiola's juggernaut had started to splutter under the incessant pressure being applied by their rivals. Tipped to follow in Arsenal's footsteps by becoming only the second team to complete a top-flight season unbeaten, a crushing 2-0 defeat to Chelsea on 8 December stopped that prediction in its tracks.

But it was to be the alleged racist abuse of Raheem Sterling by a group of home supporters that made the headlines the next day. A week after a Tottenham Hotspur supporter had been arrested for throwing a banana at Pierre-Emerick Aubameyang during Arsenal's derby victory at the Emirates Stadium, images of fans sitting in the front row of the stands hurling insults at the City forward after he went to collect the ball for a throw-in prompted Ian Wright to tweet "the bad old days are back". Sterling's subsequent Instagram post which accused certain sections of the media of helping to fuel racism confronted the issue head on. The England star cited an example of how young white teammate Phil Foden's decision to buy his mother a was presented by one newspaper compared to its coverage of black counterpart Tosin Adarabioyo – the son of Nigerian parents who was born in Manchester.

"You have two young players starting out their careers – both play for the same team, both have done the right thing, which is buy a new house for their mothers who have put in a lot of time and love into helping them get where they are," wrote Sterling. "But look at how the newspapers get their message across for the young black player and then for the young white player. I think this is unacceptable, both innocent, have not done a thing wrong but just by the way it has been worded.

"The young black kid is looked at in a bad light. Which helps fuel racism an[d] aggressive behaviour. So for all the newspapers that don't understand why people are racist in this day and age all I have to say is have a second thought about fair publicity an[d] give all players an equal chance. I am not normally the person to talk a lot but when I think I need my point heard I will speak up. Regarding what was said at the Chelsea game, as you can see by my reaction I just had to laugh because I don't expect no better."

***

A stone's throw from the many barber shops that have sprung up since The Beatles released 'Penny Lane' more than half a century ago, there is a new tourist attraction these days in L18. Tucked away just around the corner from the street that was originally named after an 18th-century slave trader, you will find the unassuming building which houses the Liverpool Mosque and Islamic Institute.

"We get so many phone calls saying we want to come in and see the mosque that the football players go to," admits Imam Shafiqur Rahman. "They're often surprised because it is a very small mosque and you wouldn't notice it if you walked past."

The jovial imam was already a popular figure in the local neighbourhood before Sadio Mané, Mohamed Salah and Naby Keïta started turning up for Friday prayers. The mosque doubles as an education centre and there was a large group of young girls politely filtering in for a lesson when I arrive on a warm July day in 2019. Removing my shoes, I am ushered into the small prayer room that appears capable of hosting no more than 20 people at a push.

"It is getting a bit tight," he admits. "On a normal day, people stand in a row but now we have to tell people to come forward and make your own row. I'd be lying if I said nobody gets excited when they meet them – of course they are icons and role models for the people that come here. They want to take pictures and it's a natural thing. If you are praying next to a Premier League footballer you want to take a selfie! But I know we have to protect them from that because they come here to get away from all of that."

Originally from Oldham, Imam Shafiq has been in charge here since he graduated from university more than a decade ago. It was there that he picked up his unlikely nickname.

"I'm really passionate about football – there's not many imams you can say that about!" he says enthusiastically. "Everyone used to call me Kolo Touré when we played football because I was a defender. It just became one of those things – I started getting Touré shirts and everything. One weekend, some of my friends went to a mosque in London and he walked in and started praying next to them. They spoke to him afterwards and told him they had a friend who was crazy about him . . . I'm not sure what made him do this but he gave them his number and told them to pass it on to me so I could get in touch."

Imam Shafiq and the Ivory Coast defender started speaking on the phone just as he was about to complete his £14 million move from Arsenal to Manchester City in 2009. Along with Togo striker Emmanuel Adebayor for £26 million and the controversial signing of Carlos Tevez from bitter rivals United, Touré was part of City's ambitious spending spree that summer. But while his brother Yaya's arrival 12 months later from Barcelona proved to be crucial for the side which would end a 44-year wait for the league title in 2012, Kolo was restricted to a bit-part role and eventually moved to Liverpool on a free transfer.

"A few days after he signed, I was doing a sermon when he walked in," remembers Imam Shafiq. "He was wearing a woolly hat – that became a famous hat for him in the mosque. It was so funny that I almost laughed during the middle of my sermon! I wasn't expecting him to come in and it was really hard to stay professional."

Touré was a regular for Friday prayers during his three years at Anfield and encouraged some of the club's other Muslim players to join him on occasions, including France defender Aly Cissokho. But the unexpected arrival of Mané one day at the start of 2017 still took the imam by surprise.

"I remember being upstairs and looking at the CCTV cameras of downstairs and I could see lots of people getting up and hugging someone who had just walked in," he says. "I was thinking, 'Who is this person?' I went downstairs and I could see he was wearing a hat and Islamic clothing so I didn't realise who it was. I went to shake hands with him and he took off his hat. That's when I saw the line in his hair and I finally recognised it was Sadio . . . After prayers he stayed behind and we went into my office for a chat. Ever since then we have been in touch."

"I try to go every Friday and he has come to my house to have some dinner," says Mané. "He's a really great guy and a big Liverpool fan."

Pictures of Imam Shafiq enjoying meals at the Liverpool forward's house are now a regular feature of his Instagram feed, although he admits those have been kept to a minimum in recent weeks.

"He's always telling me I don't like your stomach! So I started going to the gym and posted the video on Instagram, which he liked. But I stopped when he went away for the AFCON because I knew I wouldn't see him for a couple of months. He's going to be disappointed when he sees me again . . ."

Salah has also become a regular on Fridays when Liverpool are at Melwood, with both players making the 15-minute dash to the mosque before returning for their afternoon session. So far, the imam's attempts to persuade Jürgen Klopp to let him come to the training ground to conduct prayers have come to nothing. But he is working on it.

"The imam is a Liverpool fan? Haha!" laughs the manager when I raise the question with him the next day. "Mo and Sadio are always the last coming out because they have a lot of things to do. Of course we have a prayer room in the building so that's important."

A few weeks before my visit, research by Stanford University found there had been an 18.9 per cent drop in anti-Muslim hate crimes on Merseyside in two years since Salah signed for Liverpool in June 2017. That fact was proudly repeated by several Egyptians on my visit there for the Africa Cup of Nations as recognition of the wider role their favourite son is playing in society.

"He seems to have made a positive impact for Egyptian and Muslim people in England," says Cairo-based student Yussuf El Dsuky, who was working as a volunteer. "More and more people are viewing Egyptians and Muslims in general in a more positive light because of his actions so I think his impact goes way beyond football. For a country that has been struggling with tourism and our public image, he has done a lot to rectify that. When you hear about the Middle East on the BBC, usually it's bad news. But what Salah has done is to increase people's interest in a different part of the world."

Judging by the chant which became popular in the Kop just a few months after his arrival, Liverpool supporters have wholeheartedly embraced Salah's faith in recognition of the importance it plays in guiding his career. Sung to the tune of Dodgy's 1996 hit 'Good Enough', the song goes: "Mo Sa-la-la-la-lah, Mo Sa-la-la-la-lah, if he's good enough for you, he's good enough for me, if he scores another few, then I'll be Muslim too" and also includes the line "he's sitting in the mosque, that's where I want to be."

Yet while some had fully embraced the meeting of cultures, racism continued to make a high-profile and unwanted return to English football at the start of 2019 when Salah was subjected to Islamophobic abuse during the trip to West Ham in February. A few weeks later, Chelsea's Callum Hudson-Odoi – the son of a former professional from Ghana – became the second-youngest player ever to feature for England's senior side but saw his debut marred by racist chanting by Montenegro supporters towards the visitors' black players. There were similar incidents during England's Euro 2020 qualifier in Bulgaria in October 2019, while a rising number of racist incidents continued to mar the 2019/20 domestic season. Despite that, however, Imam Shafiq still believes progress is slowly being made in most UK cities.

"It has definitely improved," he says. "We have pubs and restaurants near the mosque and everyone knows that the players come down here so they come to have a look. It's nice. In the past, I would never go to a match in this kind of Islamic clothing but the last two times I have just turned up like this. There were no dirty looks and I felt welcome, which is something that you couldn't have said even five years ago. You used to be able to feel and sense the tension but that has changed. All the food is halal and I even had a steward coming up to me at half-time telling me where the prayer room was! I felt really good about that. It felt like I was at home."

The positive influences of Liverpool's Muslim superstars are clearly hitting home in a city that has one of Britain's oldest black populations. Having entered the slave trade in 1699, it soon became Europe's largest slaving port and is estimated to have carried around 1.5 million Africans to slavery in the Americas. Many of Liverpool's most famous landmarks including its town hall were financed directly by the booming industry in people before the trade was finally made illegal in the early 19th century. Increasing numbers of African sailors began to settle in the city after that and Imam Shafiq believes it is fitting that the modern Liverpool has been at the vanguard of changing attitudes. "It's a very multicultural city anyway and this has just been the cherry on the cake," he says.

In September 2018, a video of Mané helping his friend to clean out the toilets at the Al-Rahma Mosque in Toxteth after scoring in the win over Leicester went viral. In typically modest fashion, the Senegal forward seemed embarrassed to explain his actions.

"I invited my friend to drink some tea at home after the prayer and he said, 'No, I have to work, I have to wash the mosque's toilets,'" said Mané. "I told him we were going to do it together. At the moment somebody filmed us and I asked he not put it online. He swore he wouldn't do it and the next day it was on the internet. Well, it's not very serious . . ."

According to Imam Shafiq, though, that is just one example of how his religion has helped to keep him grounded.

"Sadio had to go through a lot to get to this position but is still very humble," he says. "He is giving back to the community. He knows it is important not to forget where he has come from."

Mané arranged for 300 Liverpool shirts to be delivered to his old village on the eve of the 2018 Champions League final and has also helped rebuild Bambali's school and mosque. But it is his mission to build its first-ever hospital in memory of his late father that underlines his determination to give something back.

"For sure – it's one of the reasons because of how he died," Mané explains. "Every year, we recite the Koran for my father. I try to pray for him all the time. To his memory. I remember my sister was born at home because there was no hospital in our village, which is really really sad for everyone. I wanted to build one to give people hope."

Imam Shafiq describes Mané's experience growing up as a "classic example" of the prevalent attitude many in the Muslim community have taken towards sport.

"This was a big barrier in previous generations because the imams and parents would not want their children to go into football. They looked on it as a bad thing," he says. "The son that was going into football would be treated differently from another that had gone into medicine because it wasn't seen as a worthy career. Some would even say it was against the religion. But obviously there is nothing wrong with going to football or playing it – the new generation is really trying to promote it because it can be a real force for good. It gives them hope. And energy as well. With Mo and Sadio doing so well, it seems like football has accepted Muslims and Muslims have accepted football."

***

It was always going to come down to the narrowest of margins. But 11.7 millimetres? Watching the replay afterwards as his Manchester City teammates celebrated their victory, even John Stones couldn't quite believe what he had done. The England defender's miraculous clearance was adjudged to have failed to cross the line by little more than a centimetre – or the width of a boot lace – after the ball had cannoned back towards the net following his mix-up with goalkeeper Ederson in the 18th minute of a match that would prove to be hugely significant.

Had Mané's original effort which struck the post ended up in the net, Liverpool would have found themselves 1-0 up at their title rivals having gone into the first match of the new year with a seven-point advantage. Instead, Leroy Sané's winning goal at the Etihad Stadium after Roberto Firmino had equalised Sergio Agüero's opener saw City cut the deficit to four points to revive their hopes of retaining their crown. It also ended Liverpool's run of nine successive wins and 20 league games without defeat, which had culminated in the 5-1 thrashing of Arsenal in their last match of 2018.

From being hot favourites to seal their first Premier League title after City's surprise defeats to Crystal Palace and Leicester in December, suddenly things didn't appear so straightforward.

The FA Cup loss at Wolves a few days later as Naby Keïta was selected for the first time in four matches only strengthened the suspicion that Liverpool were wobbling under the pressure. Narrow wins in their next two matches over Brighton and Crystal Palace at least maintained their lead over City, even if it required a Julian Speroni mistake to secure three points in the latter after they had trailed. But when Newcastle stunned City at the end of January in what would prove to be the last time they dropped points, Liverpool were unable to take full advantage as Leicester's Harry Maguire equalised Mané's early goal and Keïta was denied a penalty. Another draw with West Ham a week later saw the lead whittled down to just three points, before Manchester United gained some revenge for their defeat at Anfield in December with a stalemate in the return fixture at the end of February that allowed City to move within just one with 11 matches to play.

"United went into the game with injuries and had to make three changes in the first half," recalls Melissa Reddy. "Liverpool were so tentative. I don't think United could believe they had been so passive."

When Everton ground out the same scoreline at Goodison Park a week later, Klopp's worst fears had been realised. Liverpool now trailed City for the first time since the start of December having drawn three of their last four matches 0-0, including the first leg of their Champions League tie with Bayern Munich at Anfield.

"I think the players believed they were going to do it, especially in December when City started dropping points," adds Reddy. "But Liverpool had so much to lose and they started playing safe football rather than being aggressive. That came from the top down – it was by design to become more conservative. I don't think that helped because it meant they were so scared of losing that it handed the initiative to City. But I think they have learned a lot from that experience."

While Mané took his season's tally in the league to 16 in the comeback win over Burnley, Salah had failed to find the net for the fifth game in succession. That meant his early lead in the Golden Boot standings had evaporated, with his teammate now just one goal behind, Aubameyang also on 17 and Agüero leading the way on 18 goals. As the critics yet again began to circle the man who had run away with the award 12 months earlier, it only served as motivation at a critical point in the season for Liverpool.

"Mo has always had that in him," says Reddy. "He always references that Chelsea period and how he had unfinished business in England. I think he takes a little bit of joy in proving people wrong. He definitely wanted to correct the errors from the end of the season. For him to have such a watershed season scoring so many goals and for it to end so disappointingly with that injury, that gave him the desire to put things right. It was always going to be difficult given the number of goals that he scored because opposition teams were ready for him this time. But his all-round play improved and he became more of a servant to the system. That allowed people like Sadio and Roberto Firmino to shine more and get their goal tallies up."

Those qualities would come to the fore in the second leg of the last-16 tie against Bayern on 13 March. Three weeks earlier, the German champions had celebrated on the pitch after their 0-0 draw at Anfield and went into the game having thrashed Wolfsburg 6-0 in their previous match as they chased down Borussia Dortmund in the Bundesliga. But, after a cagey opening, a Bayern side containing six players aged 30 and older began to creak. Virgil van Dijk's long ball forward was brought down brilliantly by Mané just outside the area, taking out his marker Rafinha in the process. Goalkeeper Manuel Neuer had already charged out of his goal in anticipation of collecting the ball but was sent the other way by the Senegal forward's second touch as Mané spun and dispatched his shot into the empty net in one glorious movement.

An own goal from the usually dependable Joël Matip six minutes before the break when he turned Serge Gnabry's cross past Alisson allowed Bayern back into the game but this was to be a night of personal redemption for Liverpool's manager. Klopp's attitude towards Germany's most successful club had never been cordial but when they began poaching Borussia Dortmund's best players, including the £30 million purchase of Mario Götze – announced on the eve of the defeat in the 2013 Champions League final at Wembley – things quickly turned sour.

"Bayern Munich want to destroy us," alleged chief executive Hans-Joachim Watzke when Robert Lewandowski became the latest to jump ship in 2014. Five years on, it was Klopp who finally had his revenge as Van Dijk's towering header gave Liverpool a priceless second away goal, with Mané rounding things off in style when he headed home an audaciously inch-perfect cross from the outside of Salah's left boot. "We've laid down a marker tonight that LFC is back on the top level of European football," purred their manager afterwards. It was hard to disagree.

THIRTEEN

THE CHIEFS

Try as he might, Lucas Radebe could not hold back the tears. Almost 40 years to the day since Albert Johanneson's historic appearance in the FA Cup final, nearly 38,000 supporters crammed into Elland Road on 2 May 2005 to say goodbye to one of Leeds United's most iconic players at his testimonial.

It was difficult to underestimate the impact 'The Chief' had made in the decade since he and fellow South African Phil Masinga first arrived in Yorkshire. After rejecting an approach to join Manchester United having become captain of the vibrant Leeds side which somehow reached the last four of the Champions League in 2001, Radebe's influence had always extended way beyond the pitch. As well as the Kaiser Chiefs rock band who were christened in honour of his former club, a Twitter exchange in August 2019 revealed that 'Lucas' continues to be one of the most popular boys' names in Leeds, with a number of supporters getting in touch after Radebe responded to one fan who had named his son after the former captain.

But even more than his cult status in the city, Radebe became a Premier League legend who transcended club loyalty thanks to his wholehearted performances and unwavering commitment to the cause. "This is my hero," admitted President Nelson Mandela when he met South Africa's captain on a visit to Leeds Town Hall in 2001.

By then, the effects of years of injuries and repeatedly travelling back and forth to represent his homeland were already taking its toll on Radebe's body. The victim of a shooting in 1992 – a few weeks after Kaizer Chiefs had faced Steve Coppell's Crystal Palace and his future teammate Nigel Martyn in a historic pre-season match – while on his way to the local shop in Diepkloof in Soweto, the bullet miraculously entered his back and somehow missed any organs or arteries before exiting through his thigh. "There was a history of players being shot for swapping teams," he later recalled. "But I've no idea what the motive was in my case. Nobody was caught. Nobody saw who did it."

Radebe recovered sufficiently to move to Leeds with Masinga two years later. After the appearance on the wing for his debut, however, he lasted just 24 minutes on his first start in central defence against a Coventry side featuring Peter Ndlovu before rupturing the cruciate ligaments in his right knee. Never fully trusted by Howard Wilkinson – the manager who had guided Leeds to the last First Division title in 1992 – it wasn't until former Arsenal boss George Graham arrived at Elland Road in 1996 that he established himself as a regular in the first team.

Being part of Bafana Bafana's victory in the Africa Cup of Nations on home soil at the start of the year along with Masinga had helped cement Radebe's status as a national hero. Two months later, his willingness to don the gloves at Old Trafford when goalkeeper Mark Beeney was sent off in the first half of a league match against United began his burgeoning love affair with the Leeds faithful. Having started out between the sticks in his youth sides, Radebe pulled off some miraculous saves and was only beaten by Roy Keane's winning goal 18 minutes from time.

When Graham moved to Spurs at the start of the 1998/99 season, Radebe was made captain by his replacement David O'Leary and played an integral role in helping his young side finish fourth. They went one better the following year to qualify for the Champions League, with the South African's performances attracting the attention of Sir Alex Ferguson, AC Milan and Fabio Capello's Roma. "Everyone should be interested in Lucas," said the United manager at the time.

Yet his allegiances to the club which had given him his chance in European football meant Radebe never seriously considered leaving Elland Road for their bitter rivals despite the significantly improved salary on offer.

"When I first went to Leeds, I appreciated the opportunity of playing in the Premier League, even if they were lingering near the bottom half," Radebe recalls. "For me, that's one of the things that pushed me to stay at the club, as I felt very loved there because of how they looked after me. It's about the loyalty. I think if I had gone to Manchester United at that time, I wouldn't have grown as I did at Leeds, and make the impact that I did. I felt that I belonged to Leeds United."

He would later refer to the £18 million purchase of Rio Ferdinand from West Ham in November 2000 as the moment the club's adventure under former chairman Peter Ridsdale began to spiral out of control – a situation that would lead to relegation in 2004. But for a few months that season, anything had seemed possible. Despite a 4-0 thrashing by Barcelona at the Camp Nou in their opening Champions League match that saw Radebe carried off on a stretcher in the final minute, having suffered the first of many concussions in his later career, Leeds went into the final game knowing a draw against Milan would take them through ahead of the Spanish club.

A formidable performance from Radebe helped O'Leary's young side escape the San Siro with the result they needed, with Ferdinand arriving a fortnight later in what was then a world-record fee for a defender. But just as the new partnership was settling in, disaster struck during the penultimate second group stage tie against Real Madrid. Leeds had already booked their place in the last eight after ending Anderlecht's 20-match unbeaten run at home in European competition in the previous game. Yet the sight of their captain being stretchered off after 61 minutes after he had twisted his right knee making a clearance was the main talking point among supporters on their way back to Yorkshire after the 3-2 defeat.

Radebe ended up missing the victory over Deportivo La Coruña in the quarter-finals and the defeat to Valencia in the last four as the number of injuries he had suffered over the years finally caught up with him. When Ferdinand was sold to Manchester United in 2002 for £30 million, his fellow defender was out for the entire season but did manage to mark his second appearance at a World Cup finals with a goal against Spain. Radebe retired from international football a year later after Bafana Bafana's historic friendly against England and admits the air miles he racked up amassing his 70 caps had been a contributing factor to the longevity of his career.

"I had a terrible time," he says. "Most of the decisions to retire are made by players who know they have to do something to keep their careers going. Travelling back and forth on long-haul flights all the time causes injuries and eventually takes its toll on the body. And there's no appreciation of the effort you are putting in. As players you need to be treated as number one – when you retire only you have to live with your body."

As Radebe admits, the scheduling of the Africa Cup of Nations must take most of the blame for the demands placed on the continent's players at the turn of the new millennium. By then, such had been the influence of the Leeds captain that more than 30 could be found on the books of Premier League clubs, compared to just three in 1993. But if the performances of players like Radebe, Nwankwo Kanu and Coventry's Moroccan duo Mustapha Hadji and Youssef Chippo persuaded more and more club managers to recruit African players over the next decade, the prospect of losing them for six weeks in January every two years also dissuaded many.

"With the Africa Cup of Nations being played at a crucial time in European leagues, it brings up an enormous problem in terms of contradictory interests," wrote then Chelsea manager José Mourinho in the Portuguese sports paper *Record* in 2006. "The national teams are protected by legislation, the clubs are without legal power to fight for their interests. Chelsea without Drogba, Liverpool without Sissoko, Arsenal without Touré, Barcelona without Eto'o, Porto without Benni McCarthy, Benfica without Pedro Mantorras are some examples which leave us weakened and which surely push us to ask the question, 'Is it worth signing them?'"

"I won't give up on African talent and its footballing characteristics," Mourinho added. "I will continue to contribute towards its progress but never with more than one player from the same country, because I cannot be in the hands of good sense or the lack of it."

Nonetheless, by the time Radebe hung up his boots in 2005, the number of African players in England's top flight had sailed past 40, with many enjoying similarly exalted status as the Chief of Elland Road. Hadji, who arrived in 1999 and spent two years at Highfield Road before moving to Aston Villa, certainly belonged in that category too.

"It's because I was one of them," he says two decades on. "When I met people on the street or in a bar I was always talking to them – even if I didn't know their names and would never see them again! It's the best way to adapt yourself – to let people see you the way that you are rather than looking at you like a footballer. I wanted people to look at me like the man I am, not just a Coventry player."

Born in Morocco, Hadji moved to Alsace-Lorraine with his family as a child and represented France at Under-21 level before opting to play for the Atlas Lions. Along with midfielder Chippo – who spent four years in the East Midlands – the Moroccans were so popular at Coventry that supporters became fond of wearing fezzes to matches in their honour and Hadji believes that was partly down to the cult status Ndlovu had enjoyed at the club.

"He left just before me and I think for all the fans and English people seeing what he could do made it much easier for the players who came afterwards. That's why I always say to modern players that when you play somewhere it's not only about you. You have to be an example for the people who are coming after you. Moroccan players today have to be an example for the next generation. For instance, if Chippo or I or Drogba had come to England and had a bad image, then it would have made it difficult for African players to establish themselves in the Premier League."

***

"It takes a lot out of you, my heart is weak," admitted Lucas Radebe in an interview with *The Guardian* in April 2004. Having seen the majority of their highly paid stars leave the club after Ridsdale's gamble backfired spectacularly, Leeds were staring down the barrel at relegation after a disastrous season that saw Eddie Gray – Albert Johanneson's successor on the left wing – installed as the caretaker manager. Defeat against Bolton a few days later eventually confirmed the inevitable as Gray was sacked, with Radebe making just three more matches in the Championship the next season before finally calling it a day.

His final appearance at Elland Road for his testimonial saw a Leeds XI featuring Masinga and Vinnie Jones take on an International XI containing Bruce Grobbelaar in goal and a Nigerian who could also rightfully claim to have captured the hearts of supporters throughout the country. "It was brilliant playing with some of those players," young Leeds defender Frazer Richardson told the *Yorkshire Evening Post*. "I'd watched some of them when I was younger and you try and learn from them. Jay Jay Okocha was different class."

So good they named him twice, as the chant goes, the playmaker's dazzling array of skills that had enchanted Jürgen Klopp and the rest of Germany during his spell at Tony Yeboah's former club, Eintracht Frankfurt, arrived in England in 2002 as part of Bolton's cosmopolitan side. Okocha's story was a classic tale of opportunism that saw him move to Europe as a 17-year-old after impressing the coaches of German Fourth Division team Borussia Neunkirchen after going to visit his brother's friend on holiday in 1990. By the time he set foot in Lancashire, as well as embarrassing Oliver Kahn for his famous goal against Karlsruhe, he had gained a reputation as one of Europe's best free-kick takers and earned a £14 million move to Paris Saint-Germain in 1998 – an African record at the time.

Okocha – by then, like Arsenal's Kanu, already an Olympic gold medallist and African champion – was the culmination of a long history of Nigerians to have graced English football. Almost 40 have now played in the Premier League, more than any other African country. A tour party representing Nigeria's embryonic Football Association which played nine matches against some of England's most prestigious amateur teams in 1949 was also the first ever by an African football side to visit the UK. Still over a decade away from gaining independence before Ghana would lead the way under its new leader Kwame Nkrumah in 1957, the trip was designed to "help the people of Nigeria and the United Kingdom to get to know each other", according to Nigerian Governor-General John Macpherson.

"Too many of the people of the United Kingdom have had little opportunity to learn about the colonies and their peoples," he added. "There is much that we of the 'home country' can be proud of in our colonial record, and I believe that high on that list we can place our passing on of our love for games – football, perhaps, most of all."

Considering they had endured a two-week voyage from Lagos in third class while their chairman – an Englishman named Captain D.H. Holley, travelled in a first-class cabin on the Elder Dempster ship, MV *Apapa*, with his wife – defeats in only the matches where the Nigerians were required to wear boots certainly made people take notice. A 5-2 victory against Marine Crosby in their first match in front an enthralled crowd on Merseyside with ten players in barefoot led the opposition captain, Len Carney, to admit "we soon found their feet were harder than our boots". According to researcher Olaojo Aiyegbayo, some of the fans even urged the home players to take their boots off to try to compete.

A 2-2 draw in their final match against South Liverpool at the club's first game under floodlights rounded off a successful tour that had also seen the Nigerians narrowly lose to serial non-league trophy winners Leytonstone and train at Highbury. But while flying winger Ahmed Tijani Ottun would return to play in English football along with teammates Titus Okere (Swindon Town) and Teslim Balogun (Peterborough), a cartoon in the *Liverpool Echo* newspaper after the match illustrated the prevailing attitudes of the time.

"Is that a Nigerian flying down the wing?" asked one man. "No, it's a bat," came the ridiculous response from his friend. The cartoon was drawn under a banner which read: "Floodlight was necessary because it's always difficult to find a black man in the dark."

Nonetheless, Aiyegbayo believes the tour ended up being a major stepping stone for some of the country's players.

"They knew it was a great chance for them to potentially come back one day," he says. "For those who eventually came in the '70s and '80s, these are the guys that set the ground for them."

Balogun – nicknamed 'Thunder' for his powerful shot – was the most successful of those early pioneers, appearing in *Football Monthly* alongside Steve Mokone when he joined Peterborough and also playing for QPR before returning home to become coach of the Nigerian Olympic team in 1968. But it was the appearance of the second generation of players like John Chiedozie and Ade Coker which showed that times were changing, with Nigeria's expanding diaspora post-independence ensuring several other players who had grown up in England also began to emerge at the highest levels of the game.

John Salako was born in Ibadan – Nigeria's third-largest city and capital of Oyo State – but moved to Westerham in Kent with his four brothers in 1974 when his father was killed in a car crash. His mother, Jenny, had grown up in the picture postcard English village best known as being up the road from Winston Churchill's ancestral home of Chartwell and met her husband when he studied for his Master's degree in London during the 1960s.

"She wanted us to grow up somewhere more in the countryside rather than inner London so it was lovely," Salako who was ten at the time, recalls. "It was so exciting and so different. I just wanted to fit in here. I was totally engrossed with getting on with it that I pretty much totally forgot about everything in Nigeria pretty quickly. I still remember some of the Yoruba – not very much – but my elder brothers do. I really don't have any memories or hold any affection or closeness to Nigeria. It just feels like a dream. I didn't find it that hard to settle in but I remember trying to get rid of my accent. In Nigeria, other people would call us white kids but when we got to England, it was the other way around. That was a little bit confusing but it wasn't too bad."

Having first honed his football skills playing with his brothers on the streets of Ibadan, it was Salako's performances for Westerham Reds' Under-14s side that first brought him to the attention of local scouts.

"I stepped up an age group and was still scoring goals, so a guy called John Mitchell wrote to Palace and told them they had a player they should come and look at. Out of about 40 kids, myself and Richard Shaw were two of those to be picked. Palace had closed down the youth system for a few years under Ron Noades so we were two of the first to come through when it reopened. We both ended up playing in the first team for ten years."

After signing schoolboy forms at the age of 14, Salako made his debut as a substitute in January 1987 under Steve Coppell in a 1-0 defeat at home to Barnsley in the old Second Division. Also part of the Palace squad that day was Mark Bright, the son of a Gambian father who grew up in a foster home in Stoke-on-Trent and who would go on to form one of the club's most prolific strike forces with Ian Wright. Starting his career playing for non-league side Leek Town and working as an apprentice engineer, Bright had joined Palace two months earlier for just £75,000 from Leicester and finished the following season as the league's top scorer with 24 goals as Coppell's side just missed out on the play-offs.

With Salako firmly established on the left flank in Palace's multicultural side led by the former Manchester United and England winger, they made it to the two-legged final against Blackburn in May 1989 but looked to have blown their chance of promotion after losing 3-1 at Ewood Park. Two goals from Wright – who would go on to become Arsenal's record goalscorer before eventually being overtaken by Thierry Henry – ensured they achieved promotion to the top flight for the first time in almost a decade.

A year later, Salako was a crucial member of the team that recovered from being thrashed 9-0 at Anfield in September to beat Liverpool 4-3 in the FA Cup semi-final at Villa Park, only to lose the final to United after a replay. Palace followed that up by finishing third the next season, with Salako gaining some revenge for the FA Cup final defeat as he scored twice in a memorable 3-0 victory over Sir Alex Ferguson's side in their last game. It was that display that prompted Graham Taylor to select him for England's summer tour in 1991, although his international suitors initially came from an unlikely source.

"Because I was born in Nigeria I could have played for any of the home nations and my first call-up came from Wales manager Terry Yorath," Salako recalled. "I remember speaking to Steve Coppell and he told me I'd been called up. I wasn't sure what to do because I'd had three months at Swansea on loan so felt an allegiance to Wales but my heart was really with England. Steve said, 'Just wait for England. It's going to happen for you. You're good enough and if you keep going the way you are going, the England call will come.' Then the Nigerian FA came over and asked me to come to join a training camp but again I wanted to wait for England. But I kept the door open just in case that never happened. Not long after that the call came from Graham Taylor and that was it."

At the time, the question of dual nationality had yet to become the thorny issue it is today, although a number of players who had been born in the Caribbean, including Luther Blissett and John Barnes, had already represented England. Yet unlike Brian Stein, who had no option of representing South Africa when he made his debut in 1984, Salako had to make a choice.

On 1 June 1991, he became the first player born in Nigeria to represent England's senior side, replacing David Hirst as a half-time substitute in the victory over Australia in Sydney. Salako also came off the bench in the next game against New Zealand but was handed his first start against the same opponents in Wellington a few days later – one of three Palace players selected in a 2-0 win. Another start against Malaysia cemented Salako's place in the squad as he set up Gary Lineker for his fourth goal of the match, an achievement that took him to second place in England's all-time top scorers' list – one behind Bobby Charlton.

Such was Salako's impact that he was selected in the team to face Germany in a friendly in September 1991. England were on course to qualify for Euro '92 but Taylor was using the rematch of the 1990 World Cup semi-final as an opportunity to fine-tune his side ahead of the crucial qualifiers against Turkey and Poland. This time, however, England were facing a unified German side for the first time since the controversial 1938 friendly in Berlin, when the visiting players had given the Nazi salute to a watching Adolf Hitler.

Despite almost helping England take the lead when his corner was headed against the crossbar in the first half by David Platt, it was to prove a historic occasion for Salako too as his substitution for Paul Merson in the 67th minute would turn out to be his last appearance in an England shirt. Four weeks after the 1-0 defeat at Wembley and with Palace having just sold Ian Wright to Arsenal for £2.5 million, Salako injured his knee in a match against Leeds and required surgery that kept him on the sidelines for almost a year. His cruciate ligament was damaged so badly that he required a donor's Achilles tendon to repair it, making it all the more remarkable that Salako was selected in Taylor's squad for the first qualifier for the 1994 World Cup against Norway in October 1992.

His international comeback never materialised as Salako remained on the bench in a 1-1 draw, with England ending up failing to reach the finals for the first time since 1978. He was selected once more in September 1995 for the friendly against Colombia by Terry Venables, by which time he had left Palace for Coventry after suffering two relegations from the new Premier League in the space of three seasons.

Salako was a teammate of Peter Ndlovu's at Highfield Road before moving on to Fulham, Charlton, Reading and Brentford. He retired at the age of 36 having – just like Stein – never played competitively at international level. Meanwhile, Nigeria's golden generation featuring Daniel Amokachi, Kanu, Okocha and several of the players who would go on to light up the Premier League went on to reach the second round at successive World Cups, as well as winning a historic gold medal at the 1996 Olympics. But Salako insists there are no regrets about what might have been.

"I didn't really consider playing for Nigeria although I was very honoured to be asked. I felt like England was my home and that was who I wanted to play for. If it didn't happen, I think it would have been a possibility but I think it's more of a modern thing to play for a different country to enhance your career rather than showing complete allegiance to yours. The game has changed and society has changed."

It would be another 20 years before another African-born player would represent the England men's senior side in the form of Palace's Wilfried Zaha, who eventually opted for the Ivory Coast. Nigerian-born Eni Aluko blazed a trail for women's football as she won more than 100 caps before taking on racism at the FA and winning while Nathaniel Chalobah – born in Freetown, Sierra Leone but raised in south London – became the first man to play for the senior side in a competitive match during the Nations League tie against Spain in October 2018. Several players with Nigerian heritage have also gone on to play for England including Dele Alli, Ross Barkley and Tammy Abraham. But Salako admits he is reluctant to see himself as a pioneer.

"It is amazing really," he says. "Most of the other black players who have played for England have been from Caribbean backgrounds but it wasn't something I'd really thought about. It wasn't a consideration at all. I just had a dream to play for England and when I got a call-up it was the best thing that had ever happened to me."

By the time Salako finally hung up his boots in 2005, the landscape for African players in English football had changed forever. Most Premier League clubs could count at least one on their books, with many established as vital members of their respective teams. The prolific Nigeria striker Yakubu Aiyegbeni arrived at Portsmouth in 2003 as the first teenager to have scored a hat-trick on his Champions League debut and became the first African player to finish among the top ten goalscorers in the country in 2003/04 with 16. He went on to play for Middlesbrough, Everton and Blackburn over the next nine years, scoring 95 goals.

Some, however, failed to live up to the hype. Cameroon international Eric Djemba-Djemba moved to Manchester United from Nantes in 2003, linking up with Quinton Fortune – the South African who would spend seven seasons at Old Trafford as a utility player. Tipped as a potential successor to the irreplaceable Roy Keane, Djemba-Djemba ended up making only 20 appearances before being sold to Aston Villa and slipping into obscurity. "So bad they named him twice," ran the joke at the time.

Then there was Okocha. His performances for Bolton, whom he captained to the final of the League Cup in 2004, captivated supporters beyond the confines of the Reebok Stadium. As well as his supreme ability as demonstrated by two unbelievable free kicks in the semi-final against Aston Villa, the leadership and linguistic skills Okocha had amassed over his career made him the focal point of Bolton's league of nations under manager

Sam Allardyce. Playing alongside former Real Madrid defenders Fernando Hierro and Ivan Campo and Liverpool's on-loan Senegal striker El-Hadji Diouf, they ended up finishing sixth in 2005 in large part due to Okocha's influence.

"A good captain needs to be able to communicate with other members of the squad on various levels effectively," said Allardyce when he appointed him at the start of that season. "Jay Jay can converse with our multi-international squad in different languages and that is very important to us."

Okocha went on to make almost 150 appearances before leaving under something of a cloud when Bolton were relegated in 2006, beginning a spiral into serious financial difficulties that saw the club almost die altogether in the summer of 2019. He later admitted that it felt "like all that work was wasted", although anyone who watched him light up English football in those heady days would surely disagree.

***

On a beautiful day in south-west London in June 2019, Didier Drogba is holding court at the ground where he is still a king. Sporting a baseball cap turned backwards as he patiently conducts interview after interview ahead of the Soccer Aid charity match at Stamford Bridge, even four years after he last played for Chelsea and despite the presence of the world's fastest man Usain Bolt among the cast list, the former Ivory Coast striker is the man everyone wants to talk to. "I scored more beautiful goals but never one as important," reflects Drogba to one TV crew, looking off into the distance as he thinks back.

He is talking, of course, about the events of 19 May 2012, when Roberto Di Matteo's side became the first club from London to become European champions thanks in large part to Drogba's dramatic 88th-minute equaliser against Bayern Munich. After eight years' service that saw the Ivory Coast striker do more than anyone to help transform the perception of African players in English football forever, it is fitting that that Drogba will always be remembered for scoring the winning penalty in the shoot-out.

"That was a special moment for everyone," recalls Michael Essien, who was an unused substitute at the Allianz Arena that night. "Before the game, I remember Didier saying in the dressing room that we had all worked so hard to get here so now we have to give it our best shot. And then he came up with the goods in the shoot-out . . . It was a massive moment for him because he had missed the chance to take a penalty in Moscow in 2008 when he was sent off."

Four years earlier, Essien had been the driving force in Chelsea's midfield in their run to the final against Manchester United having beaten Drogba to becoming the first African to win the club's Player of the Year award the previous season. An injury crisis meant that the Ghana international played as a stand-in right-back in the thrilling semi-final against Liverpool that saw Chelsea eventually win 4-3 on aggregate thanks to two goals from Drogba, only for his red card and John Terry's penalty shoot-out miss to deny them victory against Sir Alex Ferguson's United in the Russian capital.

Both Essien and Drogba had been brought to London by José Mourinho, with the £24.4 million fee paid to Lyon for the former also eclipsing Drogba's status as Chelsea's most expensive player following his arrival from Marseille in 2004. Along with former Real Madrid midfielders Geremi and Claude Makélélé – the France international who was born in the Democratic Republic of Congo – there was an unmistakably African core to the squad assembled by Mourinho in his first spell at Stamford Bridge which underlined how much things had changed since the days of Ndlovu and Yeboah.

"It really helped," remembers Essien. "When I came there were several African guys already here. I was a bit younger than them all so they were like my big brothers – looking after me, speaking French and having a laugh away from the pitch."

Chelsea's African contingent would often wind down after a match with a trip to Peckham in south-east London – an area that was the setting for British sitcom *Only Fools and Horses* that is now home to a large proportion of families who have moved to the UK from the continent.

"I've been there a few times and to Camberwell," remembers Essien. "We used to go there for African food and there was a club we used to go to as well. It was really good to be able to relax somewhere and everyone was always pleased to see us!"

Despite scoring just ten league goals as Mourinho's expensively assembled squad won the league title in his debut season, however, it wasn't until Essien joined the club in the summer of 2006 that Drogba's influence at Chelsea began to grow. In *Commitment*, his autobiography, the striker describes a match at Manchester City in the 2005/06 season when he was booed by both sets of supporters after being named as man of the match. "What an irony," Drogba wrote. "Best player, but unloved by both sides. It really hurt."

An admission after the match that he "sometimes dived" – later claimed by Drogba to have been lost in translation in front of the TV cameras – certainly did nothing to win over some of his enemies. But while his 12 goals helped Chelsea's romp to another Premier League title, the following season sealed his reputation as one of the most important members of the dressing room. Having won two titles in his first two seasons in English football, this time Mourinho's side missed out to Manchester United but Drogba's 20 goals meant he became the first African player to win the Golden Boot, with Blackburn's South African striker Benni McCarthy in second place ahead of a certain Cristiano

Ronaldo. "It is the first time since I have been a professional that I have finished the top scorer and I think there is a lot to be proud of because throughout the year I had difficult moments," admitted Drogba when he received his award.

Just like Okocha and so many who had come before them, his trip to the top had been far from straightforward. Drogba moved to France at the age of five to live with his uncle – a professional player – before returning to Abidjan due to homesickness. That he eventually made it to Stamford Bridge via the French lower leagues was testament to the striker's sheer will and determination – traits that were very much on display throughout his time at Chelsea.

"We had lots of players with big characters who were very vocal in the dressing room and Didier was always one of the loudest," remembers Essien, who pipped his friend to the Player of the Year award that season. "If things were not going well they would always know what to say to motivate everyone. They were great leaders."

Mourinho's sudden departure a month into the 2007/08 season after he fell out with owner Roman Abramovich would have destabilised most top clubs. But, not for the last time, the squad's fighting spirit encapsulated by captain John Terry and supported by the likes of Drogba and Frank Lampard enabled them to reach the Champions League final under Avram Grant. By then, Drogba and Essien had been joined by John Obi Mikel and Salomon Kalou as the number of African players in the Premier League swelled to an all-time high of 59 – or nearly 15 per cent.

Chelsea's pursuit of Mikel, a Nigerian midfielder who had moved to Norwegian club Lyn Oslo after starring at the Under-17 World Cup, showed just how lucrative the market had become. A settlement with Manchester United eventually saw Chelsea pay £12 million in compensation to secure one of the world's best young players. The investment paid off as Mikel went on to win two Premier League titles and three FA Cups during his 11 years at Stamford Bridge, not to mention the Champions League.

He didn't make it off the bench in 2008, however, as both Drogba and Terry endured personal nightmares in Moscow. Distracted by the ill health of his maternal grandmother before the match, Chelsea's lone striker had toiled against United's central defenders Nemanja Vidić and Rio Ferdinand for the majority of the game at the Luzhniki Stadium. With the score locked at 1-1 with just four minutes of extra time to play, an argument which began when Carlos Tevez refused to return the ball for a throw-in ended with Drogba's dismissal for a pointless flick of Vidić's chin with his right hand. "Professional suicide," commented Sky TV's commentator Martin Tyler.

"I felt as if I was in a nightmare," Drogba admitted in his autobiography. "I could not believe what had just happened."

He watched from the tunnel as Cristiano Ronaldo missed his effort in the shoot-out, before Terry's penalty that would have secured victory struck the outside of the post following the captain's famous slip. Nicolas Anelka's failure to score the seventh penalty allowed United to claim a third European crown and left Drogba devastated. "One day I will win the Champions League for you," he promised Roman Abramovich's crying son in the dressing room.

Despite their growing importance in European football over the previous two decades, by 2012 only 12 African players had achieved that honour. After Bruce Grobbelaar became the first in 1984, Algerian Rabah Madjer's brilliant backheel for Porto followed three years later and then Abedi Pelé with Marseille. Finidi George and Nwankwo Kanu were part of the Ajax squad in 1995 under Louis van Gaal while Geremi won two titles with Real Madrid before his move to Stamford Bridge. Benni

McCarthy was the first of the new millennium with Mourinho's Porto in 2004, with the Portuguese also selecting three Africans – Samuel Eto'o, Sulley Muntari of Ghana and Kenya's McDonald Mariga – in Internazionale's matchday squad for their victory in 2010. Eto'o had also been part of the Barcelona side which became European champions in 2006 and again in 2009, alongside Seydou Keïta and Yaya Touré, therefore becoming the first African player to have claimed three winners' medals.

But while Eto'o would eventually spend two seasons in the twilight of his career at Chelsea and then Everton, Drogba's moment eventually arrived in the most unlikely of scenarios. When André Villas-Boas was sacked in March 2012 after losing the first leg of their last-16 tie against Napoli, the appointment of Roberto Di Matteo suddenly transformed an ageing squad which had been seriously underperforming. Drogba scored the first goal at Stamford Bridge as the 3-1 deficit against the Italians was overturned in a thrilling 4-1 victory, with the Ivorian also claiming the crucial strike in the first leg of the semi-final against Barcelona before an epic comeback in the 2-2 draw at the Camp Nou sent Chelsea through to the final.

Yet, with seven minutes to play against Bayern, it appeared they had finally run out of luck. Three African players – Drogba, Mikel and Kalou – had started the game but when Chelsea fell behind to Thomas Müller's goal, their talisman feared the worst. "For me that was it. Game over," Drogba wrote. With just two minutes of normal time remaining, however, his moment of redemption arrived from Juan Mata's brilliant corner, outleaping his marker at the near post before heading the ball powerfully into the net. Petr Čech's penalty save to deny Arjen Robben after Drogba's clumsy challenge had brought down Franck Ribéry in the area during extra time seemed to suggest it may be his night, and so it proved.

"You love being in this position," Drogba told himself as he lined up to take the penalty that would win the shoot-out.

"If you score, we win. If you miss, you miss. But you love that responsibility."

Having despatched the ball to the right side of Manuel Neuer's goal, he ran directly to embrace Čech before being smothered by the rest of his teammates. Chelsea had made history. Not only were they the first London club to win European football's most prestigious trophy but, for the first time, there had been four African players in Di Matteo's matchday squad, even if Essien didn't make it on to the pitch this time.

"We played a big part in making Chelsea what it is today and that is something I'm very proud of," he says seven years on. "We were a good mix of Brazilians, Portuguese and English players – that's what made that team so special."

Drogba would return for one more title-winning final season at Stamford Bridge under Mourinho in 2014 and end up racking up an African record 104 Premier League goals in total. Essien spent a year on loan at Real Madrid before spells in Italy, Greece and Indonesia. He is now preparing for the next stage of his career as a coach for Azerbaijani side Sabail but looks back on his time in England with great fondness.

"It was my dream come true," Essien adds. "As a young boy I always wanted to play in the Premier League so I was very excited and keen to make a good impression. Back home, we used to watch all the matches on television and it was England that everyone wanted to play. Thank God I got that opportunity and made a good impression. As an African player, you have to make a lot of sacrifices and put in the work. It's not easy to leave your family behind and go such a long way from home but we all tried to do our best and make a good career."

Their success can be measured by Chelsea's continued popularity throughout Africa. For a club which has fought hard to rid itself of an image that became tarnished by some sections of its support in the past, the role players like Drogba, Essien,

Mikel and Kalou played in changing attitudes in the stands should not be underestimated. As for the effect they had on the reputation of African players as a whole in English football, Essien is delighted to have played his part.

"It's very good," he says. "I'm proud to watch how well they are doing because we know we helped to make that happen. We were all part of the story that created pathways for the next generation."

FOURTEEN

NEVER GIVE UP

"I don't know if we can play much better," admitted Jürgen Klopp, still shaking his head in bemused disbelief. "I told the boys I'm proud of how we played. In the end, nobody is really interested – probably only football nerds will think about it – because it was about the result, and we lost 3-0."

You had to feel for Liverpool's manager. Yet another Camp Nou masterclass from soon to be crowned six-time World Player of the Year Lionel Messi appeared to have left Klopp's dream of a second successive Champions League final in tatters. A promising start in the first leg of the semi-final had seen Barcelona take the lead against the run of play through former Liverpool striker Luis Suárez, two minutes after Naby Keïta was forced off with a groin injury that would bring his first season at the club to a shuddering halt. It was a sad end to what had been a whirlwind few weeks for the Guinea midfielder. Having finally scored his first goal for Liverpool against Southampton at the start of April, he followed it up with another against Porto in the first leg of the Champions League quarter-final and started the next four Premier League games in a row.

"The goal Naby scored against Southampton delivered him," reflects Guinean journalist Amadou Makadji. "You could see how he celebrated with Sadio Mané – it was like freedom for him. There's a lot of good things to come but unfortunately he had this injury which stopped him in his progression. Psychologically he is much more confident now and not afraid of losing the ball. I think Klopp played a big part in that."

On the pitch where his idol Deco had once dazzled, however, the bitter blow of Keïta's injury was made even worse by what happened next. With just 15 minutes to play and Liverpool pressing forward in the hope of scoring a priceless away goal, Messi's tap-in after Suárez struck the crossbar doubled Barça's lead before the Argentina superstar's free kick arrowed into the top corner of Alisson's goal from more than 30 yards out. Mohamed Salah somehow struck a post at the other end when it seemed easier to score but the miss of the night was reserved for Ousmane Dembélé 20 seconds later. After combining with Messi on the break, the £120 million France forward with Senegalese and Mauritanian heritage spooned the softest of shots into the arms of the Liverpool goalkeeper with the last kick of the match. Surely it wouldn't make any difference anyway?

"I can work really well with this game," Klopp insisted afterwards. "It was a brave performance that was very passionate, very lively and, in a lot of moments, creative and direct. I will use this game to show the boys what is possible."

Few would have blamed him for not being quite so positive. Since the draw against Everton at Goodison Park at the start of March, Liverpool had won ten matches in a row but still found themselves trailing Manchester City in the Premier League title race and now staring down the barrel of Champions League elimination. Despite all the thrills and spills served up since he arrived at Anfield, Klopp seemed destined to end his third full season without any silverware once again.

Having regained the initiative in the first days of spring, City's defence of their crown was proving to be formidable. Pep

Guardiola's side beat Chelsea on penalties to win the Carabao Cup, overcame a stubborn Brighton to reach the FA Cup final and won eight successive Premier League games to set up a shot at becoming the first English team to win the domestic treble. Their hopes of adding the Champions League trophy, however, came unstuck under the watchful eye of the video assistant referee in the second leg of a thrilling quarter-final against Tottenham, with Raheem Sterling's injury-time goal deemed to have been offside by the smallest of margins after it had initially been allowed to stand.

Four days before the first leg at Spurs' new £1 billion stadium, Salah's dramatic late goal against Southampton had maintained Liverpool's challenge in the league and also ended the Egyptian's longest run without scoring since his arrival at Anfield. Keïta's header cancelled out an early strike from Shane Long but it appeared the visitors may have to settle for a point as the game reached the 80th minute. Then Mané blocked a shot from James Ward-Prowse and the ball was deftly headed into Salah's path by Jordan Henderson. Suddenly, Salah was one-on-one with Ryan Bertrand and bearing down on goal, pausing only to steady himself when he reached the Southampton penalty area before curling a trademark left-footed finish just inside the post. "Mo Salah could not pass for his goal, so go, go, go!" enthused Klopp afterwards.

It was also Salah's 50th Premier League goal in his 69 appearances in English football's top flight, making him the third quickest to have achieved the landmark behind Ruud van Nistelrooy and Alan Shearer. As if to hammer home the point that he was back in form, the Egyptian found the net again in the next league match against Chelsea with a brilliant goal from outside the area to make it 2-0 after Mané had opened the scoring. The game took place on the fifth anniversary of Steven Gerrard's infamous slip against Chelsea that had gifted City the title but any talk of a repeat was banished by Liverpool's African stars. Salah's yoga celebration, adopting the tree pose with his hands clasped in prayer across his chest, adorned the back pages of every newspaper the next day and led the speculation that he could be responding to the group of Chelsea fans who had been filmed singing "Salah is a bomber" before a game against Slavia Prague a week earlier. "I am a yoga man," he explained afterwards. "I do yoga and it just came into my mind."

Like Mané, Salah sometimes performs *sujud* – the prostration undertaken in Islamic prayer – when he scores but, according to Egyptian journalist Fady Ashraf, the reaction against his former club was an indication of the discipline's growing influence on his career.

"When the English media talked about whether he was a one-season wonder and all of that, he started to read more about yoga and how to be very calm. How to relax with the media and take himself away from everything," says Ashraf. "You can compare his quotes before and after – there is a very big difference. Salah now thinks about what he says very carefully. It is very important because in Egypt people are obsessed about football and Mohamed Salah had to be calm with the media and the fans."

"For sure he needs something like that," adds Klopp when I ask him. "To calm him down. I can imagine . . ."

The following week, Salah was named as one of the world's 100 most influential people by *Time* magazine and used his interview to discuss gender equality in the Islamic world.

"We need to change the way we treat women in our culture," he said. "It's not optional. I support the woman more than I did before, because I feel like she deserves more than what they give her now at the moment."

Salah's omission from the six nominations to be the PFA Player of the Year was something of a surprise, however, with

Mané and Virgil van Dijk up against Eden Hazard and three City players – Sergio Agüero, Raheem Sterling and Bernardo Silva – for the award the Egyptian had won 12 months earlier. After beating Cardiff to keep pace in the title race, Liverpool thrashed relegation-bound Huddersfield 5-0 in a match that saw three African players get on the scoresheet for the first time in the club's history. Salah's two goals took him to 68 in all competitions, meaning no other Liverpool player has ever scored more in their first 100 appearances. With him on 21 and Mané one behind in the race for the Golden Boot, they had become only the fourth pairing from the same club to reach the 20-goal mark in a Premier League season.

Yet as a result of City extending their winning run to 12 matches with the 1-0 victory over Burnley, Liverpool went into their 37th game of the league programme against Newcastle knowing that only three points could keep alive their chances of securing the title. It had only been three days since their defeat against Barcelona but Van Dijk's early goal seemed to have settled any remaining nerves among the visitors to St James' Park. A spirited Newcastle side under wily former Liverpool manager Rafael Benitez came back strongly to equalise through Ghana winger Christian Atsu, only for Salah to score his 22nd goal of the season when he volleyed home a superb cross from Trent Alexander-Arnold.

Salomon Rondon equalised again in the second half and the evening took another turn for the worse when Salah was struck in the side of the head by Martin Dubravka's thigh as the Newcastle goalkeeper punched away a cross. The Egyptian collapsed to the turf and seemed to lose consciousness before eventually being taken off on a stretcher in tears after a five-minute delay as he received treatment. Divock Origi was summoned to replace him and, in a role that he was to become increasingly familiar with over the next few weeks, scored the crucial winning goal four minutes from time when he headed home Xherdan Shaqiri's free kick.

"That's nearly a fairy tale," said Klopp of Origi's latest intervention. "And now we are qualified for our final on Sunday against Wolves. Of course before that we play Barcelona. But I'm not thinking of that yet. Then we will see."

The news on Salah was not so positive, however. Despite watching the final minutes of the match in the dressing room after it was decided he did not need to go to hospital, club doctors ruled that mild concussion meant he must miss the second leg against Barcelona in midweek but would be fit to face Wolves in the final league match of the season. Now all it required was for their title rivals to somehow slip up against 2016 champions Leicester in their penultimate game.

***

The City fans may not have known it at the time, but when Marc-Vivien Foé slammed home a cutback from substitute Djamel Belmadi in the 80th minute of their Premier League win over Sunderland for his second of the afternoon in April 2003, it would be the last time they would see a home player score a goal at Maine Road. Sixty-six days later and with the bulldozers still yet to roll in to demolish the 80-year-old stadium, Foé was playing for Cameroon in the semi-finals of the Confederations Cup against Colombia when he collapsed on the pitch in Lyon during the second half. Despite attempts to resuscitate him, the 28-year-old, who was playing at his home club's stadium having spent the previous season on loan at City, was pronounced dead 45 minutes later.

Foé grew up in Yaoundé and played in all of Cameroon's matches at the 1994 World Cup as a teenager. He had come close to joining Manchester United in 1998 after helping Lens win Ligue 1 for the first time. But a broken leg suffered on the eve of the World Cup in France put paid to that dream, with the powerful midfielder moving to West Ham instead for a club record £4.2 million the following year.

Until he joined on loan, City's list of African players had amounted to Johannesburg-born midfielder Colin Viljoen, who made two appearances for England during the 1970s having made his name at Ipswich under Bobby Robson. Neighbours Manchester United beat them to fielding an African player in the Premier League by almost a year when South African Quinton Fortune joined from Atlético Madrid in August 1999, with another six following in his footsteps to Old Trafford. City's signing of George Weah from AC Milan on a free transfer in the summer of 2000 finally saw the club from Manchester's east side take the plunge, with the former World Player of the Year scoring his solitary Premier League goal for the club in a 3-2 defeat to Liverpool at Anfield. Weah lasted just 11 matches under Joe Royle before returning to France, although his performances in a six-month loan spell at Chelsea the previous season suggested he still had more to offer.

City, who had recently spent a season in English football's third tier, bounced back immediately from relegation in 2001 to win the Championship title, in large part thanks to the performances of Algeria playmaker Ali Benarbia. Two years later, the former Marseille player was integral in the move to sign his international teammate Belmadi, who would go on to manage Algeria to their Africa Cup of Nations triumph in 2019. Foé had also made his way to Manchester on loan as City's multicultural squad, which also contained Cameroon teammate Lucien Mettomo, ended the season in a creditable ninth-placed finish. But the shocking death of Foé from what was later found to have been a pre-existing hereditary heart condition sent shockwaves through the world of football, not least at his former club.

"He only missed two games all season – and one of those was to be at the birth of his new baby – and won the fans over. We are all distraught," admitted City manager Kevin Keegan. FIFA president Sepp Blatter was among those to attend his state funeral in Cameroon a month after Foé's death, with new regulations subsequently introduced in an attempt to provide proper screening for players to detect heart problems. A few weeks later, Keegan announced that City had retired the No. 23 shirt in honour of their former loanee and a memorial to him was later unveiled in the garden where the pitch at Maine Road used to be. Even more fittingly, though, as City moved into their new 55,000-seater stadium that had been built for the 2002 Commonwealth Games, a new generation of African players was preparing to continue Foé's legacy.

Having drifted along in mid-table for a few years under Stuart Pearce and former England manager Sven-Goran Eriksson, the surprise purchase of the club by the state-owned Abu Dhabi United Group in August 2008 suddenly shifted the landscape of the Premier League. A raft of new expensive players including a British record £32 million for Brazil forward Robinho from Real Madrid on transfer deadline day made all the headlines, although it was manager Mark Hughes' first signing a few days after the deal to buy the club from disgraced former Thai prime minister Thaksin Shinawatra that would prove the most significant.

The son of a mechanical engineer from Bukavu in what was then known as Zaire, Vincent Kompany was born in Uccle, a suburb of Brussels, nine years after his father had arrived in Belgium as a refugee. As a student, Pierre Kompany was imprisoned in a labour camp for more than a year after joining the uprising against the dictator Joseph-Desiré Mobutu.

"We go to try to tell him to go – impossible," he remembered in May 2019, a few days after being elected as Belgium's first black mayor in Ganshoren, a district in the north-west of Brussels.

"He was strong and a big power. He put us in a military camp but he knew that he could have a problem with the European press so what he did was say that they are doing their military service."

A forged medical note from a friend who was a doctor he played football with helped smooth Kompany senior's path to Europe, although it took almost seven years for the Belgian government to finally recognise him as a citizen. By then, he had already met his wife Jocelyne Fraselle – a union leader from eastern Belgium who worked for the government employment agency – and supported his young family by driving a taxi every night. Vincent joined Anderlecht's youth side at the age of six but their early experiences were marred by repeated instances of racism.

"It was normal for us to go to youth tournaments and be called monkeys; parents shouting it," he remembered in an interview with *The Guardian* in May 2018. "That would nearly cause a fist fight with my mother. We were taught to be stronger."

Those incidents and the strong influence of his wife saw Pierre become more involved in politics, joining the Socialist party and then the Humanist Democratic Centre, a party in the centre of Belgian politics. He and Jocelyne got divorced when their eldest son was 14, only a few months after Kompany had been expelled from school and dropped from the national team squad for arguing with a coach.

"I had an edge, a different way of dealing with things," Vincent added. "My parents always revolted against inequality or unfairness, so you can imagine that when my teacher would punish someone – or me – for something that wasn't fair, I wouldn't take it."

Three years later, Kompany became one of the youngest players ever to represent Belgium in a friendly against France, also winning the *Soulier d'Ébène* (Ebony Shoe) award given to the best player of African origin in the Jupiler League during his debut season. Kompany won it again in 2005, emulating Daniel Amokachi a few years earlier, opting against leaving despite several offers from overseas. He eventually joined Hamburg for a club record €10 million the next summer but spent a year on the sidelines due to an Achilles injury.

The move to City in 2008 was an opportunity to establish himself at the heart of Sheikh Mansour bin Zayed Al Nahyan's £1 billion reinvention of the club over the next decade: a role he thrived in. Kompany was often initially employed as a defensive midfielder in his first season as Hughes guided his side to a disappointing tenth-placed finish, although they did reach the quarter-finals of the UEFA Cup, losing to Hamburg after Richard Dunne was sent off in the second leg. That summer City spent £130 million on new players, with Kolo Touré and Emmanuel Adebayor adding a distinctively African flavour to the squad. After two years in and out of the side, Zimbabwean Benjani Mwaruwari was allowed to join Sunderland on loan but in his absence City ended the season in fifth place, thanks largely to 29 goals from Carlos Tevez.

Adebayor, who trod the familiar path from Monaco to Arsène Wenger's Arsenal in 2006 for just £3 million, had his moments too. When the Togo striker scored against his former club to make it 3-1 at the Etihad Stadium only two months after his controversial move, he ran the length of the pitch towards the away fans before sliding on his knees with his arms outstretched in celebration. That earned Adebayor a two-match ban, although he later claimed that he had been provoked by racist chanting.

"I remember getting to the stadium and Arsenal fans were there. All I heard was the chant, 'Your mother is a whore and your father washes elephants,'" he told the *Daily Mail* in April 2019. "And now the same FA are trying to stop racism? I'm sorry. It doesn't work that way. Today is too late. We're tired. Enough is enough."

The arrival of Roberto Mancini and another £130 million outlay on new players including Mario Balotelli – the son of Ghanaian immigrants born in Sicily and brought up by Italian parents in Lombardy – in the summer of 2010 marked the beginning of a new era for City. Balotelli was named man of the match at Wembley as Yaya Touré's winning goal in the 2011 FA Cup final against Stoke ended the club's 35-year wait for a major honour and added the Ivorian's name to the ever-growing list of African players to have won English football's most prestigious cup competition. Since the turn of the century, only two finals have not featured at least one African international on either side, with Didier Drogba leading the way on four victories.

Under Mancini, City went on to win their first league title since 1968 as Adebayor was replaced by Sergio Agüero and the Argentina striker ended up scoring the crucial late goal in their dramatic final match against QPR. Touré would pick up two more winners' medals under Manuel Pellegrini in 2014 and then Guardiola in 2018, although the latter was soured by his lack of appearances in that final season under the Spaniard. Yet the towering midfielder still left City as one of the most decorated African players in the history of English football, also becoming an outspoken critic on the continued scourge of racism in the game.

Despite leading City to all three of their league titles, Kompany's persistent injury problems had meant his appearances were limited in the latter years of his career at City. He would even end up missing his own testimonial in September 2019 due to a hamstring twinge. The Belgian had been outstanding in the vital 2-1 victory over Liverpool at the start of the year but sustained yet another muscle strain and did not return for eight weeks. By the time City faced Leicester in the first week of May, however, Kompany was fit and ready for action. Alongside £57 million

French defender Aymeric Laporte, City had only conceded once in the wins over United, Crystal Palace and Burnley and were now within two victories of retaining their title.

No doubt keen to impress new manager Brendan Rodgers, Leicester were to prove no pushovers on an enthralling evening at the Etihad. Agüero's header that smacked against the crossbar in the first half had been the closest City had come to scoring as the visitors' defence stood firm against waves of sky-blue attacks. With 20 minutes to play and the midfield sitting deep to deny their opponents any space around the penalty box, Kompany saw his opportunity. Almost waltzing forward with the ball, he advanced to around 25 yards out before unleashing a venomous shot which dipped and swerved away from Kasper Schmeichel and into the top corner of his goal.

"I could hear people saying, 'Don't shoot, don't shoot!'" he admitted after the game. "But I've not come this far in my career to have young players tell me when to shoot. In big moments like this, I'm going to do something."

***

The morning after the night before, Liverpool's players assembled in a meeting room at a hotel in the city centre ahead of the second leg of the semi-final against Barcelona. All the talk a few hours earlier on the squad's WhatsApp group had been about Kompany's goal against Leicester, with the *New York Times* later reporting that the messages were dominated by the head-exploding emoji – defined as "a visual form of the expression mind blown, it may represent such emotions as shock, awe, amazement, and disbelief" by Emojipedia. Klopp began by asking his players if any of them wanted to discuss City's victory which had once again taken them a point clear – the 32nd time that season that the lead had changed hands in the title race.

When his question was met with stony silence around the room, he launched into a rousing speech that has since become the stuff of legend at Anfield thanks to defender Dejan Lovren.

"He said: 'Boys, believe. One or two goals, even if we don't score in the first 15 or 20 minutes, believe in the 65th, 66th, 67th minutes that we can score. Then with Anfield behind us, trust me guys, we can do it. We did it against Dortmund and we can do it tonight – just show the fucking balls tonight.'"

"In the meeting before the game he was really convinced that we could do it," adds Mané. "He pushed the boys hard to give everything possible and tried to take the pressure off us. What makes him special is that he never stops believing."

But in the absence of two of their feared attacking triumvirate in Salah and Roberto Firmino, even Klopp knew something spectacular would be required to achieve the greatest of all comebacks.

"I remember waking up the next day and thinking, 'How has it come to this?'" recalls Melissa Reddy. "It felt like Liverpool's whole season had combusted when Kompany's goal went in. You had a situation where it looked like they could end with absolutely nothing after such an amazing campaign. It wasn't until about 3 o'clock when people were starting to head to Anfield for the match that the defiance began to filter through. As kick-off edged closer, you sensed that people were thinking, 'It doesn't matter if there is no Salah, Firmino or Keïta: we can do this.' There was not even like, 'Oh well, let's give it our best shot.' There was actual belief that it would happen."

The sight of Mohamed Salah on the pitch before kick-off with the message 'Never Give Up' emblazoned in big white letters across his black T-shirt gave Liverpool supporters even more reason to feel optimistic. After his heroics against Newcastle, Origi was handed his chance up front flanked by Mané and Xherdan Shaqiri as Klopp stuck to his tried and tested 4-3-3 formation. He was rewarded when the Belgium forward tapped in after Henderson's shot was saved in the seventh minute in a move that began with Mané seizing on a poor defensive header from Jordi Alba. According to his manager, the Senegal forward's performance that evening was evidence of his growing versatility and maturity.

"Bobby and Mo were not involved but he played for three," remembers Klopp. "I'm not sure a lot of people remember him in that game because he didn't score – but he played for three players. Really. Literally. Not that he replaced him and him but he was just busy like crazy. It was unbelievable how good he was in that game. That's the thing about Sadio – I don't think even he knows how good he was in that game. That's his last big challenge. I think I've said it about him before – the only person who doesn't know that Sadio Mané is a world-class player is Sadio Mané. If he reads your book then write please: 'There's still a lot more.' Give Sadio the message there is still a lot more work to do."

Against opponents who were attempting to win their fifth European title in just 13 years and sixth in total, Liverpool could count themselves unlucky to be only one goal ahead after an action-packed first half. The introduction of Georginio Wijnaldum for Andy Robertson in a move that saw Mr Dependable James Milner filling in at left-back proved to be Klopp's latest masterstroke. Within 11 minutes of the restart, the Dutchman's two goals had drawn his side level on aggregate and Liverpool could almost smell the final. "Once Gini got the second, you knew that the game was only going to go one way," recalls Reddy.

No one could have predicted how their crowning moment of glory would arrive with 11 minutes to play, however. In an article for the Players' Tribune website a few months later, Klopp admitted that he had turned his back on proceedings just as

Alexander-Arnold stepped up to take his famous corner.

"I was talking to my assistant, and . . . you know, I have goosebumps every time I think about it . . . I just heard the noise," he wrote. "I turned to the pitch and I saw the ball flying into the goal. I turned back to our bench and looked at Ben Woodburn, and he said, 'What just happened?!' And I said, 'I have no idea!'"

Having placed the ball in the quadrant, Alexander-Arnold began to walk in Shaqiri's direction before quickly spinning on his heels and whipping in a low cross that picked out Origi as if they were communicating telepathically. Watching him sweep the ball past Marc-André ter Stegen, Barcelona's players sank to the turf in despair. More than 11,000 miles away in Nairobi, the Oduor household erupted in spontaneous joy as they realised what had just happened.

"When Divock scored the winning goal we threw our glasses in the air," admits Origi's uncle Austin Oduor. "Other people were knocking over tables. We were so excited – having come from nothing it was great to see him making the difference."

Up in the press box, former Liverpool captain Jamie Carragher leapt on to the table to celebrate what he later described as the greatest night in Anfield's illustrious history.

"The whole game was too much," admitted a dazed-looking Klopp afterwards. "Winning is difficult but with a clean sheet, I don't know how they did it."

Unusually for a man who always enjoys a beer, he had spent the minutes after the final whistle sipping from a bottle of water trying to come to terms with what his team had just achieved.

"It was a feeling that I cannot describe in words," Klopp wrote. "When I got back home, my family and friends were all staying over at our house, and everyone was in a big party mood. But I was so emotionally exhausted that I went up to bed by myself. My body and mind were completely empty. I had the best sleep of my life. The best moment was waking up the next morning and realising: It's still true. It really happened."

The rest of the city was not so restrained. After the agony of running City so close in what now seemed like would be a futile title challenge once again, the relief of reaching the Champions League final again in such dramatic circumstances at least went some way to making up for it.

"Afterwards I went for a few drinks and the amount of Liverpool fans who were still out at 2 o'clock in the morning was unbelievable," remembers Reddy. "But I think there was a deep desperation to make it count this time."

***

For a few seconds – 83 to be precise – anything seemed possible. After all, it had only been four days since Tottenham had produced a Liverpool-esque comeback against Ajax to set up an all-English Champions League final in Madrid. But just as quickly as Mané had given his side the lead against Wolves on the final day and Glenn Murray had put Brighton 1-0 up against City, Agüero's equaliser at the Amex Stadium dashed any lingering hopes of another miracle. Laporte's goal meant Guardiola's side went ahead before half-time and a brilliant goal from Riyad Mahrez – starting his first league game for five weeks – made sure of a 14th successive victory as they ended the season on 98 points.

Meanwhile, Mané scored his 22nd league goal of the season to wrap up Liverpool's ninth victory in a row and 30th in total. Yet it still wasn't enough. Their points total of 97 would have secured the title in all but two of the previous 27 Premier League seasons but Klopp was forced to admit they had fallen short. "Of course it hurts," he said. "Ninety-seven points, come on. It's a crazy number. It's the best season I ever played with a team."

At least he had the consolation of the Champions League

final still to come, while the final Golden Boot standings were also a source of personal satisfaction. Informed that Mané and Salah would be sharing the coveted top goalscorers' award with Pierre-Emerick Aubameyang after he also found the net twice in Arsenal's win over Burnley, Klopp could not help but smile. "Auba too? Do they have three boots?" he asked the TV interviewer a little incredulously. "It is good. They are all my players."

When I ask him about the achievement – later recognised by Aubameyang as "a good thing for the continent" – Klopp was still brimming with fatherly pride. "That makes for me like . . . 60 goals," he laughs.

Had the success of all three African players taken him by surprise? "Yes. I'm very often surprised by my boys, by the way," he confides. "Because I only know about potential and the rest is imagination and dreams and stuff like that. My dreams! And then . . . wow! I couldn't even have dreamt of that."

There were three weeks to prepare for the meeting with Spurs in the final and Klopp gave his players a few days off to relax before they reconvened in Marbella for a training camp. City wrapped up their historic treble after thrashing Watford 6-0 in the FA Cup final – Kompany's final match for the club. He announced the next day that he would be taking over as Anderlecht's player-manager after 11 years that had yielded 12 trophies in all. "The legacy he left behind is great, not only for City but the Premier League, and I think everyone should appreciate what he's done for English football," said his City and Belgium teammate Kevin De Bruyne in tribute.

Most of Liverpool's squad had gone on holiday to recharge their batteries after an exhausting season, although Salah still seemed to be recovering as they flew to Spain. Alex Oxlade-Chamberlain – back to fitness after almost a year out injured – captured a video of the double Golden Boot winner stretched out asleep on the floor of the aeroplane wrapped up in a blanket and posted it to Instagram with the caption "Egyptian kings need sleep too".

"Like a baby! He's sleeping like a baby," laughed the England midfielder into the camera. As various other giggling players come to row 20 to take a look for themselves, Oxlade-Chamberlain posted another message: "Did you know that the Egyptian king can't be woken up and will remain unfazed sound asleep until he is ready to wake?"

Joking aside, though, Salah's physical condition had been a concern for Liverpool's manager going into what would be the defining match of the season. The start of Ramadan on 5 May meant it had already been nearly three weeks since he and the rest of the Muslim players in the squad including Mané, Keïta and Shaqiri had eaten during daylight hours. It was an issue that usually comes around in the build-up to international tournaments, depending on the calendar. This time, with Eid al-Fitr – the festival marking the end of Islam's holy month – not taking place until two days afterwards, the scheduling of the match at 9 p.m. European time on 1 June meant that their preparation to face Tottenham would surely be severely hampered by their religious obligations. According to Klopp, however, the players had devised a plan that would satisfy everyone by postponing their fast for a few days before one of the biggest matches of their lives.

"At the first moment when we had the situation of course we had to find a solution but we did that. They found a way to do it in a proper way," he admits. "You cannot do it for four weeks. It's like this. There are exceptions – you can extend Ramadan and do it later."

"You have a choice," confirms Imam Shafiq, who was consulted by Mané about what to do. "It's fine to miss a few days if necessary. But Sadio and Mo are usually very strict about fasting because they believe it makes you a lot stronger. If you're doing something for God then he returns the favour."

***

Some of the 63,000 supporters at sparkling new Wanda Metropolitano Stadium in Madrid's eastern suburbs had barely taken their seats after the pre-match build-up. But there was Mohamed Salah, waiting patiently with his hands on his hips to take the penalty as Spurs players continued to surround the same referee from last year's final, Damir Skomina of Slovenia. Even the most diehard Liverpool fan would have admitted it was a soft decision, although the law at the time was clear: If the ball strikes an arm in an "unnatural position" inside the box then there can be only one outcome. This time, the luck already seemed to be on the side of the team from Merseyside.

Racing on to a hopeful punt forward by Henderson, Mané's cross intended for Salah at the back post had initially struck the chest of Moussa Sissoko before cannoning up on to his outstretched right arm. The France midfielder's immediate reaction was to turn to the referee, as if expecting the worst, and his fears were confirmed immediately as Skomina pointed to the spot. Only 22 seconds had been played. As Salah prepared to begin his run-up, he wiped away the sweat in his beard before swooping in to hammer his penalty just to Hugo Lloris' right. The ball flew past the Tottenham goalkeeper's despairing face, seeming to accelerate as it ripped into the net. Salah spread out his arms and slid knee-first towards the celebrating Liverpool fans behind the goal. A year on from the nightmare against Real Madrid in Kiev, he had taken his opportunity with aplomb.

"Oh 100 per cent," says Klopp when I ask him if the penalty against Spurs was a cathartic moment. "It's his character. He wants to be decisive. He wants to win these things."

In the build-up to the final, Salah had been asked if he dreamed of scoring the winning goal. "Not just dream," he replied. "I hope it becomes a reality and I score in the final, then win the Africa Cup of Nations too."

With the continental tournament taking place in his homeland that summer, the prospect of becoming the first Egyptian to win the Champions League had increased Salah-mania to new levels before the final. But his goal meant he had just become only the fifth African player to score in Europe's most important match, joining an exclusive club that also includes Mané, Samuel Eto'o and Drogba.

"The pressure that they have is much more than we have here," acknowledges Klopp. "They are the heroes of their country because they are the best player and they really look up to them. But you also get criticism from everywhere when you are not at your best, which happens to everyone because we are all human beings. They are really under pressure and dealing with that is not easy. But the older they get and the more experienced they get it becomes easier to deal with. For Mo, for sure, it's more difficult."

Perhaps unsurprisingly, Tottenham's players took time to react after falling behind so early on and rarely threatened Alisson in Liverpool's goal before half-time thanks to a typically imperious performance from Van Dijk, who would go on to be named man of the match to go with his PFA Player of the Year award. A reshuffle by manager Mauricio Pochettino saw the Londoners pile on the pressure in the second half as the Brazilian made crucial saves to deny Son Heung-min, Lucas Moura and Christian Eriksen. Origi had been introduced from the bench in the 58th minute for a flagging Firmino to give his side fresh legs in attack. But as the game headed into the last five minutes, just one goal separated the teams and the 30,000 Liverpool supporters inside the stadium could only watch and pray.

Then Liverpool won a corner and Milner's cross flicked off

the head of Son at the near post. Van Dijk tried to volley the ball towards goal, only to hardly make contact. A weak clearing header allowed the Dutchman to challenge Moura in the air, with the ball falling perfectly into the path of Joël Matip to lay it off for Origi with the most delicate of touches. Taking control of the ball with his right foot to set himself, the super-sub lashed his left-footed shot across Lloris and into the net. It was all over.

"All the pressure was distilled into that moment when the ball fell to him," says Reddy. "But he was as cold as ice in the way he took the chance. Then he celebrated like it was a Sunday league game, not the Champions League final."

At first, there had been no real emotion on Origi's face before he was mobbed by what seemed like Liverpool's entire playing and coaching staff in front of thousands of ecstatic supporters. The final whistle sounded a few minutes later and the two goalscorers were among the first to embrace on the pitch, with Klopp hardly able to control his emotions on the touchline. His record of six successive defeats in major finals had been consigned to history as Liverpool sealed their sixth European crown. "It was an intense season with the most beautiful finish I ever could have imagined," he admitted in his post-match interview.

After Henderson had lifted the famous trophy, a delighted Mané celebrated by jumping into the huge Champions League canvas that was covering the pitch. "I think I'm still dreaming," he reflected the following day. Back home in Senegal, Liverpool's victory was also greeted with delight.

"It was the same as if the national team had won something," Saer Seck recalls. "At the end of the game, even in my house, everyone was hugging and jumping around. We were all Liverpool fans and Sadio did not walk alone!"

Less than 24 hours later, Merseyside police estimated 750,000 people lined the streets of Liverpool to welcome home their heroes on an open-top bus tour of the city. Only the Everton fans stayed away. The players had barely slept, having stayed up until the early hours before catching a flight back to Merseyside.

"We had a party after the game that was very intense in the way that everyone wanted to find a space where you can be alone with friends and family," remembers Klopp. "But even they ask you about the match. I'm not very good in these moments to be honest. I don't want to speak too much – it's difficult when they all have questions. Then the celebrations in the city were world class and we went home and had a little kitchen party. The next day I was sitting in front of the television watching all the YouTube videos about it because I wanted to see all the views of it. Then I packed my suitcase and went on holiday – it felt like I was flying without flying. With my personal history as well . . ."

For Salah, Mané and Keïta, though, the season was still not over. In honour of their new status as the first players from Egypt, Senegal and Guinea to win the Champions League, all three received royal welcomes from their international teammates when they met up for the Africa Cup of Nations a few weeks later. While Mané and Salah were afforded guards of honour, the Guinea squad went even further, preparing a special cake for Keïta – who had been ruled out of the final due to injury but still received a winner's medal – with the message: "Le Syli felicite Naby" (The Syli – Guinea's nickname – congratulate Naby) and also serenaded him with a rendition of 'You'll Never Walk Alone'.

"We are so proud," reflects Makadji. "Naby's story is like every young person's in Guinea – from a poor family and not having any money. Having to fight for their passion. Now young players at home can say, 'If Naby did it, why not me?' He has given them hope."

EPILOGUE

"One of my aims in setting up Diambars was to win the World Cup," says Saer Seck intently. "I don't want to go there to be a spectator or just to reach the quarter-final. I don't want to watch the final on TV. We want to be part of history."

We are sitting in a lobby on the third floor of the Senegal team's hotel, a heavily fortified compound situated next to an Egyptian army base not far from Cairo International Airport. Having arranged to meet Seck, the vice-president of the Senegalese FA who founded his youth academy in 2003 thanks to funding from Patrick Vieira, I first had to negotiate my way past armed police flanked by mounted machine guns as they sweltered in their uniforms under the unforgiving June sun outside. The team liaison officer who came to escort me into the hotel just so happened to be called Mohamed Salah and confided quietly that he thought Sadio Mané and co. would overcome his namesake in the final of the Africa Cup of Nations a few weeks later to win their first-ever title.

"It's definitely about time," continues Seck, who is Senegal's chef de mission in Egypt. "We have the players and they know it's a big chance to win that first star. But winning the World

Cup is the long-term aim. I have a generation of boys at the moment who were born in 2005 and 2006 . . . they are really amazing. We know we have to be a bit more organised, work hard and keep our players focused. We have enough talent and physical capacities to achieve it and hopefully we will."

With temperatures in excess of 40 degrees at that time of year, many had questioned the wisdom of switching the 2019 edition of the tournament to North Africa after Cameroon was stripped of the hosting rights in October 2018. Led by the player who had just won back-to-back Premier League Golden Boots and scored a penalty in the Champions League final, the Pharaohs were immediately installed as favourites to win their record eighth continental crown in the first tournament to have been held at the end of the domestic season in Europe.

For years, the Confederation of African Football (CAF) resisted calls to move the biennial competition from its traditional date in January but had finally relented under growing pressure from the clubs. A record number of teams – 24 – were also taking part as minnows Burundi, Madagascar and Mauritania made their finals debut. My own small contribution to the Burundian cause had involved transporting 46 pairs of boots that had somehow ended up being stranded in London two days before their opening match against Nigeria. After three hours with customs at the airport, during which I became on first-name and smoking terms with most of the officials having initially been asked to pay $6,000 in tax, I was eventually allowed to enter the country with the boots. Not that they did the team captained by Saido Berahino any good: despite the presence of the former West Brom striker who had once been called up by England's senior team without winning a cap, they lost all three group stage matches and failed to score a single goal.

Led by Mané, Kalidou Koulibaly of Napoli and Everton's Idrissa Gueye, Senegal were a different proposition altogether.

Gueye – who would join Paris Saint-Germain for £30 million a few weeks later – was one of six Diambars youth products in coach Aliou Cissé's squad while another three, including Mané, came from Mady Touré's Génération Foot.

"The academy system is very strong and it is helping to grow the exportation of players to Europe," admits Seck. "We've been doing that for many years but the difference now might be that they can reach a high level. We have Sadio, we have Idrissa and Kalidou Koulibaly. We do not have plenty of people – only 14 or 15 million, which is nothing compared to somewhere like Nigeria with 200 million – but in Senegal every child is playing football. And playing and playing and playing."

Inspired by Senegal's performance at the 2002 World Cup, Seck – a former midfielder who played as an amateur in France – set up Diambars after making his own fortune as an industrial fisherman, with a little help from Vieira.

"When Arsenal played, everyone would watch on the television," he remembers of the former Arsenal captain. "Patrick often came back to visit and talk to the kids. He would send us balls and shirts from Arsenal for the best kids who were performing well. We used him as a role model. I don't know how many times Idrissa Gueye spoke to him when he first moved to France with Lille but he was a real inspiration for him. He still calls me to hear the news about the academy – when we won the cup he called me to congratulate us. I'm very proud – it's part of my social involvement. It's not a matter of money for me. We are a non-profit organisation so I don't make a single penny . . ."

Both academies now have senior sides firmly established in Senegal's top flight, with Diambars having picked up their first league title in 2013 with a team of teenagers. In June 2019, the side that beat Génération Foot in the cup final to stop them winning the double had an average age of just 17. Unsurprisingly,

Seck – who invests any profits made from transfers back into the academy – admits his phone never stops ringing.

"Five minutes before I came to meet you, I had a message from a club in Turkey saying they want two players," he says. "Yesterday it was Standard Liège. The day before Bordeaux . . ."

The success of Mané and Koulibaly has only increased demand from Europe, although Seck believes his young players are still not treated with the same respect as the rest of the world.

"People are certainly paying more attention to them," he nods. "But they are not considering Africa to be part of football's economic model. I'm sorry but when you want to buy someone who could be the next Sadio Mané or even a lesser player for less than €500,000 and Vinícius Júnior from Brazil goes for €61 million, it's disrespectful of Africa. We asked for €1 million for the player who was voted the best player at the last African Under-20 tournament and we were told we were crazy. This boy in five years will cost €100 million. This is where Africa must be respected by European football. When you are Brazilian, even if you are an average player you cost about €3 million. The best African players cannot cost a third of that."

I ask him whether he thought that was a legacy of history in a country that was one of Africa's biggest slave hubs for almost 400 years.

"Yes without a doubt," Seck agrees. "It's not only about football. It's about the whole perception and consideration of Africa due to slavery and a dominant economic relationship. People still continue to think that with really poor money you can get anything you want in Africa. We are fighting but it is really something very difficult. Most of the academies have had no investment and are really happy with small amounts just to pay our staff. But we have to keep fighting to change the mindset of European clubs and FIFA. Why is Africa still not respected despite the fact we have had Sadio and everyone who came before him like George Weah, Samuel Eto'o, Didier Drogba – players who have made history in Europe and the Champions League?"

A few weeks later, Mané's dream of rounding off his spectacular season by leading Senegal to their maiden AFCON title was thwarted in the final by an Algerian side led by a resurgent Riyad Mahrez. Egypt's surprise elimination against South Africa in the last 16 curtailed any predictions that the tournament would act as a shoot-out between Salah and Mané in their quest to become the first African to win the Ballon d'Or since George Weah. Instead it was Mahrez who stole the show.

Inspired by his role in helping Manchester City secure an unprecedented domestic treble, a stunning free kick from their captain in the last minute of the semi-final against Nigeria had led his country to the brink of winning the competition for the first time since 1990. Coached by former City midfielder Djamel Belmadi, Algeria took advantage of Koulibaly's absence due to suspension by opening the scoring in the second minute through Baghdad Bounedjah and never looked like letting it slip.

"Sometimes I watch the video and think: 'Wow, what have I done?' It is unbelievable," Mahrez later reflected. "It is something that will stay forever."

***

The 2018/19 Premier League season was historic for African players. As well as the 66 shared between Sadio Mané, Mohamed Salah and Pierre-Emerick Aubameyang in winning the Golden Boot, they contributed 117 – 11 per cent – of the total number of goals scored, with at least one African player making an appearance for 15 of the 20 clubs. In total, almost 300 African internationals have now graced the Premier League since Peter Ndlovu became the first in 1992 as the continent has emerged as one of the most lucrative sources of talent in the multi-million pound industry that football has become in the 21st century.

They have certainly come a long way since Arthur Wharton made the journey from Accra to Staffordshire more than a century earlier. From Steve Mokone and Albert Johanneson to Lucas Radebe and Didier Drogba, each has his own unique story of battling against the odds to achieve their dream, even if it has sometimes come at huge personal cost. But the opportunities today's superstars enjoy would not have been possible if it wasn't for pioneers like Wharton or Johanneson, who confronted discrimination and racism head on in their quest to play the sport they loved.

Of course, the story continues to evolve. Two decades after Christopher Wreh made history as the first African player to win the league title, Arsenal's purchase of Ivory Coast forward Nicolas Pépé from Lille for an eye-watering £72 million at the start of August 2019 was the fifth time a Premier League club had broken the continent's transfer record in as many seasons. He was soon followed by another Génération Foot product in the form of 20-year-old Ismaila Sarr, who joined Watford from Rennes for £30 million at the end of the summer transfer window. Both struggled to make an impact initially, with Pépé having to wait until the second week of December to score from open play as Arsenal ended a ten-match run without victory under caretaker manager Freddie Ljungberg. In January, Mbwana Samatta ensured Tanzania became the 100th different nation with a Premier League goalscorer and also found the net for Aston Villa at Wembley as they were beaten in the Carabao Cup final by Manchester City.

Meanwhile, Liverpool's blistering start to the 2019/20 season as they attempted to end the 30-year wait to be champions of England saw Mané and Salah inspire Jürgen Klopp's side to an astonishing 20 wins from their first 21 matches of the new campaign – a record in all of Europe's top five leagues. In recognition of their achievements in 2019, seven Liverpool players had dominated the Ballon d'Or shortlist, with five

Africans among the 30 nominees. The only one not playing for a club in the Premier League was Koulibaly of Napoli, while Mahrez could lay claim to have won more silverware than any of the other contenders. A few weeks earlier, however, there had been a hint that it wouldn't be Africa's year.

"Cristiano Ronaldo, Lionel Messi and Van Dijk – which is your choice?" asked the reporter on the red carpet at FIFA's The Best ceremony in Milan.

Sporting a typically garish silk double-breasted jacket and with his hands in his pockets, Samuel Eto'o shrugged his shoulders and sighed.

"The best ones for me are Mohamed Salah and Sadio Mané," he said before starting to chuckle to himself. "But they are not here."

With that, Eto'o strode off before his interviewer could even react. It had only been a few days since the Cameroon striker's retirement after scoring nearly 300 goals during his glittering career in which despite winning three Champions League titles, the closest he had come to being recognised as the best player in the world was in 2009 when he finished fifth behind Messi.

"It's difficult to understand how he never won it with the impressive career he had," admitted José Mourinho, Eto'o's former manager at Inter Milan. "He was the best striker in the world for several years and I think he deserved a Ballon d'Or. But these are things out of our control."

Eto'o had his own theory. "We are only good to denigrate our own brothers. We are not respected," he told French broadcasters RFI on his retirement. "It's a fact. I hope I'm wrong, but the next Ballon d'Or will be neither Mané nor Salah. There is no explanation that Mané, Salah or Aubameyang, the top three scorers of the Premier League last season may not even be among the top five."

Almost a quarter of a century since Weah's landmark triumph at AC Milan, incredibly the Liberian remained the only African ever to be selected as one of the best three players in the world.

Arsène Wenger and Drogba – who somewhat ironically had been given the honour of hosting the Ballon d'Or ceremony at the start of December – were also among those to throw their weight behind Mané in the weeks leading up to it. Even Messi himself seemed to agree. As the Barcelona superstar received his FIFA award in Milan, he revealed that he had picked the Senegal forward as one of his three votes ahead of erstwhile rival Ronaldo.

"If you look at where I've come from, it shows I've come quite far," Mané reflected in an interview with the Sunday Times that week. "Without being for a long time at an academy, I got here. All I can say [to kids] is to keep working hard and go for your dream."

Eto'o's prediction proved to be correct, however. Once again, there was no African in the top three as Messi was crowned for a record sixth time, with Virgil van Dijk in second place and Cristiano Ronaldo third. The presence of Mané, Salah and Mahrez in fourth, fifth and tenth respectively did represent the continent's strongest-ever showing in the sport's most prestigious individual honour, even if the final result provoked outrage among many Liverpool supporters and beyond.

"For me this Ballon d'Or is for Sadio Mané, there is no doubt about that," argued his Senegal teammate and Crystal Palace midfielder Cheikhou Kouyaté the next day. "Listen, if Sadio was a Brazilian or a European there would not have been any debate. Maybe it's not just football that they look at because there is no way three people had a better season than him."

Mané's breathtaking performance in the 5-2 evisceration of Everton in the Merseyside derby two days later certainly underlined his claim. Divock Origi also scored twice almost 12 months on from his sensational return to the first team in the same fixture as Liverpool put five goals past their rivals for the first time in almost 40 years and manager Marco Silva was subsequently sacked. Not to be outdone, Salah and Naby Keïta – making his first league start of the campaign after yet more injury problems – combined to devastating effect in a 3-0 win against Bournemouth to extend Liverpool's unbeaten run in the league to 33 matches. As Klopp had predicted, they weren't finished yet.

Liverpool ended the year by beating Flamengo in the final of FIFA's Club World Cup in Qatar thanks to Roberto Firmino's goal in extra time. Having scored his first Premier League goal of the season in the victory over Bournemouth, Keïta was rewarded with his third successive start in further proof that the midfielder was slowly beginning to find his feet on Merseyside before injury struck again. The 4-0 thumping of second-placed Leicester on Boxing Day and a narrow win over Wolves rounded off their miraculous 2019 that had seen Klopp's side conquer the world and move to within touching distance of ending their domestic title drought.

After 44 matches - a run stretching back to the defeat against City in January 2019 and five short of Arsenal's record - Liverpool's unbeaten run in the Premier League was finally ended by Watford on 29 February, 2020 thanks to two goals from Sarr in a virtuoso display.

"Ismaïla is a gazelle, so he needs time," Mady Touré had told me of his latest protege a few weeks earlier, before throwing in another of his bold predictions. "What I can say is that Ismaïla is a little like Cristiano Ronaldo. And Ronaldo is his idol. They have quite a similar way of playing. I said Sadio would blow up in England and I can tell you that Ismaïla will do the same. He will even win a Ballon d'Or too."

A few days after Sarr's heroics in the 3-0 victory at Vicarage Road, Liverpool's reign as European champions was ended by Diego Simeone's Atlético Madrid after a thrilling second leg which took place just before the global sporting calendar came to a shuddering halt due to the coronavirus pandemic. Needing only six points to be crowned champions for the first time since 1990, the red half of the city had to keep the champagne on ice for just a little longer.

At least Mané already had the consolation of being named Africa's best player at the start of the year. Taking place in the Red Sea resort of Hurghada, where a certain Sergio Ramos had been welcomed to much fanfare during a family holiday in the summer, fittingly Eto'o had been chosen to host the ceremony which was also attended by Wenger and various African legends. But Salah's decision not to join Mané on the private jet laid on by Liverpool was a clear indication that the player who had finished as runner-up to his teammate in the previous two years had finally broken his duck. With his uncle Ibrahim watching on from the VIP seats, Mané was confirmed as only the second Senegalese winner of the award after El-Hadji Diouf in 2001 and 2002.

"To be honest, I would love to play football more than to be in front of many important people to speak because football is my job, I love it, but speeches are not, by the way!" he joked in English.

"It is a big day for me . . . I don't really know how to say it but I would love to thank all the Senegalese people. They have been with me all the time and they push me to do better. Also the people from my village. I have come very far, Bambali is a very small village and I am sure they are watching on the TV."

Back home, the party had been going on all day. A YouTube video later showed the whole village watching on in the darkness as their hero was crowned, before breaking into the chorus of the song which had been penned by Génération Foot's honorary president, Youssou N'Dour, in tribute to their hero. "Mané! Sadio! Mané! Sadio!" N'Dour later said Mané's achievements had earned him "a golden place in the heart of all Africans".

"I'm very honoured because Youssou N'Dour is a legend," admits Mané. "He is someone who always tries to encourage everyone and make a big impact for the young generation in Senegal. His partnership with Mady Touré at Generation Foot is helping boys to become professional players, which is really important for our development."

Salah was also quick to send his congratulations to his teammate via Instagram, with Mané's sponsors New Balance unveiling billboards bearing the slogan "Rise of a Lion" to mark their launch of a new pair of personalised boots celebrating his coronation. Six years on, Touré's prophecy had almost come true.

"I think it's an immense joy for Sadio," he reflected. "It's also an immense joy for Génération Foot. But none of that has come as a surprise to me. I told you he was in the vein of Neymar and Messi. And now Sadio has almost won the Ballon d'Or. I'm telling you, the fact he has been named as the best player in Africa will spur him on. That's his objective. Sadio always told me he would become one of the best players in the world. Now he is among them."

I ask Mané a few months later whether he remembers his mentor's original prediction?

"Yes I can remember it," he smirks. "People were saying, 'what the hell is he talking about?!' But Mady is like a Dad to me. We sometimes speak on the phone and he always has good advice for me. When he was in the academy he said to me just before I signed my first contact with Metz, 'Sadio, in 2012 there is an African Nations Cup - you can play of the first team at Metz for two months and then you will be in the national team that becomes African champions!' He has always believed in me and told me that I'm going to win the Ballon d'Or. That's so important. It's why I always say - never stop dreaming. It's what I've tried to do from the beginning. I think everything is possible in football so why not? I'm really proud and grateful to be mentioned, especially considering where I have come from."

APPENDIX

African international players who have appeared in the Premier League by 2019/20

Divided by country plus the club and year that they made their debut

Algeria
Mehdi Abeid – Newcastle United 2014
Nadir Belhadj – Portsmouth 2008
Djamel Belmadi – Manchester City 2002
Ali Benarbia – Manchester City 2002
Nabil Bentaleb – Tottenham Hotspur 2013
Hamer Bouazza – Watford, Fulham 2006
Madjid Bougherra – Charlton Athletic 2006
Kamel Ghilas – Hull City 2009
Adlène Guedioura – Wolves 2009
Rafik Halliche – Fulham 2010
Riyad Mahrez – Leicester City 2014
Moussa Saïb – Tottenham Hotspur 1997
Hassan Yebda – Portsmouth 2009
Islam Slimani – Leicester 2016
Sofiane Feghouli West Ham 2016
Rachid Ghezzal Leicester 2018

Angola
Manucho – Manchester United 2008

Benin
Rudy Gestede – Cardiff City 2013
Stéphane Sessègnon – Sunderland 2010
Steve Mounie – Huddersfield 2017

Burkina Faso
Bertrand Traore – Chelsea 2015

Burundi
Saido Berahino – West Brom 2011
Gaël Bigirimana Newcastle 2012

Cameroon
Benoît Assou-Ekotto – Tottenham Hotspur 2006
Timothée Atouba – Tottenham Hotspur 2004
Sébastien Bassong – Newcastle United 2008
André Bikey – Reading 2006
Eric Djemba-Djemba – Manchester United 2003
Roudolphe Douala – Portsmouth 2006
Eyong Enoh – Fulham 2012
Samuel Eto'o – Chelsea 2013
Marc-Vivien Foé – West Ham United 1998
Geremi Njitap – Middlesbrough 2002
Joseph-Désiré Job – Middlesbrough 2000
Lauren – Arsenal 2000
Jean Makoun – Aston Villa 2010
Stephane Mbia – Queens Park Rangers 2012
Patrick M'Boma – Sunderland 2001
Lucien Mettomo – Manchester City 2002
Valéry Mézague – Portsmouth 2004
Allan Nyom – Watford 2015
Salomon Olembé – Leeds United 2003
Alexandre Song – Charlton Athletic 2005
Rigobert Song – Liverpool 1998
Franck Songo'o – Portsmouth 2005
Somen Tchoyi – West Bromwich Albion 2010
Pierre Womé – Fulham 2002
Joel Matip – Liverpool 2016
Gaeten Bong – Brighton 2017
Andre Zambo-Angussia Fulham 2018
Alan Nyom – Watford 2015
Eric Maxim Choupo-Moting Stoke 2017
Clinton N'jie – Spurs 2015

Cape Verde
Cabral – Sunderland 2013
Pelé – Portsmouth 2008

Central African Republic
Frédérick Nimani – Burnley 2009

Congo
Lucien Aubey – Portsmouth 2007
Christian Bassila – West Ham 2000
Thievy Bifouma – West Bromwich Albion 2013
Amine Linganzi – Blackburn Rovers 2009
Christopher Samba – Blackburn Rovers 2006

Congo DR
Benik Afobe – Bournemouth 2015
Yannick Bolasie – Crystal Palace 2013
Gianelli Imbula – Stoke 2015
Hérita Ilunga – West Ham United 2008
Elias Kachunga – Huddersfield 2016
Gael Kakuta – Chelsea 2009
Lomana LuaLua – Newcastle United 2000
Dieumerci Mbokani – Hull 2015
Arthur Masuaku – West Ham 2016
Chancel Mbemba – Newcastle United 2015
Youssouf Mulumbu – West Bromwich Albion 2008
Arnold Mvuemba – Portsmouth 2006
Michel Ngonge – Watford 1999
Shabani Nonda – Blackburn Rovers 2006

Egypt
Ahmed Elmohamady – Sunderland 2010
Ahmed Fathy – Sheffield United 2006
Gedo – Hull City 2013
Hossam Ghaly – Tottenham Hotspur 2006
Mido – Tottenham Hotspur 2004
Mohamed Salah – Chelsea 2013
Mohamed Shawky – Middlesbrough 2007
Amr Zaki – Wigan Athletic 2008
Trezeguet – Aston Villa 2019
Mohamed Elneny – Arsenal 2015
Ramadan Sobhi – Stoke 2016
Ahmed Hegazi – West Brom 2017

Equatorial Guinea
Emilio Nsue – Middlesbrough 2016
Pedro Obiang – West Ham 2016

Gabon
Daniel Cousin – Hull City 2008
Pierre-Emerick Aubameyang – Arsenal 2017
Mario Lemina – Southampton 2017
Didier Ndong – Sunderland 2016
Bruno Ecuele Manga – Cardiff 2018

Gambia
Modou Barrow – Swansea City 2014

Ghana
Albert Adomah – Middlesbrough 2016
Junior Agogo – Sheffield Wednesday 1997
Patrick Agyemang – Queens Park Rangers 2011
Christian Atsu – Everton 2014
Andre Ayew – Swansea City 2015
Jordan Ayew – Aston Villa 2015
Derek Boateng – Fulham 2013
Kevin-Prince Boateng – Tottenham Hotspur 2007
Michael Essien – Chelsea 2005
Emmanuel Frimpong – Arsenal 2011
Asamoah Gyan – Sunderland 2010
Elvis Hammond – Fulham 2002
Richard Kingson – Birmingham City 2007
Nii Lamptey – Aston Villa 1994
John Mensah – Sunderland 2009
Sulley Muntari – Portsmouth 2007
Alex Nyarko – Everton 2000

Quincy Owusu-Abeyie – Arsenal 2004
John Paintsil – West Ham United 2006
Baba Rahman – Chelsea 2015
Jeff Schlupp – Leicester City 2014
Lloyd Sam – Charlton 2004
Tony Yeboah – Leeds United 1994

Guinea
Mohammed Camara – Derby County 2007
Titi Camara – Liverpool 1999
Kaba Diawara – Arsenal 1998
Kamil Zayatte – Hull City 2008
Naby Keita – Liverpool 2018
Ibrahima Cisse – Fulham 2018

Ivory Coast
Serge Aurier – Tottenham 2017
Eric Bailly – Man United 2016
Sol Bamba – Cardiff 2018
Ibrahima Bakayoko – Everton 1998
Jeremie Boga – Chelsea 2017
Wilfried Bony – Swansea City 2013
Guy Demel – West Ham United 2011
Aruna Dindane – Portsmouth 2009
Didier Drogba – Chelsea 2004
Seydou Doumbia – Newcastle 2015
Emmanuel Eboué – Arsenal 2004
Emerse Faé – Reading 2007
Jean-Phillippe Gbamin – Everton 2019
Gervinho – Arsenal 2011
Steve Gohouri – Wigan Athletic 2009
Max Gradel – Bournemouth 2015
Salomon Kalou – Chelsea 2006
Jonathan Kodjia – Aston Villa 2019
Arouna Koné – Wigan Athletic 2012
Lamine Kone – Sunderland 2015
Abdoulaye Méïté – Bolton Wanderers 2006
Nicolas Pépé – Arsenal 2019
Abdul Razak – Manchester City 2010
Yannick Sagbo – Hull City 2013
Jean Seri – Fulham 2018
Olivier Tébily – Birmingham City 2002
Cheick Tioté – Newcastle United 2010
Kolo Touré – Arsenal 2002
Yaya Touré – Manchester City 2010
Lacina Traoré – Everton 2013
Wilfried Zaha – Manchester United 2013
Didier Zokora – Tottenham Hotspur 2006

Kenya
Victor Wanyama – Southampton 2013

Liberia
George Weah – Chelsea 1999
Christopher Wreh – Arsenal 1997

Mali
Yves Bissouma – Brighton 2018
Kalifa Cissé – Reading 2007
Fousseni Diabate – Leicester 2017
Samba Diakité – Queens Park Rangers 2011
Mahamadou Diarra – Fulham 2011
Moussa Djenepo – Southampton 2019
Frédéric Kanouté – West Ham United 1999
Jimmy Kébé – Reading 2007
Modibo Maïga – West Ham United 2012
Bakary Sako – Crystal Palace 2015
Mamady Sidibe – Stoke City 2008
Mohamed Sissoko – Liverpool 2005
Yacouba Sylla – Aston Villa 2012
Djimi Traoré – Liverpool 2000
Molla Wague – Watford 2017

Morocco
Nordin Amrabat – Watford 2015
Salif Diao – Liverpool 2002

Oussama Assaidi – Liverpool 2012
Sofiane Boufal – Southampton
Marouane Chamakh – Arsenal 2010
Youssef Chippo – Coventry City 1991
Manuel da Costa – West Ham 2009
Karim El Ahmadi – Aston Villa 2012
Talal El Karkouri – Sunderland 2002
Tahar El Khalej – Southampton
Nabil El Zhar – Liverpool 2006
Mustapha Hadji – Coventry City 1999
Hassan Kachloul – Southampton 1998
Noureddine Naybet – Tottenham Hotspur 2004
Abdeslam Ouaddou – Fulham 2001
Youssef Safri – Norwich City 2004
Romain Saiss – Wolves 2018
Adel Taarabt – Tottenham Hotspur 2006

Nigeria
Julius Aghahowa – Wigan Athletic 2006
Ola Aina – Chelsea 2016
Ade Akinbiyi – Norwich City 1993
Hope Akpan – Reading 2013
Shola Ameobi – Newcastle United 2000
Daniel Amokachi – Everton 1994
Victor Anichebe – Everton 2005
Sone Aluko – Hull City 2013
Celestine Babayaro – Chelsea 1997
Leon Balogun – Brighton 2018
Efan Ekoku – Norwich City 1992
Emmanuel Emenike – West Ham 2015
Dickson Etuhu – Sunderland 2007
Kelvin Etuhu – Manchester City 2007
Finidi George – Ipswich Town 2001
Brown Ideye – West Bromwich Albion 2014
Odion Ighalo – Watford 2015
Kelechi Iheanacho – Manchester City 2015
Carl Ikeme – Wolverhampton Wanderers 2011
Alex Iwobi – Arsenal 2015
Blessing Kaku – Bolton Wanderers 2004
Nwankwo Kanu – Arsenal 1998
Obafemi Martins – Newcastle United 2006
John Obi Mikel – Chelsea 2006
Victor Moses – Wigan Athletic 2009
Ahmed Musa – Leicester 2016
Wilfred Ndidi – Leicester 2016
Victor Obinna – West Ham United 2010
Peter Odemwingie – West Bromwich Albion 2010
Jay-Jay Okocha – Bolton Wanderers 2002
Isaac Okoronkwo – Wolverhampton Wanderers 2003
Seyi Olofinjana – Stoke City 2008
Danny Shittu – Watford 2006
Sam Sodje – Reading 2006
Isaac Success – Watford 2017
Taye Taiwo – Queens Park Rangers 2011
Ifeanyi Udeze – West Bromwich Albion 2002
John Utaka – Portsmouth 2007
Taribo West – Derby County 2000
Yakubu Aiyegbeni – Portsmouth 2003
Joseph Yobo – Everton 2002

Senegal
Demba Ba – West Ham United 2010
Habib Beye – Newcastle United 2007
Henri Camara – Wolverhampton Wanderers 2003
Aliou Cissé – Birmingham City 2002
Papiss Cissé – Newcastle United 2011
Ferdinand Coly – Birmingham City 2002
Mohamed Diamé – Wigan Athletic 2009
Salif Diao – Liverpool 2002

Lamine Diatta – Newcastle United 2007
Djibril Diawara – Bolton Wanderers 200
Souleymane Diawara – Charlton Athletic 2006
Papa Bouba Diop – Fulham 2004
El Hadji Diouf – Liverpool 2002
Mame Biram Diouf – Manchester United 2009
Papy Djilobodji – Sunderland 2016
Khalilou Fadiga – Bolton Wanderers 200
Abdoulaye Faye – Bolton Wanderers 200
Amdy Faye – Portsmouth 2003
Idrissa Gueye – Aston Villa 2015
Magaye Gueye – Everton 2010
Diomansy Kamara – Portsmouth 2004
Cheikhou Kouyaté – West Ham United 2014
Sadio Mané – Southampton 2014
Kader Mangane – Sunderland 2012
Alfred N'Diaye – Sunderland 2012
Badou Ndiaye – Stoke 2017
Dame N'Doye – Hull City 2014
M'baye Niang – Watford 2016
Oumar Niasse – Everton 2015
Henri Saivet – Newcastle 2015
Diafra Sakho – West Ham United 2014
Lamine Sakho – Leeds United 2003
Ismaila Sarr – Watford 2019
Ibrahima Sonko – Reading 2006
Pape Souaré – Crystal Palace 2014
Armand Traoré – Arsenal 2007

Sierra Leone
Al Bangura – Watford 2006
Albert Jarrett – Watford 2006
Kei Kamara – Norwich City 2012

South Africa
Shaun Bartlett – Charlton Athletic 2000
Kagisho Dikgacoi – Fulham 2009
Mark Fish – Bolton Wanderers 1997
Quinton Fortune – Manchester United 1999
Mbulelo Mabizela – Tottenham Hotspur 2003
Phil Masinga – Leeds United 1994
Benni McCarthy – Blackburn Rovers 2006
Aaron Mokoena – Blackburn Rovers 200
Steven Pienaar – Everton 2007
Lucas Radebe – Leeds United 1994
Tokelo Rantie – Bournemouth 2015
Eric Tinkler – Barnsley 1997

Tanzania
Mbwana Samatta – Aston Villa 2020

Togo
Emmanuel Adebayor – Arsenal 2005
Yoann Folly – Southampton 2003
Moustapha Salifou – Aston Villa 2008
Floyd Ayite – Fulham 2018

Tunisia
Yohan Benalouane – Leicester City 2015
Radhi Jaidi – Bolton Wanderers 2004
Wahbi Khazri – Sunderland 2015
Mehdi Nafti – Birmingham City 2005
Hatem Trabelsi – Manchester City 2006

Zambia
Emmanuel Mayuka – Southampton 2012
Collins Mbesuma – Portsmouth 2005

Zimbabwe
Benjani – Portsmouth 2005
Bruce Grobbelaar – Liverpool 1992
Peter Ndlovu – Coventry City 1992
Marvelous Nakamba – Aston Villa 2020